CW00530232

ISBN 978-0-332-96398-3
PIBN 10716314

FB &c Ltd, Dalton House, 60 Windsor Avenue, London, SW19 2RR.
Company number 08720141. Registered in England and Wales.

For support please visit www.forgottenbooks.com

THE

Publications

OF THE

Thoresby Society

ESTABLISHED IN THE YEAR MDCCCLXXXIX

VOL. XXVII

FOR THE YEAR 1919

TESTAMENTA LEODIENSIA

WILLS OF LEEDS
PONTEFRACT, WAKEFIELD, OTLEY
AND DISTRICT

1553 to 1561

EXTRACTED AND EDITED BY

GEORGE DENISON LUMB, F.S.A.

A Vice-President of the Thoresby Society, Member of the Council of the Yorkshire Archæological Society, the Yorkshire Parish Register Society, the Leeds Philosophical and Literary Society, etc.

PRIVATELY PRINTED FOR THE THORESBY SOCIETY

LEEDS, 1930

PREFACE.

THIS volume of wills is extracted from the 14th, 15th, 16th and 17th books of the registered copies at the York Probate Registry, extending from the year 1553 to the year 1561. It is the result of numerous visits to York during the last seventeen years.

The earlier wills, contained in vol. xix, published in 1913, numbered 547.

This volume contains 543 wills of testators residing in Leeds and the adjacent towns and villages. The inhabitants had much in common in professions and trades, in intercourse and kinship.

As stated in the preface to vol. xix, the wills were copied in the register books from dictation, and the peculiarity of spelling, repeated in successive wills, indicates that they were written by the same clerk, and in addition, apparently there was no accurate collation.

The preface contains remarks on the distribution of the estates of deceased persons, and other matters to which reference is recommended, and therefore are not repeated here.

The thanks of the Society are due to Mr. Jesse A. Myers for kindly undertaking the laborious work of preparing the indexes, and to Mr. W. B. Crump, M.A., for explanatory notes in the index of subjects.

G. D. L.

LEEDS, *April*, 1930.

ERRATUM

Page 177. *For* roddes *read* coddes.

Testamenta Leodiensia.

EXTRACTED FROM THE *PROBATE* REGISTRY AT YORK.

---

*P*ERCIVAL LYNLEY, OF *P*ONTEFRACT.

(xiv. 10 b.)

In the name of God Amen: in the yere of oure lorde God a thousand fyve hundreth fiftie and thre, the xxij day of Aprile. I P'cevall Lynley, of Pontefracte, seke in bodie and holl of mynde and memorie, make this my last will and testament in mann' and forme followinge. Firste I bequeath my saull vnto almightie God, to oure ladie sancte Marie and all the holie company of heaven, and my bodie to be buried where it shall please God to take me to his mercie. Also I bequeath to Thomas my sonne my best jackett and to Thomas and John my sons my towe beste dublette. Also I bequest to John my sonne my varrant curtall nagge. Also I bequeath to Jennet Anderson x[s] and my jackett. And the Residue of my goode vnbequeathed over and besides my wives parte I giue vnto Thomas Lynley and John Lynley my sonnes and Jennet Lynley my doughter, whome I make myne executors of this my last will and testament. Also I constitute and make William Lynley, of Dunynglawe, and Thomas Gawthorpe, of Tadcaster, supvisors of this my last will. Thes beinge witness', S[r] Giles Scott, vicare of Tadcaster, Amer Denton, Robert Bikerton, Roger Pickeringe, Henrie Mawe, Robert Henrison, and Thomas Elles, with other as Thomas Gawthorpe.—[*Proved* 6 *June*, 1554, *by Wm. Lynley and Thomas Gawthorpe, curators of Thomas Lynley, John Lynley, and Jane Lynley, minors.*]

GEORGE LOWCOKE, OF ABERFORTH.

(xiv. 11 a)

In the name of God Amen: the last daye of November, the yere of oure lorde God a thousande fyve hundrethe fiftie and thre. I Georgie Lowcoke, of Abberforth, holl of mynde and seke of bodye, ordaneth and maketh this my testament and last will in forme and manner thus followinge. First I bequeath my soull to Almightie God and to all the celestiall company in heaven. Secundlie, my bodie to be buried in my pishe church yerde in Abberforde. Thirdlie, I bequeath to William myne eldest sone that power rayment that belongeth to my bodie. The reste of my goode, my dette paid and my buriall dischardged, I giue frelie to Agnes my wif and to Thomas, William, and Mathue, my children, to be equally devided emonge them all, whome I make Executors of this my testament and last will. Recordes herof, Robert Smith and Leonarde Lowcoke, with other.—[*Proved* 13 *June*, 1554, *by the widow, grant reserved to the other executors, minors.*]

William Pickard, of Menston.

(xiv. 16 a.)

In Dei nōie Amen: the xxvj^th day of February in the yeare of o^r lord God a thowsand fyve hundryth fiftie and thre. I Wiłłm Pickard, of Menston in the countie of Yorke, beinge of good and perfite memory, makes this my Last will and testament in man' and furme folowinge. Firste I comende my soulle vnto Allmightie God my maker and redemer, and to o^r Ladye Sancte Mary and to all the holy company of heaven, and my body to be buryed within my ꝑishe churche yearde of Otley. Item I will that my dettꝭ be paide and my body honestly brought furthe of my holle goodꝭ. Item I will that the Residewe of my said goodꝭ be equallye devided betwixt Jenett my wyffe and Xpofer my sonne, whome I maike my full and lawfull executors of this my last will, thes beinge wytnes, Anthone Steade, Richard Parker, James Roodꝭ, wth other moo. Item I maike Xpofer Pykerd my brother and William Pickerd his sonne the suꝑvisorꝭ of this my last will and testament.—[*Proved* 6 *March*, 1555.]

Christopher Allan.

(xiv. 23 b.)

This ys the will of Xpofer Allane, written the xth day of February in the vj yere of the Reigne of Edward the sixt. First I bequithe my sowle vnto the father of heaven, and my body to be buryed wythin the churche or churche yearde of Waikfeild, moreover I doo maike my twoo sonnes my hole executorꝭ of all my goodꝭ, my debtꝭ paid and I brought forth of my goodꝭ, my will is that all my tackꝭ shall goo to my twoo sonnes, that is to Johne Allane and Bryane Allane, to bring them vppe w^thall. Moreover I doo maike Richard Allane and Roger Allane the suꝑvisorꝭ of my will. My will ys that Richard Allane and Roger Allane shall haue the gou'naunce of my twoo sonnes, and thare goodꝭ and tackꝭ the wiche I haue geven vnto them. Dettꝭ that I the said Xpofer Allan doth owe: In primis to Mr Bayles v^li, to Roger Allane xij^s, and to the said Roger xv^s. I thinge that I owe Francꝭ Graunt xx^s. Dettꝭ that I the said Xpofer ys owne: Item Anthony Franke xij^s viij^d, Robert Tempest iij^s iiij^d, Johne Tempest iij^s iiij^d, Richard Sharp x^s viij^d, Thomas Sotheren v^li, Richard Achinson x^s viij^d, Henry Todde x^s viij^d, Johne Leke x^s viij^d, Brian Walker v^s, Robert Eden vj^s viij^d, Richard Barber ij^s vij^d, Johne Smythson xx^s. I for gyve rest, Johne Laike of Normanton iij^s iiij^d, Johne Cowꝑ xxx^s, and of that I haue as moche of him as drew xij^s so ther is bott xviij^s. Also I did pay vnto s'r Johne Tempest by the councell of my maister v^li, and that was that I shulde have one Lease of the Erel shyngꝭ for x yeres whan ys pattane bare effect, that is to saye whan my M^r pattane was expressed and done the wch v^li Richard Ellys delyu'ed for me vnto the said Sr Johne Tempest at Doncaster and at the same tymes I the said Xpofer did go for the said Sr Johne wth my M^r to the borders of Barwycke of my nowne proper costꝭ and chargꝭ having no penny of the Kingꝭ wages.—[*No grant.*]

Robert England, of Gildersome.

(xiv. 30 a.)

In the name of God Amen: the yere of o^r Lord god a thowsand five hundrithe fiftie and five, the xx^ti daye of Marche. I Robert England, of Gildersu' w^t^in the ꝑishe of Batleye, of good and hoole mynd, dothe make this my last will and Testament as hereafter dothe appere. First and principallie I give and bequethe my sowle to God almightie the father eternall, and to o^r^ blissed ladie sancte Marie the glorius Virgin, and to all the hollie companye of heaven throughe the moost dredde and most mornfull Lorde dere Jesus Christe, and my bodie to be buried in the ꝑishe churche yerde of all hallowes at Batleye. Also I give and bequethe to the Churche of Batleye xij^d^. It'm I give and bequicthe to Elisabethe England, my sonne doughter, one yonge whie stirke and she to be put to the moost profecte of the madyn. It'm I give and bequiethe to Agnes my doughter one cowe or xx^s^ of moneye besides her childes porc̃on. It'm I give and bequethe vnto William my sonne one howse and one crofte wch is nowe in the vse and occupac̃on of Henrie Longley and Elyn his wief, and also the feld land that the said Henrie dothe occupie w^t^ towe doyles in Nepshawe painge the Lordes rent for the said doiles. Furthermore the foresaid Henrie shall enioye and occupie the foresaid howse and Tenement the space of iiij yeres after my dethe painge v^s^ in a yere vnto the foresaid William my sonne at the iiij yeres end, then the said William my sonne shall enter vnto the foresaid howse duringe his naturall Liffe. It'm I give and bequiethe vnto John my son one donne horse or a marke of moneye besides his childes porc̃on. Furder I make Elisabethe my wief my hole executrix, to have the thirde of all my goddes after that my dettꝭ be paid, painge thes my v children ther childes porc̃ons. Thes be the names of my children that shall receave my goodes: James, William, John, Robert, and Agnes, to have ther p'tes as it shall come to more over the reverc̃on of my nom̃e ꝑte after the funerall expens' be paid shall retorne vnto Eliz' my wief, William, John, and Agnes, also that thes my three children shall have thes my legacies that as herebefore rehersed, and that Adam my son and heire shall have my landes as testifiethe above wryten, further Adame my sonne and beire shall give Agnes my doughter xx^s^ of lawfull moneye at my desier, and so Eliz' my doughter that is maried havinge her childes porc̃on shall have one iron ronghe to give vnto his son Robert after her deceasse. Thes beinge wytnesse, Willfraye Rayner and James Croft, w^t^ other moo.—[*Proved 2 May*, 1565.]

THOMAS BURTON, CLERKE.

(xiv. 35 a.)

In the name of God Amen: the xxix daye of Aprill in the yere of o^r^ lord God 1555. I Thomas Burton, clerke, sumtyme fellowe in the Trinitie colledge in Pomfracte laite suppressed, of hoole mynde and saif memorie, thankꝭ be vnto almightie God, makes this my last will and testament in manner and furme followinge. Firste I bequethe my sowle vnto almightie God my onelie Sauior and Reademer, to o^r^ blissed ladie sancte Marie, and to all the Celestiall companie of heaven, and my bodie to be buried in the churche yerde of Metheleye so nye vnto my father and mother as maye convenientlie be, and at the daye of my buriall to have masse and derige songe wth all other suffrages therunto belonginge. It'm I give to the Repac̃ons of Meatheley churche iij^s^ iiij^d^. It'm I will that at the daye of my buriall to be distributed vnto the pow^r^ people xl^s. It'm I give to Richard Hauthame, to Richard Spence, and to Thomas Slakke my godsonnes, everie one of them iiij^d apeice. It'm I give to everie one of my brother Cherles children, of Badley, v^s a peece. It'm I give to my brother Cherles wief an angell noble. It'm I give to my sister fortune and her children equallie to be deuided emongst them xl^s. It'm I give to my brother Robert children everie one of them xiij^s iiij^d a pece. It'm I give to Eliz' Atkinson, my brother William doughter, iij^s iiij^d. It'm I give to everie of my brethren William and Ellis children v^s a peece. It'm I give to Richard Burtonne, sonne vnto my brother William, frelie vnto him and his heires of his bodie lawfullie begotten my howse in Pomfracte w^t all the appurteñnce therunto belonginge for ever. And yf yt fortune the aforesaid Richard to diseace w^towte yshowe then I woll that it goo to Robert Burton, son to my brother William aforesaid, and to his beires of his bodie lawfullie begotten and so furthw^t all the rest. Also I do give to William and Ellis wiefes ather of them an angell noble. It'm I give to my brother Sr Richard Burton my best cappe, my worset jacket, and my sarcenet tippet. It'm I give to my suster Agnes Smithe x^s. It'm I give to Sr Roger Marshall, to Sr Johnne Dickson, and to Sr Johnne Soresbie everie one of them iiij^s a peece. It'm I give to the buildinge of Meatheleye Brigge xx^s. It'm I give to everie one of the brethren and sisters in the Trinitie colledge in Pomfracte w^t ther too s'runtℯ xij^d a peece. It'm I woll that my brother Sr Richard Burton be my Superuisor of this my last will and testament to see that it be fulfilled, and he to have for his panes my old riallℯ. The residewe of all my goodes not above given, my debtℯ paid, my legacies fulfilled, and my funerallℯ discharged, I give to William Burtunne and Ellis Burton, my brethren, whome I do make m̃y full executors of this my last will and testament, to dispose for the healthe of my sowle as shall please almightie God and them. Thees wytness', Sr Antonie Askh'm, p'sonne of Metheleye, Sr Richard Shanne, Gilbert Nunnes, and Robert Gamble, w^t other.—[*Proved 12 May*, 1555.]

George Cawood, of Newton Kyme.

(xiv. 50 b.)

In the name of God Amen : I George Cawode, of the perishe of Newton Kyme, in perfect mynde and good rememberaunce, in the firste day of September in the yere of our lord god a thowsand fyve hundrythe fyftie and foure, make my Testament and last will in man' and furme folowinge. Fyrste I bequythe my soulle to almighti God my maker and to his onely sonne J'hu Chryste my Lorde and Redemer, in whome I put my hole hope and truste of my saluacyon throughe the meritℯ of his blyssid passion. Also I bequythe my body to be buryed in the kirke garthe of the forsaide Newton. Also I bequythe for the adorninge of the Churche xij^d. Also I bequythe to Alison my wyffe the hole intereste of my fermeholde for terme of her Lyfe so that she kepe her self widowe, and after hir wydohode o^r terme of her lyfe I bequythe to Christofer my sonne my hole intereste therof. Also I bequythe to Agnes my dowghter xx^s, to Janet my doughter xx^s, to Katheryne my dowghter xx^s, to Richard Wyley my nevie iij^li v^s viij^d to be payd by the bandes of Christofer Cawod my sonne at his mariage. Also I bequythe to Sicile my dowghter xx^{s} for her childes portion wth the wch she was well contented and satisfied before the wytness^{s} of this will. Also I bequythe to eu'y god childe I haue iiij^{d}. Also I bequythe to eu'y cotage wthin the pishe iiij^{d}. Also I bequythe to Richard Cawodde a frese cote, to Johne Baringh'm, to Thomas Wrey, and to Johne Wrey, of Clifford, as moche frese as shalbe sufficient to maike eu'y one of them an honest cote. Also I bequythe to Alison my wyfe all my other goodę bothe moveable and vnmoueable, whome I maike ful executrix of this my last will; and ou'seers of the same, Christofer Cawod, Thomas Carbot, and Willm Wylkinson, my sonnes, to whome for thare paynes I bequythe xx^{s} a pece. Wytness^{s} hereof, Johne Arthington, Richard Shipley, and Johne Vicars. —[*Proved* 11 *Oct.*, 1554.]

RALPH HORSMAN, OF MONK FRYSTON.

(xiv. 56 a.)

In the name of God Amen: written at Monke friston the xth daye of November in the yere of oure lorde God a thousande fyve hundrethe liij, that I Rauf Horsman, of the said towne, holl of mynde and goode and pfite remembrance, thankę be vuto God, beinge seke in my bodie ordaneth and makith this my last will and testament in manner and forme followinge. Firste I bequeath my soull vnto god almightie, oure ladie sancte Marie, and to all the celestiall company of heaven, and my bodie to be buried within the churche of oure blissed ladie at Monke friston aforsaid if it shall please god to call me to his mercie at this present tyme. Item I bequeath vnto Katheryn my wif my best bounde wayne, foure of the best yockę and teames, a ploughe and foure of my best oxen, towe kie, and my blake horse, and vnto my said wif in full recompence and satisfaction of her thirdę of all my landes, tenementę, and Leases at Hilton all suche leases as I haue in the lordshippes of Friston, Hamleton, Hadelsais, and Birkyn duringe here naturall lif. And if it shall fortone the saide Katheryne to die before the said leases or any of theme be determyned and ended, or that she will not contente here self with this said legacie, then I will that all the said leases shall go to the onlie vse and proffett of Leonarde my sonne, and she to take that at the lawe will appoynte here. Item I giue vnto William my sonne all my leases that I haue at Hilton. Item I giue vnto Leonarde my sonne all the annuall rentę, issues, and proffettę grovinge or comynge of all my landes at Hilton aforesaid duringe the space of xj yeres next and imediatelie followinge after my deathe, and also vnto the said Leonarde I giue iij^{li} vj^{s} viij^{d}. Item I giue vnto John Horsman my brother half an old aungell. Item I giue vnto Sr Richarde Jennynge iij^{s} iiij^{d}. Item I giue vnto Sr William Gibson ij^{s}. Item I giue vnto John Meth'm xij^{d}. Item I giue vnto John Lambert iiij yewes and viij^{s} that are in his hande. Item I giue vnto Adam Lambert a whitheded quye that hath had but one calf and ij yewes. Item I giue vnto Agnes Carnabie vj^{s} viij^{d} and one yewe. Item I giue to everie serunte that shalbe with me the daye of my death viij^{d}. Item I giue vnto all myne owne children and to William Nutt and Alice Nutt tenne sheppe whiche is in Robert Beaman kepinge at Gateforde. Item I will that Laurence S^{r}u'nte of Mash'm shall have the governance, ruyll, and kepinge of Leonarde my sonne and all his goodes to he come to his full adge of xxj yeres, and the said Laurence to haue for his paynes takinge about the premisses one old aungell and a gold rynge that was myne vncles, whiche rynge he shall haue but duringe his naturall lif, and after his decease I giue it vnto William my sonne if he shalbe then livinge, and if he be deceased then to the next of my kynne beinge men or men children. Item I will that Alan Horseman, of Hilton, shall haue the governance, rewll, and kepinge of William my sone and all his goodes to he come to the adge of xxj yeres, and the said Alan to haue for his paynes takinge aboute the premisses one old aungell. Item I will that the said Laurence and Alan shall haue to there proper vses all the annual rentꝭ, issues, proffettꝭ, comyng or growinge of all my landꝭ and leases at Hilton solonge as they shall fynde my sonnes at Scole notwithstandinge my former legacie of the said annuall rentꝭ to them before graunted. Forthermore I will that if the said Laurence and Alan shall thinke it convenient when my said sonnes shall come to laufull yeres of discretion to putt theme to be prenticꝭ with the assent and consent of the suꝑvisore of this my will and testament, then imediatelie after my said sonnes be bounde prenticꝭ I will that the aforsaid annuall rentꝭ shalbe converted and go to the onelie vse and proffett of my said sonnes equally to they come to there full age. Item I giue vnto William my sonne tenne of the beste oke trees in the garth. Item I giue vnto Leonarde my sonne all my bookꝭ if he shall chaunce to be learned and be preste, or els to any childe that William my sone shall haue to be learned and be preste, or els to any child of the said Leonarde that shalbe preste. Item I will that Jennet my doughter and all here goodꝭ shalbe at the rewll, governance, and kepinge of Richarde Beckwith, of Nutwithcote in the ꝑishe of Mash'm, here grandfather, to she come to age of xx yeres or els be maried, and he to haue for his paynes takinge an olde aungell. And if the said Richarde will not haue here then I will that John Horsman my brother haue here and all here goodes as is aforsaid with the aungell that my said father in lawe shulde have hade, and if the said Richarde Beckwith will take vpon hyme the rewll of my saide doughter then I giue to his wif half an olde aungell. Item I giue vnto Isabell my suster vj^{s} viij^{d}. Item I giue vnto John Mettam wif iij^{s} iiij^{d}. Item I giuc vnto William Nutte thirtie of the best trees in the garthe after terme of the beste of all the saide trees be taken forth if the said William Nutte do not vex or troble nor aske accomptꝭ of my executors for rentꝭ of his landꝭ or reꝑacions of his bowses, and if he vex or troble them then this legacie to be void. Item I will that everie one of the ꝑsons afore named that shall haue the Rewll and governance of my saide children shall fynde sufficient sureties to be bounde for the redeliverie of all my childer's goodes as everie one of theme shall come to ther laufull age as is aforsaide. And further I will and desier that the suꝑvisors of this my will shall forsee that it be substancially done and that this my will shall not be approbate withoute they be at the approbacion therof. Item I giue vnto William Wilson, of Monkefriston, and to Ottuell Metcalf, whom I ordre and make the suꝑvisors of this my testament and last will, and they to se as moche as the lawe will admitt theme that my children haue ther right in everie behalf and either of theme to haue for ther paynes to be taken in and aboute the same one old aungell, and ther chardges to be borne at all tymes. Item I will that if theye that hath the rewll and kepinge of my said children have any vexacion or troble in or aboute theme that they haue there costes and chardges borne at all tymes. The Residue of all my goodes not bequest, my dettę paid and my funerallę dischardged, I giue and bequeath theme vnto William and Leonarde my sonnes and Jennet my doughter, whome I ordre and make my full and laufull executors of this my last will and testament that it be fulfilled in everie article with effecte. Thes beinge witnesses, William Wilson, Sr William Gibson, preste, Sr Richarde Jennynge, preste, Laurence Servante, and Alan Horseman, with other moo.—[*Proved 25 April, 1554, by Richard Beckwith, Alan Horsman, and Laurence Servante, guardians of the children of deceased during minority.*][1]

———

William Nelstrop, of Huddlestone.

(xiv. 61 b.)

In the name of God Amen: the eight daye of Septembre in the yere of oure lorde gode a thousande fyve hundrethe fiftie and thre. I William Nelstrope, of Huddilston in the p̱ishe of Sherborne, holl of mynde and of p̱fitt remembrance, makę this my testament and last will in manner and forme followinge. Firste I giue and bequeath my soull to almightie God, requiring oure ladie sancte Marie and all the holie company of heaven to be mediators for me, and my bodie to be buried within the p̱ish churche yerde of all sanct in Sherborne nye vnto my father and mother. Item I giue and bequeath vnto the blissed sacrament for my tithes negligentelie forgotten iij^{s} iiij^{d}. Item I giue to Wilfride Nelstrope my sonne a blake cowe grete with calf. Item I giue to the saide Wilfride one acre of whete and one acre of barlie to be sowene this next yere. Item I will that Henrie Nelstrope my sonne in full recompensacion of certan goodes geven vnto hyme by the late vicare of Ledsame, Mr Wilkynson, and other his frendes, which stoke of goodes and the proffetę therof I haue alwaies hetherto receyved and converted to myne owne vse shall haue viijth oxen, one yren bounde wayne, the best thre kien, ij quyes, and a yonge baye mare and seven store shepe. And I confesse and declare this to be his owne propre goodes geven vnto hyme by his forsaid frendes. Item I giue to Lionell Nelstroppe, William Laiklande, Chr̃ofer Wikynson, and to William Nelstrope the yonger everie on of them a yonge quye. Item I giue to Elen and Anne Nelstrope my doughters everie of them a yewe and a lambe. Item I giue to William Nelstrope, Anthony sonne, one yewe lambe. Item I giue to Sr John Talio^{r} xij^{d}. Item I giue to Sr Robert Blaunche xij^{d}. Item I giue to Richarde Henrison and to Sr Mathewe Smythson to either of theme iij^{s} iiij^{d}, who I ordane, constitute, and make sup̱viso^{r}s of this my last will and testament to se the same p̱formed and fulfilled. The Residue of all my goodes, my dettę and legacę paide and my bodie honestlie brought forthe, I giue to Elisabethe my wif who I make my sole executrix of this my last will and testament. Witnesses herof, Sr Mathue Smythson, my curate, Sr John Talio^{r}, Sr Robert Blaunche, prestę, John Foxam, Laurence Turpyn, Robert Burman John Denes, with other.—[*Proved 21 April, 1554.*]

(1) For the will of John Henrison of Gipton, proved 13th Ap^{r}il, 1554, see *ante*, vol. xv, p. 53.

THOMAS JOHNSON, OF HAZLEWOOD.

(xiv. 63 b.)

In the name of God Amen: I Thomas Johnson, of Hessilwode, beinge somewhat deseased in my bodie, nevertheles holl and ꝑfitt in my memorie, the xxij daye of Aprile in the yere of oure Lorde god a m^{l}v^{c}liij, make this my last will and testament in manner and forme followinge, that is to saye. First I bequeath my soull to almightie God and to the meritꝭ of Christꝭ passion, oure redemer, and my body to be buried in the church of Heslewode before the chauncell dores. Also I bequeithe to v power people everie of theme ij^{d} and ther dynner at the daye of my buriall. Item I bequeath my grett caldron of brasse to Christabell my doughter to here mariedge and to be delyu'ed vnto her the daye of her mariedge or els if she shall forton to die before she be maried then I will that the same caldron shalbe disposed emong my thre children or doughters Elisabeth, Dorothie, and Philipe. Item I bequeath to Chr̃ofer Settle and my doughter his wif xl^{s} in money or els xx^{tie} shepe which of theme he will choise, and also a milke cowe for his porc̃on and hers. Item to John Settle, the same Chr̃ofer sonne, a yewe and a lambe, and to Robert Settle, his other sonne, a nother yewe and lambe. Item to the said Chr̃ofer I giue my best grene cote. Item I bequeath to my wif Agnes ij brase pottꝭ, one of the best sorte and a nother of the secunde sorte. Item to my doughter Elisabeth a brase pott next the beste pott, and to Dorothie and Philipe either of theme a brase pott. Item I bequeath to Dorothie, my eldest doughter, for her full portion of my goodes, tenne gymber shet [*sic*] and one quye stirke. Item I bequeath to my doughter Chr̃obell and Elisabeth either of theme a mattres with a coverlett and a pare of shettꝭ and a bolster. Item all my pewther vessell to be devided indifferentelie betwene my wif and my foure doughters Chr̃obell, Elisabeth, Dorothie, and Philippe. The Residue of all my goodes not bequeathed, after my dettꝭ, legacies, and funerall expenses paid and dischardged, I gine and bequeath to my saide wif and foure yonger doughters, whome I make and constitute to be my executors of this present will at the oversight and survio^{r} of my Mr Sr William Vaviso^{r}, knyght, whome I make and ordane to be survio^{r} of the same and to se all thingꝭ mynistred accordinge to this my will. Thes be the dettꝭ that I owe: First to Roger Dyuley v^{s}. To Anthony Wharton for corne viij^{s} ij^{d}. Item to Richarde Gryme for a rente of half a tith to be due for a half yere at Lambmes. Witnesses, Sr William Vavaso^{r}, knyght, Rauf Wren, Esquier, and Sr John Mores, prest, with other moo as Laurence Atkynson and John Woode.—[*Proved* 24 *April*, 1554, *by the widow, grant reserved to the children.*]

PERCIVAL FRANK, OF PONTEFRACT.[1]

(xiv. 64 a.)

In the name of God Amen: I Parcivall Franke, of Pontefracte in the countie of [York], gentleman, beinge holl of mynde and ꝑfite remembrance, xxvj daye of Auguste in the firste yere of the Reigne of oure moste Soveraign ladie Marie by the grace of God of Englande, Fraunce, and

(1) He heads the pedigree in *Dugdale's Visitation*, ed. J. W. Clay, vol. iii, p. 178.

Irelande quene, defender of the faith, doth make this my last will or testament in this manner and forme followinge. Firste I bequeath my soull to Almightie God my redemer and Savio^{r}, and my bodie to be buried wher it shall please myne executors. Also I bequeath to Jane my wif a lease of Castleforth yngꝭ and Allerton yngꝭ duringe the yeres contened in the said leace, and after the decesse of my wif the said leace to remayne to my children. Also I gine to the said Jane the copie of my house with all thingꝭ therto belonginge and after her decesse to my children. Also I giue to the said Jane my lease that I haue by Lionell Craggꝭ of the close called the preyle and my wif to paye to John Ricarde wif, of Pollington, called Agnes Ricarde, xxxiij^{s} iiij^{d} by yere duringe fyve yeres, and if she die within the said yeres then I will that Oswald Ricarde, of Hecke, haue the rest of the saide if any be vnpaid, and to putt it to such vse as they and I haue hade covcacion of and the first payment to begyne at suche tyme as my wif dothe entre to the saide close called the preyle. Also I bequeath to my suster Jennet Walles a bill lienge in my Caskett at Barwike to receyve all thingꝭ contened therin of Robert Browne, of Horneclif, that is to saye, three barrellꝭ of salmon and xxxiij^{s} iiij^{d} in money, and my suster to paye all suche chardges as I haue been at aboute her waters at Barwike as it shall appere by a booke. Also I bequeathe to my ser̃unte Elisabeth Skynner xij^{d}. Also I bequeath to my curate Sr William Chamber xvj^{d}. The Residue of all other my goodes not bequeste I will that they be at the ordre of Jane my wif, Henrie and John my sonnes, Jane and Isabell my doughters, whome I make my holl executors joyntelie together. Also I will that Oswald Ricarde and William Adam shalbe the ꝑvisors of this my will and either of theme to haue for ther paynes takinge v^{s}. In witnes herof, Sr John Barker, vicare of Pontefracte, Sr Richarde Rideall, preste, Thomas Edrington, alderman, John Jackson the elder, William Calbeke, Robt. Bleysbie, and my curate S^{r} Wiłłm Chambre.—[*Proved 26 April, 1554, by the widow, grant reserved to the children.*]

Robert Turpin, of Towton.

(xiv. 70 b.)

In Dei nõie Amen: the viijth daye of Auguste in the yere of o^{r} Lorde god a thowsand fyve hundreth fiftie and one. I Robert Turpyn, of Towton in the countie of Yorke, husbandman, hoole of mynde and of good memorye, loved be god, maketh my laste will and testam^{t} in manner and forme following. Furst I give and witte my soule to allmightie God, to our blessed Lady sanct Marye, and to all the celestiall companye of heaven, and my bodye to be buryed within the parishe churche or churche yerde of Saxton. Also I give and bequeth all my goodes, my dettes paid, to Eliz. Turpyn my wife, George Turpyn, Alexander Turpyn, and Frauncys Turpyn, my chylder, whome I ordeyn and make my full executors of this my last will and Testamente, and theye to bringe me furthe honestlye and dispose for the healthe of my soule after their discretions. In wytnes hereof, George Parkar and Alexander Lacockꝭ, wth other moo.—[*Proved 18 Jan., 155(? 4), by Alexander Laicockꝭ, Thomas Turpyn, and Robert Turpyn, guardians of children during minority. Grant reserved to the other executor.*]

William Scoles, of Thorpe on the Hill.

(xiv. 75 a.)

In Dei nõie Amen: the xxij^{tie} daye of Auguste in the yere of our Lorde God, 1555, wytnessethe that I Wiłłm Scoles, of Thorpe of the hill in the parishing of Rothwell in the Coũtie of Yorke, Clothyar, hole and perfite of mynde and memorye, makes this my laste will and testamente in manner and forme following, that is to saye, furst I bequeathe and geve my soule vnto Allmightie god, and my bodye to be buryed w[t]in the Churche yerde of the hooly Trynitie in Rothwell aforesaid. Allso I bequeth to the holye sacramente their xij[d]. Item I bequeth to the poore people of the said parishing in Almes xij[d]. It'm towardes the building of Metheley bridge vj[d]. It' I bequeth to Wiłłm Scoles and John Scoles my sonnes my broode lowme w[t] horne wheles, baretrees, and yeares ꝑteyning the same, and allso two paire of the beste sheres vppon condicõn that if the said Wiłłm and John do learne and teache there yonger bretherne there occupacõn, otherwise that said Wiłłm and John my sonnes shall not clayme nor taike the same lowme, sheres, and other the p'misses perteyning the same as my parte of this my laste will w[th]out the goodwill of Jennet Scoles now my wife. Also I bequethe vnto Richarde Scoles and Vmfrey Scoles my yonger sonnes other ij paire of sheres. Also I bequeth to Jennet Scoles my doughter one greate panne to be taken after the deathe of the same Jennet Scoles my said wif. Allso I will and give by this my last will and testamente the residewe of all my goodes moveable and vnmoveable vnto the same Jennet Scoles my said wyf, my dettes, childes porcõns, and the funerall charges and expenses y'of paide and donne according to the lawes of this realme. In wytnesse wherof I the same Wiłłm Scoles vnto this my laste will and testamente haue setto my marke the daye and yere abouesaide in the p'sence of Wyłłm Gascoyne thelder, Wyłłm Gascoigne the yonger, Laurence Gascoigne, Raif Scholes, George Scoles, John Armington, and others than and theire being presente.—[*Proved* 31 *Oct.*, 1555.]

John Bradley, of Leathley.

(xiv. 92 a.)

In Dei nõie Amen: the yere of our Lord God m[l]ccccccliij and the furst day of M'che. I John Bradlaye, of Leithlay, seeke of bodye and hole in mynde withe perfite remembraunce, make this my laste will and testament as hereafter dothe followe. Furste and before all thingꝭ I give and comyt my soule to Allmyghtye God, to our ladye sanct Marye, and to all the holye company of heaven, and my bodye to be buryed in my ꝑyshe churche yerde of Leathelye aforesaid. Allso I will that my cosyn Thom's Bradlay shall haue the order of my sonne James Bradleye till he come to lawfull yeares so that the goodꝭ and childe parte of the said James shall still remayne wth his moth' duryng the said terme, and the said Thom's Bradley to haue his costꝭ and chargꝭ borne when he dothe labor in ony matters of the said James. Allso I will that my children shall have there childes porcõus according to the dew order of the lawe. Allso I will that Margaret my wyfe and James my sonne shall be myne executors jointly together, and after my dettꝭ paid and fun'all chargꝭ borne, my sade wyfe and my said sonne to devyde the reste of my goodꝭ equally bequixte them.

These witness's, Myles Walkar, clarke, p'son there, Wyllm Sadler, Thom's Forrest, iunior, P'sevall Mason, Thom's Bradley, Omfrey Hodgesonne, wythe other mo.—[*Proved* 4 *Dec.*, 1553 [*sic*]].

THOMAS HORNER, OF WESTON.

(xiv. 93 a.)

In Dei nōie Amen: the yeare of our Lorde m[l]cccccliiij and the xxviij[th] day of Aprell. I Thom's Horner, of the pishe of Weston, hole of mynde and p'fite memorye, ordenythe and makę this to be my laste will and testament in manner and forme as dothe followe. Furst I bequeathe my soule to Allmightie God, and my bodie to be earthed within the churche yarde in Weston. Allso I give to my dame Banton one stone of wolle. It'm to Jennet Hewit one stone of wolle. It'm to Jennet Mawson one stone of wolle. It'm I give to Agnes Banton iij[s] iiij[d]. It'm I geve to Izabell Wodde, of Myddleton, iij[s] iiij[d]. It'm I give to the mending of the hye waye vj[s] viij[d] at the discrecon of my m[r] and my curate. It'm I give to Thomas Standforthe my best paire of hoosen. It' to lytle Henry vj[d]. It'm to euery one of my m[r] s'vauntę iiij[d]. It'm to Henry Oldered, of Denton, one hole rayment at the discrecon of my m[r] Banton. It' George Mawson iiij[d]. It'm to Richard Oldred wyfe ij yardę of white-clothe. It'm to Agnes White ij yardę clothe. It'm James Braywhait iiij[s]. It'm to Agnes Thomas iiij[d]. It'm Water Steid wyfe iiij[d]. It' to Bollande wyfe iiij[d]. It'm to Harryson wyfe iiij[d]. It'm to Agnes Wodde iiij[d]. It'm to my curate iij[s] iiij[d]. It'm to s' Thom's, of Denton, vj[d]. It'm to Willyam Thomson wife vj[s] viij[d]. It'm to Thom's Plomland vij[s] being in the handę of Wilłm Slater, of Denton. It'm I geve to my syster Thackwarye vj[s] viij[d], and to ether of her childer vj[s] viij[d] yf my goodę will extende so farre. The residew of my goodę vnbequest I give to Costan Banton and to Samson Horner my brother sonne, whome I do make myne executors of this my last will, and they to dispose it for my soules helthe at the discrecon of [*sic*]. These being witnesses, Edwarde Mawson, Thomas Standforth, and Rycharde Thomas, w[th] other mo.—[*Proved* 4 *Dec.*, 1554.]

RICHARD EMSON, OF BARKSTON.

(xiv. 96 b.)

In the name of God Amen: the x[th] day of Januarye in the yeare of our lorde God a thowsande five hundrethe fiftie and thre. I Richarde Emson, of Barkston w[th]in the parishe of Sherborne, hole of mynde and of good remembraunce, makę this my testament and last will. Furst I bequeathe my soule to God Almightie and to our ladie sainct Marie and to all the celestiall companye of heaven, and my bodie to be buried whereas it shalle please God. It'm I geve to the blessed Sacramente xij[d]. It'm I geve to euerye one of my breather ij[s]. Also I geve to Thomas Dowkar my blewe jacket. It'm I geve to my mades'unte xij[d]. It'm I geve to Thomas Emson my sonne all suche goodę as shall come and discende vnto me by the last will of John Emson my father. It'm I will that if it fortune Alice my wyfe to dye before my sonne Thomas Emson shall come vnto lawfull age, that my brother John shall haue the custodie of my said sonne and all his goodę during his mynorytie. The residue of all my goodꝭ, my dettꝭ paid, I give to Alice my wife and to Thomas Emson my sonne, who I make my executors. These being witnesse, John Whaledell, John Paele, and [*sic*].—*No proof given.*

JOHN THWAITES, OF PONTEFRACT.

(xiv. 96 b.)

In the name of God Amen: I John Twaitꝭ, of Pontefracte in the countie of Yorke, yoman, the iiij[th] day of November in the yeare of our lorde God a thowsande five hundrethe fiftie and foure, hole of mynde and good remembrance, dothe ordeine and make this my testamente and last will in manner and forme that hereafter followithe. Furst I geve and bequeathe my soule in to the handꝭ and mercye of Allmightie God my maker and redemer, and to the prayer of sainct Marie the mother of our saueyor Jesus Christ, and to all the bolie companie of heaven, and my bodie to be buried w[th]in the parishe churche of Allhallows in Pontefracte nighe vnto my father. Further I will that of all suche takes and leases w[ch] I the said John Twaittꝭ had withe Jo͞hne my mother that my parte therof holy to remaigne to Izabell my wyfe and Richard my sonne after my disseas, and to haue and occupie my said ꝑte of the said takes withe the said Jo͞hne my mother duringe all the terme and yeares of the said takes. It'm I give my best hoose to Robert Sawndꝭ the younger. It'm I will that all the other my raymente be given to the poore at the discre͞con of Johne my mother and Izabell my wife. The residewe of all other my goodꝭ not bequest, my dettꝭ paid, and the funerall expens' maide the day of my buriall, I give to the [said] Izabell my wif and Richard my sonne, whome I make of this my last will my full executors to dispose my said goodꝭ to the honour of god. These being witnesses, S[r] Roger Frykeleye, preiste, Nycholas Lenthorpe, Henry Hebillthaite, withe other moo.—[*Proved* 13 *Dec.*, 1554, *by the widow. Grant reserved to the son, a minor.*]

WILLIAM COWARD, OF PONTEFRACT.

(xiv. 96 b.)

In Dei no͞ie Amen: the xxiiij[te] day of Februarye in the furst yeare of the raigne of our soueraigne Ladie Marie, quene of Inglande, Fraunce, and Irelande, Defendor of the faithe and also next vnder christ the Supreme heade of the Churche of Inglande and Irelande. I Wil͞lm Cowarde, of Pontefracte, seike in bodie and hole in mynde and remembraunce, makithe this my last will and testament in manner and forme following. Furst I geve my soule to God Allmightie my maker and redemer, and to all the blessed company in heaven, and my bodie to be buried w[th]in the churche yearde of Alhallowes in Pontefrett, or ellꝭ where yt shall please god. Also I bequeth my leasses of my mylnes to Nycholas Cowarde my brother and my pyckꝭ and chessellꝭ. Also I bequeathe to Anne my doughter my kowe. Also I geve to Emmot my doughter my white nag. Also I give to Wil͞lm my sonne the greate borde that I bought of Wil͞lm Huntenden. Allso I geve to Wil͞lm my sonne my closse. Also I geve to Jo͞hnet my wife the surrendre of my closse that I have of Wil͞lm Nels-throp. Allso I give to Anne my doughter my cownter. Allso I give to Raynolde Gibson my s'vaunte a windell of wheate and my buckskyn dowblet and a hatchet. Allso I give to John my brother my blewe cote. Allso I give to Roberte Lyster my brother in lawe my white cote. Allso I give to Nicholes my brother my trusse bed. Allso I give to Anne my doughter a greate arke. Also I give to Emmot my doughter a greate salting fat. Also I geve to Sr Anthonye Flemyng xij^d. Allso I give to Xpofer Wynsesse my bay meare and my bay nag. Also I give to my vnkle Wiłłm Clif my best dowblet. Also I give to Wiłłm *P*erson ij^s and to be honestlie aparelled. Allso I give to the poore people iij mettę of corne. All the rest of my goodę vnbequeathed, my dettę paid, my funerall expens's made, I give to Wiłłm my sonne and Anne my doughter, whome I ordeyne and make my executors. Witnesses herof, Thom's Ederington, Wiłłm Schallę, Thom's Rodwell, Wiłłm Cliffe, Anthonye Flemyng.—[*Proved* 13 *Dec.*, 1554, *to the widow, guardian of the children. minors.*]

John Watson, of Wakefield.

(xiv. 97 a.)

In the name of God Amen: the xij^th day of Julye, the yeare of our Lorde god 1554. I John Watson, of Wakefeilde, carier, wth in the countie of Yorke, ꝑfite of mynde and knowledge, makithe this my laste will and testamente in forme as here followith. Furst I geve my soule to Allmightie God, and my bodie to be buried in the Churche yarde of Wakefeilde or els where it please Allmightie God; secondely I give vnto Anne Burton my s'vande ij^s, the rest of all my goodę bothe moveable and vnmoveable I give vnto Agnes my wife and Nicholes my sonne to be devided betwixt them by even porc̃ons, whiche I make my lawfull executors, and they to discharge my dettę and funerall expens's and all other thingę. It'm I will that Wiłłm Grethed, Nycholes Rayn', and John Grethed be suꝑvisors of this my last will. These being witnesses, John Dowson, Robert Townende, of Wakefeild, and Sir Wiłłm Bawl, preiste.—[*Proved* 13 *Dec.*, 1554.]

William Plafford, of Barkston.

(xiv. 97 a.)

In the name of God Amen: the xxviij^te day of October in the yere of our Lorde god m^lccccl. I Wiłłm Plafforde, of Barkston, hole of mynde and memorie, make this my last will and testament after manner and forme following. Furst I witte my soule to God allmightie and to our ladie sanct Marie and to all the holie company of heaven, and my bodie to be buryed within the parishe churche yarde in Sherborne. I witte to my curate to pray for me iiij^d. I witte Wiłłm and Roberte my sonnes all my worke howse. I give to Alexandre my sonne vj^s viij^d. I wit to Edmonde my sonne half an acre of harlie when it is sowen. I give to Agnes my wife one litle blacke cowe and my house that I dwell in now withe all ap'teñncę belonging to the said house as longe as she lyvithe, and after her decease to John my sonne as right heare vnto the same. I give vnto Agnes my doughter a cuppborde. I wit to Jenet my doughter a brode panne. I wit to Isabell my doughter a greate cawdron, and I will that John Plafforde my sonne be suꝑvisor of this my last will and testamente, and to se that euerye one of my childer haue there right. The residewe of all my goodę not bequeathed, my dettę paid and my will fullfilled, I give and bequeathe vnto Agnes my wife and Wiłłm my sonne, whome

I make my executors of this my last will and testamente. Witnesses herof, Willm Polle and John Quardaill and John Plaisse.—[*Proved* 13 *Dec.*, 1554, *by the son. Grant reserved to the widow.*]

William Lister, of Leeds.

(xiv. 113 b.)

In the name of God Amen: the xxij° daye of January, anno D'ni 1554. I William Lister, of Leedes, being of hoole mynd and good remembrance, makith my last will and Testament in maner and furme followinge. First I give my sowle vnto Almightie Gode my maker and redemer, o^r ladie sancte Marie, and to all the blissed companie of heaven, and my bodie to be buried in the Churche yerde of Sancte Peter in Leedes. Also I give to Robert Lister my father my best jackett, my best doublet w^t hoose and showes. Also I give to Julian my wief and to her children all my hoole goodes that I the said William Lister haithe or may have, aswell xiij^s that Robert Calbecke dothe owe vnto me as all other goodes and tackkꝭ of landes, saving onelie I will that ymediatlie after that my wief do take any ma' to husband that then one litle cloose caulled haire pightill shall remane to my sayd children all yeres to come and all profettꝭ therof, and Briand Lister to have the oversight herein, and allso I make my wief my full executrix to se my children and my goodes vsed according to this my last will. Thes being wytnes, Briand Lister, Robert Lister, William Lawson, and Robert Symson.—[*Proved* 22 *June*, 1554.]

Alice Midgley, of Headingley.

(xiv. 117 a.)

In the name of God Amen: the xiiij^th daye of June in the yere of o^r lord God 1553. I Alice Migheleye, of Heddingleye, widowe, w^tin the ꝑishe of Leedes, hole of mynde and bodie and of good memorie, makes this my last will and testament in maner and furme followinge. The first I give my sowle to Almightie God my maker and redemer, and my bodie to be buried w^tin the church or churche yerde where yt shall please god that I shall die. Also I give to Eliz' my doughter five markꝭ. Also I give to Alice my doughter five m'kꝭ. Also I give to Sr John my sonne [*sic*], also I give to Jennet my doughter vj^li xiij^s iiij^d lent to her husbande Richard Saxton at mydsomer before the greete sweete. Also I give to everie s'uant dwellinge in my howse at the daye of my deathe one sheepe. Also I give to Robert Myghleye xx^s. Also I make John Kent my hoole executor to bringe me honestlie furthe of my goodes and to dispoose for my sowle as he shall thinke best to whoome I give the residew of all my goodes vnbequest. Allso I make George Marshall my brother the suꝑuisoure of this my last will and testament to se that all thingꝭ be doone accordinge to the premiss'. Thes beinge wytness', Chr̃ofer Hobson, Nicolas Claughton, Lawrance Rawson, John Hebetson, Lawrance Webster, Thomas Rawson, w^t other moo.—[*Proved* 6 *April*, 1554.]

Agnes Bound, widow, of Otley.

(xiv. 120 a.)

In Dei nõie Amen: I Agnes Bounde, widowe, of Otleye in the countie of Yorke, do make, constitute, and ordane this my last will and testament in maner and furme followinge, the fifte daye of Marche, Anno D'ni 1554, s'e'd'm computaconem Ecclie Anglicane and in the first and secund yeres of the Reignes of *P*hillipp and Marie, &c. Firstt I bequiethe my sowle to the marcie of my redemer Jesus Christ, and my bodie to be buried in the Churche mold of Otleye aforesaid, besechinge o[r] blissed ladie sancte Mary and all the fare feloshippe of heaven to praye for me, and I will y[t] my debtę shalbe paid of all my hoole goodes. That done and my bodie brought furthe after the custome of neighborehead I bequieth to Dorithe Sikes one bedde and a bedde cloose. Also I bequiethe vnto Jenet Webster, of Foston, one brasse pott. The residewe of all my goodes moveable and vnmoveable not bequested and all dettę owne to me, my debttę paide, my funerall expn's's deducted, I give to Dorithe my doughter, whome I make my sowle executrix of this my last will and testament. And the right worshipfull my M[r] M[r] Francis *P*almes I make oversear of the same. Thes beinge witnes, S[r] Anthonie Jackeson, clerke, George Wharton, of Otleye, and Thomas Dunwell, of the same, yoma', the day and yere abouesaid.—[*Proved* 18 *April*, 1555.]

WILLIAM SCALES, OF *P*ONTEFRACT.

(xiv. 125 b.)

In Dei nōie Amen: the xxv[th] daye of Marche in the first and secund yere of the Reigne of *P*hillippe and Marie by the grace of god Kinge and Quene of England, France, Neapolis, J'r'lm, and Ierland, Defendors of the fathe, prince of Spane and Cicilie, Archduke of Austrie, Duke of Millan, Burgond, and Brabant, Countess' of Adspurge, Flanders, and Tiroll. I Wilłm Seailles, of Pontifract, seke in bodie and good and ꝑfyte in remembrance, makethe this my last will and testament in maner and furme folowinge. Firste I give and bequieth my sowle to God Almighti my onelie maker and redemer, and to the blissed companie of heaven, and my bodie to be buried w[t]in the ꝑishe Churche yerde of Alhallowes in *P*ontifracte or ellę where yt shall please God. It'm I give to euerie one of my seven children seven poundes Tenne shillings for ther childes porcõns of my goodes, And yf yt fortune any of them to die then ther ꝑte to retorne and remane to thuse of them that be livinge. It'm I give to Lionell my brother a cote and iij[s] iiij[d] in moneye. It'm to Antonie my brother a coote. It'm to Francę my brother a Coote. It'm to Richard my brother a cote yf they be good to my wicf and my children. It'm I give to Thomas my sonne my burgage. It'm I give to Boniface Savage my freese gowne. And I woll and desier the said Boniface to be the Superuisor of this my will and testament. All the rest of my goodes bothe moveable and vnmoueable and leasses and tackes vnbequiethed, my debtę paid, my funerall exp'ns's maid, I give to Jennet my wief whome I ordanc and make my sole executrix. Wytnesse hereof, Thomas Holgate, maior of the same Towne, Bonniface Savage, William Holgate, and William Gretehead, and Anthonie Fleminge, preste.—[*Proved* 29 *April*, 1555.]

WILLIAM RAWLING, OF *P*ONTEFRACT.

(xiv. 136 a.)

In the name of God amen: I William Raulinge, of Pontefracte w[t]in the countie of Yorke, Cordiner, hole of mynde and ꝑfite rememberaunce, the secunde of December in the firste yeare of the reigne of our most sou'ande Ladye quene Marye by the grace of God of Ingland, Fraunce and Irelond quene, doothe maike this my last will or testament in this man' and forme folowinge. Fyrste I bequithe my soule to Almyghtie God my redemer and savior, and my bodie to [be] buryed in my ꝑishe churche yearde of All Sainetes at Pomfret. Also I bequithe to Margaret my wyfe x^{s} wiche is in the handꝭ of my brother Johne Rawlyn. Also I bequithe to my saide wyffe foure stones of talowe wiche is in my brother handꝭ for the wyche talowe I haue paid him. Also I will that my doughter Elesbeth shall haue for hir childes portyon xl^{s}. Also I bequithe to my brother Johne foure stones of talowe wiche he haith in his custodie. Also I bequithe to Xpofer Wilbarne a blew jacket and a fusthane dublet. Also I bequithe to Robert Raulyn iij^{s} iiij^{d} wiche is in my brother Johne handꝭ. Also I bequithe to Johne Smythe iij^{s} iiij^{d} wiche is in my brother John handꝭ. Also I bequethe to Edmonde Raulin iij^{s} iiij^{d} wiche is in my brother Johne handꝭ. Also I bequithe to my brother Robert Raulyn my violet jacket. The resydew of all other my goodꝭ not bequest, dettꝭ and portions dischargid, I will that they be at the ordere of Margret my wyffe, whome I maike my hole executrix. In wytnes herof, my brother Johne Rawlyn, bruyster, and my curett o' Willm Chamber and s^{r} Richard Rydall, w^{t} other moo.—[*Proved* 10 *May*, 1554.]

ROBERT BEMUNDE, OF THORPE ON THE HILL.

(xiv. 136 b.)

In the name of God Amen: the sevent day of Aprill, the yere of owre Lorde god a thowsand five hundrethe fyfte and iiij. I Robert Bemunde, of Thorp of the hill in the ꝑishe of Rothwell, holle of mynde and good remembraunce, thankꝭ be to God, maikꝭ this my last will and testament after this furme folowinge. Firste I bequith my soull to god Almyghti and to o^{r} ladie sainete Marye and to all the celestiall company of heaven, and my body to be buried in the churche yearde of the blyssyd trynite of Rothwell. Item I bequithe vnto the blessed sacrament of the alter viij^{d}. Item to Raiffe Roidhouse xx^{s}. Item to Johne his sonne an iron chimney. Item to Robert his sonne my beste jaket and best howse [? hose]. Item to Agnes Radhowse my doughter iij^{s} iiij^{d}. Item to Elsabethe and Jennet my doughters all my woll spone and vnspone. Item to Thomas Rodhowse a yowe and a lambe. Item to Charles Prest iij^{s}. Item to Methlay bryge ij^{s}. The residew of my goodꝭ, my dettꝭ paide and funerall expencꝭ mayde, I gyve to Johne my sonne and Elsabeth and Jenett my doughters, the whome I maike my executors. Thes witness's, Mr William Gascoinge, thelder, William Scholꝭ, Rayffe Scoles, Johne Armitage, w^{t} others.—[*Proved* 10 *May*, 1554.]

JOHN EMSON, OF NEWTON KYME.

(xiv. 141 a.)

In the name of God Amen: I John Emson, of the ꝑishe of Newton Kyme, in ꝑfite mynde and goode remembrance, the xxij daye of January in the yere of oure lorde God a thousande fyve hundreth fiftie and thre, makꝭ my testament and last will in manner and forme followinge. Firste I bequeth my soull to almightie God my maker and to his onelie sonne

Jhu christe my lorde and Savior, in whome I putt the holl hope and truste of my salvacion throughe the merites of his blissed passion, and my bodie to be buried in the church yerde of the aforsaid Newton Kyme. Also I bequeath my lande in Southmylforth felde and my medewe to John my eldest sonne. Also I bequeath the intereste of my farmhold to Anne my wif for terme of here lif, and after her tyme to John myne eldest sonne and William my yongeste sonne for the space of towe yeres indifferentalie to be occupied betwene theme, and afterwarde to the forsaid William my holl intereste therof. Also I bequeath to Thomas my sonne a blake stott and a brended. Also I bequeath to Thomas Emson my godson all my shepe that I haue with his father. Also I bequeath to Richarde my sonne an oxe and a cowe havinge the vse of theme all redie. Also I bequeath to John my eldeste sonne the yongest graye maire and to William my sonne a bay stagge. Also I bequeath all my other goodes both moveable and vnmoveable to Anne my wif, to John, to Richarde, to Thomas, and William my sonnes, whome I make full executors of this my last will. Witnesses herof, Richarde Shipley, Georgie Cawode, and Couenant Stevenson. —[*Proved* 28 *June*, 1554, *by Agnes, the widow, John, Thomas, and William, Richard being dead.*]

John Blathwate, of East Keswick, Husbandman.

(xiv. 142 a.)

In the name of God Amen: in the yere of oure lorde God a thousande fyve hundreth fiftie and towe, the xij[th] daye of Julie. I John Blathwate, husbandman, of Estkeswike within the pish of Harwode, make my will and testament in this forme followinge. First I bequest my soull to God Almightie that created and bought it, and my bodie to be buried within the holie sanctuarie at Harwode church. I will to my wif Elisabeth and to my thre doughters, Elisabeth, Isabell, and Dorothie, the goode will of my farmhold duringe the terme of my yeres as my lease specifieth; if my wif Elisabethe departe within my terme of yeres it to remayne to my doughter Elisabeth; if Elisabeth departe and die I will my forsaid farmhold to Isabell; if Isabell die I witt it to Dorothie. Wher I ame dettable to Richarde Appleyerde thre pounde of his portion or barne parte I will it shalbe maid forthe iiij[li], my bodie buried and funerall chardges dispatched and my dette paid, and if my parte of my goodes, my dette to be paid and that leaves of my parte of the goodes to be devided to my wif Elisabeth and to my thre doughters. Also I ordan and make my wif Elisabeth and my thre doughters myne executrices for to se the pformance of this my will and testament after the order of the lawe for the health of my soull. Witnesses, John Plesington, Nicholas Rowley, John Sutton, William Preston, clerke, with other.—[*Proved* 9 *July*, 1554, *by the widow. Grant reserved to the three daughters.*]

Anthony Mawde, of Otley.

(xiv. 146 a.)

In Dei nōie Amen: the xiiij[th] daye of Marche in the yere of oure lorde God a m[l]v[c]lj. I Anthony Mawde, of Otteley, of holl myud and good remembrance, make this my laste will and testamente in manner and forme followunge. First I bequeath my soull to almightie God my maker and redemer, and my bodie to be buried in the churche of Otteley. Item I giue and bequeath to Jennet my wif all my holl landę in Otteley and Farneley, both copiehold and frehold, duringe here widuehede paynge yerlie to Dorothie Mawde my doughter the some of foure markę duringe the lif of the said Dorothie if it chaunce she amend not of here dissease. And if it chaunce that she amend I will that she shall haue asmoche money rune of the pffettę of the said landes as other of my children shall haue to there portions and no more. Also I will that my said wif shall kepe my thre sonnes at scole vnto such tyme as they shalbe able to be apprentice. Item I will that my said wif shall paye to everie one of my children the some of sex shillingę and eight pence of the proffettę of the said landes at suche tyme as they shall marie or be lowsse of prentishipe. And if it chaunce that my said wif marie then I will that all the proffettę of all my land shall go to the proffet of my childer at the discression and order of my supvisors vnto suche tyme as my sonne William come to the full adge of xxj yeres. Item I giue and bequeath to everie one of my bretherne and susters vj^s viij^d. Item I giue to William Fletcher vj^s viij^d. Item I giue to Elisabethe my serunte and Agnes Burnet either of theme a gymber lambe. Item I giue to everie one of my god children iiij^d. Item I giue xx^s to power people in Otteley wher moste nede is. Item I giue to John Lyndley, of Farneley, my wynter cote. Item I will that my lease whiche I bought of Gerrot Whetley be sold and the pffet therof to paye my dettę at the order of my supvisors. The Reste of my goodes, I honestlie brought forthe, my dettę paid, my legaces and funerall expenses dischardged, I giue to Jennet my wif and vnto all my childrene salvinge William and Dorothie. And I make my said wif, John and Nicholas my sonnes, Anne and Jennet my doughters, my executors of this my last will and testament. Also I make William Mawde my father and Chrofer Mawde and Chrofer Waid my supvisors of this my last will and testament to se it pformed and I bequeath everie of theme iij^s iiij^d for ther paynes. Thes witnesses, George Pullan, Chrofer Cave, Chrofer Waid, and other moo.—[*Proved* 11 *August*, 1554, *by John, son of deceased. Grant reserved to Jane, Nicholas, and Ann, children.*]

John Nettleton, of Leeds.

(xiv. 147 a.)

In the name of God Amen: the xixth daye of Julie in the yere of oure lorde god a m^l v^c liiij. I John Nettleton, of Ledes in the countie of [York], by the visitacion of God seke of bodie but by his grace of good and pfite memorie, doth make, ordan, and constitute this my last will and testament in manner and forme followinge. Firste I bequeath my soull to the grete mercie of the almightie lorde J'hu christe, trusting by the meritę of his passion to be one of those that shalbe saved. And I bequeth my bodie to be buried within the pishe churche of Ledes. Also I bequeath to Jennet Nettleton, Agnes Nettleton, and Sibill Nettelton, my doughters, nowe vnmaried, to everie one of them twentie markę in full satisfaction and payment of there holl childer portions of all my goodes. Also I will and bequeathe that Jennet my wif shall haue all my landes and tenementę duringe her naturall lif, and after here decease my close called Scott mylne close boundinge of the rige in Vodehousę nerę Ledes to the vse of Thomas Nettleton my sonne and his heres for ever after the custome of the manner, and my other closse lienge betwene Knowstrope and hill housebankꝭ to the vse of the said Thomas and his heres paynge therfore twentie markꝭ of good and laufull money of England, wherof vj^{li} xiij^{s} iiij^{d} to be paide to Sibill my said doughter and the other vj^{li} xiij^{s} iiij^{d} to be equallie devided betwene Anne, Jennet, and Agnes, my doughters, imediatelie after the decease of Jennet my wif, or within one half yere then next after. Also I bequeath my best cote or jackett to William Mighley, my next jackett to Thomas Nettleton my sonne, and to Robt Nettleton my brother one other jackett or dublett. The Residue of all my goodes and cattallꝭ, my dettꝭ paide, funerall expens' deducte, I giue and bequeath to Jennet my wif, whome I do make and ordan my full executrix of this my last will and testament, in the presence of Richard Sympson, John Heyton, Thomas Cowꝑ, William Hargrave, Robt Settill, Richarde Walge, William Waide, William Cowper, with other.—[*Proved* 14 *August*, 1554.]

———

ROBERT WARD, OF LUMBY.

(xiv. 163 a.)

In the name of God Amen: the x daye of December in the yere of o^{r} lord god a thowsand five hundrithe fiftie and fower. I Robert Warde, of Lamebie w^{t}in the ꝑishe of Shereburn, hole of mynde and of good Remembrance, makꝭ this my Testament and last will in manner followinge. First I give and bequieth my sowle to almightie god, requiringe the blissed virgin Mary and all the hollie companie of heaven to be mediators for me, and my bodie to be buried w^{t}in the churche earthe of all Sanctes in Shereburn. It'm I give to my Curet for tiethes forgotten xij^{d}. It'm I give to the churche workꝭ iij^{s} iiij^{d}. It'm I give to Sr Robert Blaunche iiij^{d}. It'm I give to Hewghe Atkinson x^{li}, one Quarter of Barleye, and one Barewane. It'm I give to Johnne Atkinson ij Bushelles of malte. It'm I give to the same John ij Bushellꝭ of haver. It'm I give to Thomas Richardson ij Bushellꝭ of Barleye. It'm I give to William Atkinson one Quarter of Barleye. It'm I give to Johnne Mowes ij bushellꝭ of Barleye. It'm I give to Lancelot Witleye ij Bushellꝭ of Barleye. It'm I give to Johnne Warde the Lease of my farmeold at Lumbey after the decease of Margaret my wief. It'm I give to Johnne Warde ij Bushellꝭ of barleye. It'm I give to Johnne Warde the doughter of Jenkin Warde ij Bushellꝭ of Barleye. It'm I give to Agnes Browne ij Bushellꝭ of Barleye. It'm I give to Hewghe Atkinson and to his heires for ever one beast gaite in Lumbeye pastures, the whiche I bought of Johnne Owldret. The residue of all my goodes, my debte and legacꝭ paid and my bodie honestlie brought furthe, I give vnto Margaret my wief and vnto Johnne Warde, Alice Warde, and to Margaret Ward, whoo I make myne executors. Wytness' hereof, Mathewe Smitheson, my curet, Sr Robert Blaunche, Johnne Battell, John Watkin, and John Warde, w^{t} other.—[*Proved* 25 *May*, 1555.]

———

WILLIAM WOODHOUSE, OF SHERBURN.

(xiv. 178 a.)

In the name of God Amen: in the yere of oure lorde god 1554 and the xiiij daye of Marche. I Willm Woodhouse, of Shereborne, being hole of mynde and of perfite remembraunce, thanckes be vnto allmightie god, being diseased and sicke in my bodye, ordeynes and makes this my laste will and testamente in manner and forme following. Furst I bequethe my sowle to God, ore ladie saincte Marie, and to all the Celestiall Companye of heaven, and my bodie to be buryed within the Churche yerde of All hallowes of Shereborne, nere vnto my grandfather. Also I bequethe to the blessed Sacramente for tithes and oblacons forgotten ij^s. It'm I bequethe xx^s to be distributed to poore people the daye of my buryall. Also I bequethe my sonne John to my brother John Calverd, and to haue the rewle, governaunce, and keping of hym to he come to his laufull age of xxj^ti yeres, and to haue his porcon and all his goodes with hym. Allso I bequeth to my brother Thomas Thorneton my sonne Thomas, and to haue hym and all his porcon and goodes to he come to his full age of xxj yeres if it shall please hym to take hym. Also I give and bequethe to my vnkle Wm Willson and to Thomas Thorneton the residewe of all those yeres that shalbe vnexpired and vnronne at the daye of my dethe, of all those landes and tenementes that my brother Thomas ded geve me by his laste will, and theye to paye the yerelie Rente therefore. And I will that my wife shall paye aleven poundes for thre yeres Rente by past at the making thereof of the said Landes. Also I give to Thomas my sonne and Agnes my doughter the yerely rentes and proffettes growing or comyng of Edwarde Hallele house wch I haue by copie of the Courte for certeyne yeres yet enduring. Itm. I geve vnto John Thailer prest, to praye for my soule and all Christen soules, xij^d. The residewe of my goodes, my dettes paid and funeralls discharged, I give and bequethe them to Agnes my wife, John, Thomas, and Wm Woodhous, my sonnes, Agnes and Isabell my doughters, whome I make and orden my full executors of this my laste will and testamente. And if my said wyfe shall fortune to be withe childe, then if god sende it into the worlde, then I will it shalbe full executor withe all other afforesaide. These witness', Thomas Morret, Symon Barmby, John Hillome, with others and Thomas Thorneton.—[*Proved* 18 *October*, 1555, *by the widow. Grant reserved to the children.*]

THOMAS WILLIAMSON, OF MICKLEFIELD.

(xiv. 200 a.)

In the name of god Amen: in the yere of our lorde a thowsande fiue hundrethe fiftie and foure, the xxvth daye of Januarye. I Thomas Wyllmson, of Mikelfeilde in the pishe of Shereburne, of hoole mynde and remembraunce, makithe this my laste will in manner and forme following. furst I bequeth my soule to Allmightie god and to our Lady sanct Marye and to all the celestiall company of heaven, and my bodye to be buryed in the parishe Churche yerde of Shereborne. Allso I ordeyne and make my wyfe and my two children, Henry Willmsonne and John, my full executors. And if it please god that my wife be wth childe it shalbe as forderly in the goodes as any of the other. And allso I give to the blessed Sacramente vj^d. Item I give to Sr John Taylar viij^d. It'm I give to Sr Robert Blaunche iiij^d. It'm I give to Richard Willmson my sonne xx^s. And allso I will that Mr Henry Gascoigne haue Richarde my sonne and the xx^s to the behove of the said Ric. my sonne to he come of lefull [age]. The residewe of all my goodes not bequests, my dettes and my funerall expens's maid aboute my buriall, I give them to my wife and to my two children Henry Willmson and John. Recorders hereof, Henry Gascoigne, gentleman, John Hawghton, John Robson, and John Walkar. —[*Proved* 14 *November*, 1555, *by the widow. Grant reserved to the children.*]

RALPH STANDFIELD, OF OTLEY.

(xiv. 206 a.)

In the name of God Amen: the eight day of Julye in the yere of our lord god 1555. I Rauf Standfeild, of Otleye in the Countie of Yorke, yoman, being of hoole mynde and stedfaste memorye, makithe this my last will and Testament in manner and forme following. Furst I bequethe my soule to the mercye of my Redemer Jesu chryste, and my bodye to be buryed in the Church yerde of Otteleye aforesaid, beseching o[r] blessed Lady St. Marye and all the sanctes in heaven to praye for me. Allso I will that my body be brought fourthe after the discrec̃on of Alice my wyfe and Christopher my sonne wth the Councell and aduyce of S[r] Christopher Wayde, clarke, and John Dycconson. It'm I bequethe to Nicholas Daide iij ewes and allso to Jenet Smythe iij ewes, and to Elyn Haddilscie one ewe and one lambe or elles one calf. Also I will that Alice my wyfe and Chr̃ofer my sonne shall haue all my landes and ten'tę equally deuyded betwix' theme so longe as she shall lyve and after her decease to remayne hoolye to the said Chr̃ofer. Allso I do give all my goodes moveable and vnmoueable, and all the dettes owing to me, to my said wife and Chr̃ofer my sonne, equallye to be deuyded betwix' them saue onely xx[tie] markes, whiche my said wife shall dispose vnto the children of my two doughters at suche tyme as she shall thincke conuenient necessary and requysite, vpon condic̃on that nether my said doughters nor their husbandes shall vex, trowble, or sewe for any other childes porc̃on my executors iointlye nor seuerallye, and if they be not thus contente nether they nor there children to haue any peny but as they shall recover by the lawe. Allso I make my executors Alyce my wyfe and Chr̃ofer my sonne of this my laste will and Testamente, and S[r] Xpofer Wayde and John Dycconson supervisors of the same, geving vnto ether of them viij[s] for their paynes taking, and allso as oft as nede shall require their reasonable costes and charges to be borne in all thinges concerning the fullfillyng of this my last will and Testamente by my said executors. Thes being witnes, Sr Anthonye Jackson, clarke and curate of Ottley, Sr Xpofer Waide, clarke, and John Dicconson, wth other moo.—[*Proved* 13 *August*, 1555.]

ROBERT WALTON, OF PONTEFRACT.

(xiv. 206 b.)

In Dei nõie Amen: the xvij[th] day of [*sic*] A[o] Dni 1555. I Roberte Walton, of Pontefracte in the Countie of Yorke, clothedryver, do make my testam[t] and laste will in manner and forme following. Furst I bequethe my soule to Almightye god, to our Ladye sainct Marye, and to all the blessed companye of heaven, and my bodye to be buryed in the Church yerde of Englisthorpp right ouerthwarte the Churche porche. It'm I bequeathe to the highe Aultare of my parishe Churche in Pountefracte for my Tythes neglygently forgotten xx[d]. It'm I will that a coumbe of wheate and a coumbe of malte shuld be delte amongest poore folkes at the markit crosse of Pontefracte the next market day after M'ty'mas daye. I praye my wyfe to bestowe more Allmesse at her discrecon where she and Sr Thomas Huntington shall thinke moste nedefull. It'm I give vnto Thomas and John Warde to eche of them a jacket clothe desiaring them to make labor for to get a new leasse in my house of Mr Hunte, and yf theye can not get it than to breake the matter to Mr Nicholes Sayvell and to Mr Furnes desiaring them to breake this matter to Mr Sayvill, knight, and put him in remembraunce of me and my poore wyfe and my children. I will that my wyf send hym ij capons. It'm I give my brother Leonarde the graye hoose clothe and the yelowe wch I had withe me at this tyme. It'm I give to my brother Medleye my dagger. It'm I will that Edwarde Watton give vnto Thomas Yuce viijs. It'm I give vnto John Stagge a pair of hoose clothe. It'm I give to Thom's Graue, of Lynne, for discharging of me of a certeyne Stewardshippe of a cockit ais he knowethe xijs whiche Mr Graye, of Bury, oweth me. It'm The rest of all my goods not bequeathed, leasses and tackes, in farmes and landes now in my occupying, I will that all together wth all my substaunce be equallye deuyded in iij partes, whereof I give to my wyfe the thirde pte and the other ij partes to be equalye deuyded betwix' my foure children. It'm I give vnto Robert my sonne a Burgesseshippe lying in bondgaite in Pountefracte. It'm I will that he and his porcon of my goodes rem' in the custodye of Sr Thomas Huntington, p'son of Ackworthe, my speciall good freinde. It'm I will that Henry my sonne remayne still with his mother till he be iij yeres olde and than my brother Leonarde to haue hym and his parte of my goodes. It'm I will that Anne shalbe at the keping of my two systers Beatrix and Elizabethe, and theye to receyve her porcon, laying on sufficient sureties to paye her the same agayne whan she shall come to laufaill aige. It'm I will that Margaret and her parte shulde remayne still wth her mother, and in case be that any of my forsaid children shulde dye I will that his or her parte shulde be equallye deuyded amo'gest the rest of my children. Fynally I make my wyfe my sole executrix, she to receyve my dette and paye my dette. It'm I will that Sr Thom's Huntington, person of Ackworthe, shulde be supervisour and he to haue for his labour a paire of hoose clothe of Westron Carseye. Wytness', Mr. Phillyp Silke, psonne of Englisthorpe, Xpofer Bowling, Wylłm Burdon, Godfraye Cooke, wth other.—[*Proved* 12 *August*, 1555.]

Robert Rowley, of East Rigton, Husbandman.

(xiv. 207 a.)

In the name of God Amen: in the yere of or Lorde God 1553, and in the vijth yere of Kinge Edwarde the vjth. I Roberte Rouley, of the eist Righton in the countie of Yorke, husbandman, makethe my laste will and Testamente, being of hoole mynde and not sicke in mann' and forme following. Furst I bequethe my soule to Allmightie God, our Lady saint mary, and to all the hoolye companye of heaven, my bodye to be buried in Bardesaye Churche yerde. Item I will that my executors give iiijd to foure poore men. It'm I will Thomas Rouley, sonne of Xpofer Rouleye my sonne, whose soule god pardon, haue thre pounde in full paymt, satisfaccon, and recompence of his childes parte, and all other legaces and promises of goodes to hym by me mayd. It'm I make Nycholes Rouley my sonne executor, and he to delyuer my sonne Thomas Rouleye his barne parte as he haithe p'mysed me, twentie nobles whan the said Thomas thinckes good, and haue nede therof after my deathe. It'm I give the residew of all my goodes, my dettes paid, all expens's allowed, to the said Nicholas my executor to his vse and to dispose at his discretion. In witness' hereof, Xpofer Marshall thelder and John Haireclyf.—[*Proved 5 August,* 1555.]

JOHN SKIPTON, OF *P*ONTEFRACT, ALDERMAN.[1]

(xiv. 208 a.)

In the name of God Amen: the ixth daye of June in the yere of our Lorde God 1555. I John Skipton, of Pontefracte within the countie of Yorke, alderman, makithe my laste will and Testamente in manner and forme following. Furst I bequethe my soule to Allmightye god my maker and Redemer, and my bodye to be buryed in the pishe Church of Pontefracte aforesaid. It'm I bequethe to the highe waye namede Bondgate vj^s^ viij^d^, and to Beighall brig vpwarde vj^s^ viij^d^. It'm I bequethe to either myne apprentic̷ xiij^s^ iiij^d^, and to either of them a yowe and a wether shepe. It'm to Willm Richardson vj^s^ viij^d^. It'm I give to Henry Skypton and his heires for euer one hous in Pontefracte next vnto Tatams house rented yerely at vj^s^. It'm I give to Thomas Skipton, sonne of John Skipton my sonne, one house in *P*ont' aforesaid nowe in the tenure of Henrye Hewit, and to his heires for euer. It'm I bequethe to Willm Skipton sonne of Wyllm Skipton laite dwelling in *P*ont' in a streate there called roper gaite, nowe depted, one howse in the same strete wth thapp'tennc̷, nowe in the tenure of Thomas Heptenstall, to hym and his beires for euer. And I will that Leonarde Helaghe shall haue thorder and gou'naunce therof and allso to lette, take, and receive the rentes and profett̷ therof comynge and arysing, making the said Wyllm accompte therof whan he shall come to full aige. It'm I give to Willm Skipton my sonne all my copieholde lande not surrendred and the hous that he nowe dwellithe in wth v acres belonging to the same of lande, and also one close called Denvell cont' iij acres, also one close lying in the northe feilde conteyning half an acr' lying betwix' the landes of the laite monasterye of Pountfracte on the northe and the landes of Wyllm Ellys of the southe, two acres and a half of Lande in the north feilde and half an acre in the myddle taythx, and allso one house wth thapp'tennc̷ vpon monckhill in the tenure of John Jackson, and one laithe wth a garthe nowe in the tenure of Robert Childe, to haue and to holde all the closes, landes, houses wth thapp'tennc̷, to the said Wyllm Skipton and to his beires for euer. Item I give vnto John Skipton, my yonger sonne, one house wth thapp'tennc̷ in Pontfracte wherin I dwell, one howse wth thapp'tennc̷ nowe in the tenure and occupacon of wid' Tatam, wth ij acres of lande p'chased of Henry Furnis lying nere the well close head. Allso one close called *P*arke close lying betwix' the landes of Roberte Malet of the east and the landes late Rich'de Rydiall of the west. Allso one close in feryfriston lying betwix the cowe close at Ferybrig of the east and the landes of Sr Wyllim Vavasour of the west, wth thre acr'

(1) The will of his widow is given on p 66.

and one rode of lande p'chased of Thomas Wentworth lying in shooell broodes, and allso one house wth app'tennce in the Bayly now in the tenure of Thomas Barker. To haue and to holde all the said landes, closes, and howses wth thapp'tennce to the said John Skipton to hym and his heires for euer. It'm I giue and bequeth to my said sonne John Skypton and to his heires for euer one house in Pontfracte lying in the Baylye and one acr' of lande lying on the gallowe hill purchased of Thomas Wentworth. It'm I give vnto my said sonnes Wyllm Skipton and John Skipton twentie poundes to be deuyded betwix' them. It'm I bequethe to Wyllm Spence, my syster sonne, if he be lyving, vj^li^ xiij^s^ iiij^d^, to be paid by my sonne John Skipton. It'm I give to Effphm Hodgeshon my god doughter iij^s^ iiij^d^, a yowe and a wedder sheepe. It'm I give to John Skipton and his heires, sonne of Richarde Skipton my brother, deceassed, one house in Pountfract in the ledder m'kite now in the tenure of [*blank*] Spence, condicionally that he nor his beires shall not alyene nor sell the same. It'm I give to Johannet Dingdaile iij^s^ iiij^d^, a yowe and a wedder sheppe. It'm to John Richardson my godsonne a yowe and a lambe. It'm to Johannet Hurst xij^d^. It'm to Esabell Hurst xij^d^. It'm to Robert Walton, sonne of Robert Walton, deceassed, iij^s^ iiij^d^. It'm to Willm Helaighe, sonne of Leonarde Helaighe, iij^s^ iiij^d^. It'm to Emmot Firth ij^s^. It'm to Alice Shann my s'vaunte ij^s^. It'm to Wyllm Wyllson ij^s^. It'm to Anne Skipton, doughter of my son John Skipton, xx^s^. It'm to Agnes Skipton, doughter of Wyllm Skipton, deceased, vj^s^ viij^d^. It'm I give to Johannet Hodgeshon, doughter of Wyllyam Hodgeshon, deceased, vj^s^ viij^d^. The Residewe of all my goodes and catalles moueable and vnmoueable, my dette and legacies paid and my funeralles discharged, I give them frely and hoolye to Agnes Skipton my wyfe, whome I make sole executrix of this my laste will and testamente, and further that my said executrix shall during her naturall lyfe haue, holde, occupie, and allso taike and receive the rente and profette of all my said landes, closes, houses, whatsoeuer theye be before bequethed and not bequethed during her said lyfe. Also I make Richarde Wilbore of Pont', alderman, James Brokesbank, Robert Vsher, and Wyllm Norton supvisours of this my wyll and testamente, to see all thinges done according to the trewe meanyng therof, and euery of them to haue a pece vj^s^ viij^d^. These being witness', Nicholas Carlyll, Edward Rusbye, Leonarde Helaighe, Richarde Tatam, Lyonell Mexboroughe, Roberte Poole, Willm Wyllson, and John Tailer, w^t^ other moo. Item I give vnto my said sonnes Wyllm Skipton and John Skipton, and to their heirs for euer, five acr' of errable lande lying and being in the northe feilde of Pount'fracte, purchaside of Roberte Eldesleye, to be equally deuyded betwix them. These witness', Richarde Wilbore, of Pount'fracte, Alderman Richard Tatam, Robert Poole, Edwarde Rusbye, Willm Richardson, and Robert Shiplaye.—[*Proved 29 July*, 1555.]

KATHERINE APPLEYARD, OF THORP ON THE HILL.

(xiv. 190 b.)

In Dei nōie Amen: A^o^ D'ni 1554, the fyrste day of October. I Katheryn Appleyerde, of Thorpe on the hill, beinge at this present tyme seke of bodye, holl and pfyte of mynde and remembrance, maketh this my laste will and testamente in maner and forme following. Fyrst I bequeath my soull vnto God allmightie, to our lady sancte Mary, and to all the blyssed companye of heven, and my body to be buried w^th^in the churche yerde [of] Roythwell. Item I bequeath vnto the hygh alter of Roythwell for forgotten tythes xij^d^. It'm I bequeath vnto the vse of the said churche of Roythwell xiij^s^ iiij^d^. Item I bequeath to be delte emonge the poore folkes at the day of my buriall vj^s^ viij^d^. The reste of my gooddes and cattels moveable and vnmoveable, my dettę and legacies paid and my buriall honestely furth, I bequeath vnto Wiłłm Leghte and John Burnell, whome I make my executors of this my laste will and testamente, and also I make Mr. Wiłłm Gascogne, esquier, the eldest, the supvysor of this my laste will, &c. Thes beinge wytnesses, Wiłłm Gascogne, senior, armiger, Johannes Beamonde, Johannes Clif, Eliz. Townende, p me Wiłłm Foster.—[*Proved* 3 *April*, 1555.]

ROBERT PAWSON, OF FARNLEY.

(xiv. 239 a.)

In the name of God amen: the xxvij day of May in the yere of our lorde God a Thowsande fyve hundrethe fyftie and foure. I Roberte Pawson, of Farneley in the countie of Yorke, whole of mynde and of good and pfite remembrance, maketh and ordeyn this my last will and testament in maner and furme folowinge. Firste I bequithe my sowle to God Almightie my Creator and redemer, desiringe our blyssed ladie and all the hollie sainetę in heaven to pray for me and wth me that my soull may reste imongę the elect people of God in heaven, and my body to be buryed w^th^in the churche yearde of Otley, my pishe churche, and also my mortuary to be paid as the Lawe will. Item I will that my goodę shalbe devided in thre partes, that is to say, one p'te to my selfe, an other pte to my wife, and the thirde pte to my children. Item I give to Grace my doughter xx^s^ towardę her mariage, and x shepe wiche is hir owne, and also one kirtill. Item I give to Anne my doughter a girdill and ij shepe, and the same girdill to be in hir mother kepinge so longe as she kepis hir my wiffe. Item I give to William my sonne all my workinge gear p'teninge my occupacion, and foure dusson of shepe ledder. Item I give to Mr. Johne Fawkes my maister my best syluer spone desiringe him to be good m^r^ to my wiffe and my children. Also I geve to maister Richard Fawkes iij^s^ iiij^d^. Item I geve to Anthony and Olin' my sonnes aither of thame twoo shepe and to Christ'er and Johne my sonnes aither of them a whye and also to the said Anne my doughter a gowne and a kirtill. Item I geve to Margaret myne aunte certayne close, and to Jenet my aunte a peticote and a napperon, and I geve to Dorothe Dibbe a gimmer, and to Anne Jeffray a yowe and a lambe, and also if Elizabeth my wife be wth childe at my deathe I will that the same childe haue it porcion of my goodę as other of my children haith. Item I gyve xij^d^ to a mendinge of the highe waye betwixt Otley and Farneley, and I owe other xij^d^ wiche Richarde Pawson gave to the same vse. The residewe of my goodę I honestlie broughe furthe shalbe equallie devided emongę my children, and I maike the said Eliz' my wyffe and William my sonne my executorę, and I desier Nicholas Pawson and William Dibbe to be my supvisores, desiringe them to se this my said will fulfilled in all causes. Thes be wytnesses, Thomas Dunwell, Thomas Cave, Johne Teale.—[*Proved* 12 *May*, 1555, *by the widow. Grant reserved to the son.*]

Ellis Rayner, of Birstall.

(xiv. 242 b.)

In Dei nōie Amen: the xxiiijth daye of Auguste in the yere of our lorde God 1553. I Ellys Rayner, of the ꝑishing of Burstall, of hoole mynde, makithe my laste will in forme following. Furst I bequethe my soule to God Allmightie and to the companye of our blessed Ladye sainete Mary and to all the saintes in heaven, and my bodye to be buryed in the Churche yarde of Burstall of the hoolly apostles Peter and Poolle. In p'mis the hous and croft withall the lande therto belonging that I purchased at Wyscardhill which is nowe in the tenure and occupacōn of Costyn Fowler, I gyve it hoolly to Wyllm Rayner my sonne and his heires for euer. Item the house and crofte wthall the landes yrto belonging in lytle Gomersall nowe in the tenure and occupacōn of Wyllm Lang, I give them hoollye to George Rayner my sonne and his heires for ever. It'm I will that all my hoole goodes be set in thre partes, one parte to bring me fourthe at the tyme of my buriall to contente all manner of dettes and paye all my dettes, and another p'te of my goodes and landes to my wyfe according to the lawe, and the laste parte I give to all my children savinge Wyllm and George my sonnes shalbe contente wth suche lande as I haue given them. And allso John my sonne shall haue no hoill parte but some thinge to be rewarded wthall at sight of Marmaduke Rayner, Lyonell Rayner, Thom's Goodall, and Peter Stublaye, wch iiij men I desire and put in truste for me to be suꝑvisors of this my laste will. Fynallye I make Elizabethe my wyfe, Wyllm and George Rayner my sonnes, my full and laufull executors after my deceasse, desiaring my fore naymed suꝑvisors to be good to my wyfe and my children as my speciall truste is in them. Moreouer yf any thinge remayne of my parte of goodes, all dettes and dewties contente and paid, I will that my suꝑvisors devyde it to my youngest children at theire discrecōns as they thincke moste nede. These men being wytnes, Thomas Gom'sall, Thomas Clarkson, Robert Norton, and Barnerde Lylle.—[*Proved* 19 *July*, 1555.]

Anthony Hammond, of Scarthingwell, Esq.[1]

(xiv. 246 b.)

In the name of God Amen: the xxvjtie day of Auguste in the yere of our lorde God a thousande fiue hundrithe fyftie and thre, be it knowen that I Anthony Hamonde, of Skarthingwell of the parishe of Saxton in the countie of Yorke, Esquier, being sicke of bodye and hoole of mynde and p'fite of Remembraunce, ordeynith and maketh this to be my laste will and testamente in manner and forme following. Furste I giue and bequethe my soule to God allmightie most hartelye beseching hym to take me to his greate mercye so that my soule maye remayne wth our ladye sancte Marye, the mother of our saueyour Jesu christe, and all the blessed company in heaven, and my bodye to be buryed wthin the parishe Church where it shall please allmightie God to call me to his greate mercye.

---

(1) He heads the pedigree in *Dugdale's Visitation*, vol. ii, p. 441. He bought Scarthingwell.

Also I give to the proctor of the parishe Churche of Saxton for my offeringes and tithes forgotten xij^{d}. Also I give to poore folkes wthin the parishes of Saxton, Sherborne, Fenton, and Kirkbye, iiij^{li} vj^{s} viij^{d} to be distributed at the discrec̄on of my executors. Also I will that Margaret Hamonde my wyfe shall haue for and in the nayme of her Jointer of Dower of all my landes and other her Estates in the same landes one yerely annuytie of twentie poundes to be paid quarterlye duryng her lyfe naturall to be received at the hands of my sonne Wyłłm Hamonde and his heires, and also my chamber wthin my manor of Skarthingwell wch she will choise. And also that she shall haue mete and drincke for her self, her maid, and one man s'v'nte, withe fierwood necessary in her chambre at her pleasure, at the onelie costes of my said sonne Wyłłm Hamonde and his heires duringe her naturall lyfe. And for the ꝑformaunce of this Estate I will that my sayd sonne Wyłłm Hamonde and one sufficient suertye wth hym shalbe bounden by his dede obligatorye in the some of one thowsande m'kes to my sonnes in lawe Bryan Leedes and Henry Yonge. Also I give and bequethe to Jefferaye Metcalf my s'unte yerely during his lyve naturall xxvj^{s} iiij^{d} to be receved at the handes of my said son Wiłłm Hamonde yerely, to be paid at the Feastes of Martynmes and *P*entecoste by euen porc̄ons. And for defaulte of paymente of the said yerely rente of Annuytie of xxvj^{s} viij^{d} or any parcell therof to distreyne vpon all my landes lately bought of Sr George Cornewaill, knight. And also I give vnto Thomas Crostwhaite my s'unte one annuytie of the yerelye Rente of xiij^{s} iiij^{d} during his lyfe naturall, to be Receyved at the handes of my said sonne Wyłłm Hamonde yerely at the feastes of M'tynmes and Pentecroste by euen porc̄ons. And for defaute of paymente of the saide yerely annuytie or rente of xiij^{s} iiij^{d} or any percell therof to be vnpaid at the feastes before expressed to distreyne vpon all my lands lately purchased vpon s^{r} George Cornewaill, knight. Also I give vnto John Storre one other of my s'untes the house and garthe that he nowe dwellith during his lyfe naturall withoute any rente paying for the same. Also I will that Wyłłm Hamounde my sonne immediatlye after my discease shall make and assure to Bryan Hamounde one of the yonger sonnes of my said sonne Wyłłm Hamounde and to the heires mayles of the said Bryan laufully begotten of landes and tentę of the clerely valewe of ^{xxtie} m'kes lying and being wthin the parishe of Kirke Fenton, and for defalte of heires of the said Bryan Hamonde to remayne to the right heires of me the said Anthonye Hamonde. And that my said sonne Wyłłm Hamonde shall haue the custodye and keping of the said Bryan Hamonde and the order and receyte of the said landes till he come to the age of xxj^{ti} yeres. And to kepe the said Bryan at Scholes of lerning and Innes of courte. And if my son Wyłłm Hamonde do dye, as god defende, before the said Bryane come to the age of xxj^{ti} yeres That then the said Bryane Hamonde shalbe in the custodye of Bryan Leedes his vnkle. Also I geve vnto John Hamonde my nevey the yerely rente or annuytie of xl^{s} during his lyfe naturall yerely to be receyved at the handes of my execut' so that he wilbe ordered by them or elles not. Allso I give vnto Wyłłm Hamonde the yonger xl^{s} yerely during his lyfe naturall to be recevyed at the bandes of myne executors. Also I will that my children in lawe, Henry Yonge, Thomas Yonge, and Frances Leedes, shall haue euery one of them xxvj^{s}

viij[d] by thandes of my executors. Also I giue and bequethe to Thomas Longleye my s'unte for his diligent s'uice xl[s]. Also I give and bequethe to Dorothie Yonge twentie m'kes to be paid at the daye of her maryage by thandes of myne executors. Also I will that Eliz' Hamonde, doughter of my sonne Wyllm Hamonde, shall haue of my gyfte one hundrethe m'kes towardes her maryage to be receyved at the bandes of myne executors. Also I give to Bryan Hamonde one hoole complete harnes the beste but one, and all my other harnesses and Implementꝭ of warre I give vnto Wyllm Hamonde my sonne during his lyfe and after his decease to Remayne hoolye to Anthonye Hamonde. Also I give vnto my welbelouid wyfe Margaret Hamonde one siluer salte and a cover, one lytle silner cuppe wth a cover, and a siluer pece and vj siluer spones of the best that is dayly occupied w[ch] I haue delyuered her wth my handes. The residewe of all my plate and my cheyne of golde I give to Wyllm Hamonde my sonne to have the occupac̃on therof all his lyfe, and after his decease to remayne vnto Anthonye Hamonde, sonne and heire of my saide sonne Wyllm Hamonde. Also I will that the residewe of all my s'untꝭ to whome I haue bequethed nothing, shalbe rewarded at the discretion of my executors. Also I geve and bequethe to Bryane Leedes my sonne in lawe xl[s]. Also I give to Thomas Crosthwhaite my s'unte xxvj[s] viij[d], whome I make supvisors of this my laste wyll and testamente for there paynes to see all thinges in my said wyll fulfilled. The residue of all my goodes not bequeathed, my dettes paid, my legacꝭ and funerall expens' paid, I give vnto Margaret Hamonde my wyfe and Wyllm Hamonde my sonne, whome I make my hoole executors of this my laste will and testamente. Geven at Skarthingwell the daye and yere aboue written. Wytnesses hereof, Thomas Crostwhaite, Jefferaye Metcalfe.—[*Proved 2 Nov., 1555.*]

Christopher Taylor, of Westerton.

(xiv. 255 b.)

In Dei nõie Amen: the viij[th] day of October in the yere of o[r] lord 1554. I Chr̃ofer Taylor, of Westerton w[th]in the pishe of Wodkirke, hole of mynd and of good remembrance, ordeyn and make this my last will in man' and fourme folowing: first I wil my soule to God Almightie, trusting throughe the gloryous intercessio' of the most blissed virgyn our lady S[t] Mary and all the Celestiall Companye of heaven, and my body to be buryed w[t]in the halowed ground where it shall please God to call me. Also I gyve to John Taylor, my elder sonne, all my land in Rodwell and one house in Wodkirke y[t] John Fadyn dwelleth in, and the said John Taylor to maike one yerelye obbyt at the pishe Churche at Wodkirke at the feast of St. John Baptist for eu'more for his grandfather soule and his grandmother soule and all Christen Soules, at the w[ch] obbyt the pish preist shall have viij[d] and to other p'stꝭ other viij[d] betwene theym and the Clarke, and v[s] to be delt to the poore in bread. Also I gyve to Eliz' and Margret my daughters two ky betwene theym the best y[t] thei will choyse. It' I gyve to W[m] Taylor, sonne of Thomas Taylor, one kowe w[ch] is at John Huntꝭ. Also I gyve to Eliz' and Margret Tailor, daughters of Thomas Taylor, either of theym x[s]. Also I gyve to George and Rafe my sonnes, Jenet, Eliz', and Margret my doughters, eu'y of them v[s] w[ch] was geven to theym by their grandfaither; all this to be taiken of my hole goodde$s$. Also I gyve to Thom's Speight sonne of John Speight iij^{s} iiij^{d}. Also I will y^{t} my goodes be devyded in three p'te, one to my wyfe, an other to my childer, and the third p'te I gyve to John Taylor, my yongest sonne, George Taylor and Rafe Taylor, whome I make my executors, and they to distribute for my soule as they and their friende thinke best. I will y^{t} John Taylor, my yongest sonne, shalbe halfe executor wth the said George and Rafe. Also these to be supuisors of this my will, Edward Tailor, Gilbt Brown, John Grene, and John Hunt. Theise being witnesses, John Lee, yonger, and Willm Lee. Dette y^{t} I owe: First to John Nettleton, dyar, iiij^{s} vj^{d}. Dette owen to me, first, Thom's Bradley xliij^{s} iiij^{d}, John Grene xx^{s}, Henrie Wynterburn vj^{s}, Gilb't Feighfeild ij^{s}. It' to Gilbt Feighfeild, windill of ry. It' to Rycherd Bothe a wyndill of rye. It' to James Winkinson a secke of haver.—[*Proved* 11 *June*, 1555, *by George Taylor. Grant reserved to the other executors, minors.*]

James Clayton, of Birstall.

(xiv. 260 a.)

In Dei nõie Amen: the xxviijth day of Marche in the yeare of oure lord 1555. I James Clayton, in the pishe of Kirstall [Birstall], of hole mynd, maiketh my last will in fourm folowing: first I bequythe my soule to god Almyghtye and to the feloushippe of oure blessed ladye St. Mary and to all S^{te} in heaven, and my body to be buryed in the Church yeard of Kyrstall [Birstall] of the holye Apostles Peter and Paule. First I gyve to lytle Agnes Haylay a chimneye of iron, one yong quie styrke, and one ewe and a lambe, whiche goodes shalbe and remayn in thandes of Thom's Clayton my sonne to set forward to hir pfytt tyll she come to thage of xvjth yeres. Also I gyve to Jenet and Eliz' Pogson to either of theym an ew and a lambe. Also if James Clayton my sonne chalence for any p'te of my goodes then I will y^{t} Thom's my sonne gyve to hym vj^{s} viij^{d} and wth y^{t} he shalbe contented. Also I gyve to John Pogson wif xv^{s}, whereof v^{s} is in his bandes. Also I gyve to John Halay an ew and a lambe. And Thom's my sonne shall gyve to my daughter Halay wife one wyndell of rye. Finallye the rest of all my goodde$s$ y^{t} remaynethe, all many^{r} of dette and duties content and paid, I gyve theym holye to Thomson Clayton my sonne and also the take and good will of my farmehold and mylne (by the lycence of my Mr Sr John Nevill), trusting his M^{r}shippe wilbe good M^{r} to hym as he haithe ben vnto me at all tymes. And I maike Thom's my sonne my full executor of all my goodes and to fulfill this my last will. These being wytnes, Nichols Brocke, Gilbt Haldworthe, Willm Byus, John Pogson, Willm Taylor, Willm Peyrson, Lynoell Rayner.—[*Proved* 9 *July*, 1555.]

Stephen Wise, of Farnley.

(xiv. 268 b.)

In the name of God Amen: the xvjth day of Marche in the yere of o^{r} lorde a thousande fyve hundreth fiftie and foure. I Stephen Wise, of Ferneley, of good Rememberaunce, maketh this my last will and testament in maner and forme followinge. Firste I bequeith my soule to God Almightie and to o^{r} blessed Lady and to all the sanctes in heaven, and my body to be buried w^th^in the churchyerd of Sancte Peter at Ledes. Item I bequeith to the hie altare for forgotten tithes or oblac̄ons yf there be any behinde vnpaid xij^d^. It'm I will that all suche costę as shalbe maid the day of my buriall to be maide at the discrecon of my wief and Wiłłm Judson my brother in Lawe and my debtę paid and my funerall expens' done. The residue of all my goodę moveable and vnmoveable I gyve and bequeith to Margaret my wief and to the children accordinge to the Lawe. Item I maike my executors of this my last will and testament Margaret my wief and Wiłłm Judson my brother in Lawe. Theis beinge witnesses, Thomas Gibson, chapleyn, Wiłłm Crooke, Wiłłm Chapmā, Wiłłm Judson, with other.—[*Proved* 13 *Aug.*, 1554.]

John Linley, of Middleton.

(xiv. 268 b.)

In Dei nōie Amen: I John Lynley, of Midleton within the ꝑishe of Rothwell, of a hole mynde and good Rememberaunce, maketh this my last will and testament the xxviijth daie of Auguste in the yere of our Lorde god m^li^v^c^liij after this maner and forme folowinge. Firste I bequeith my soule to almightie god and to our Lady Sancte Mary and to all the celestiall company in heaven, and my body to be buried within the churche yerde of Rothwell. Also I bequeith vnto my wief my fermeholde, all my goodę moveable and vnmoveable, after my disecase. Item I bequeith vnto Anne Lynley a quye styrke of thre yere olde and a gymer lame. Item I bequeith to Wiłłm Lynley all my best eloise to be arayed cleane ouer. Item I have boughte of Wiłłm Bushope a quarter and a half and fyve strokę of Rye and paid for and to be deliu'ed betwixte this and all halowines. Item I bequeith vnto euery one of my god children iiij^d^. Item I bequeith to the churche to bye anowrnamentę iij^s^ iiij^d^. Item I bequeith to my mother iij yerdę of marbyll clothe. Also I make Jenet my wief my full executrix of this my last will and testament. Thes being wittenes, Wiłłm Walker, James Walker, Wiłłm Lynley, Henry Hall, wth other.—[*Proved* 13 *Aug.*, 1554.]

Benedict Wasche, of Kirskell, Adel.

(xiv. 269 a.)

In the name of God Amen: the xth daie of Auguste in the yere of o^r^ Lorde God a thousande fyve hundreth liij. I Benedic Wasche, of Kirkstall w^th^in the ꝑishe of Addle, seke in Body but ꝑfite of memory, maketh this my last will and testament in maner followinge. Firste of all I gyve my soule to God Almyghtie, and my body to be buried w^th^in the churche yerde of Sancte John Baptiste at Addell. Also I assigne my fermehold in Horsfurthe nowe in the tenure of Wiłłm Cave to Johane my doughter. Also I gyve and assigne to Eliz. my doughter one fermehold in Rawden nowe in the teno^r^ and occupac̄on of Hawxfurthe wief. My funerall expens's maid and my dettę paid, The Residue of my goodę I gyve to Jane my wief, whome I make my full and lawfull executrix of this my last will to se it truelie executed and fulfilled. Recordę of my will, Wiłłm Foster, Richard Waite, and Wiłłm Lupton, clerke.—[*Proved* 13 *Aug.*, 1554.]

Richard Waith, of Arthington.

(xiv 269 a.)

In Dei nōie Amen: the xv^th^ daie of Octobre in the yere of our lorde god a thousande fyve hundreth fiftie and thre. I Richard Waith, of Hardingto' of the parishe of Addill, of hole mynde and good Rememberaunce, maketh this my Last will and testament in this fourme followinge. Firste I bequeith my soule to god almightie and to his mother our blessed Lady Sancte Mary and to all the faire felowship that is in heaven, and my body to be buried w^th^in the churche yerde of Addill. Also I bequeith to Thomas my sonne all my tentures and two paire of sheares. Also I gyve to Nicholes my sonne two oxen. And I bequeith to Laurens my sonne an oxe and to Thomas my sonne an oxe and to thre of my doughters euery one of them a cowe. Also I bequeith to Elizabeth my doughter a brode pan, and also to Alice my doughter a panne and a pott, and to Jane my doughter a panne. Also I gyve to Nicholes my sonne an arke that is in the seller and all the geere that belongeth to ploughe and wayne. Also I bequeith to John my sonne an arke whiche doith stande in the house and a fatt stot or a cowe or the price of them. And I bequeith to Mawde my doughter a whie that is wth John Waite, of Hemenbrughe. Also I gyve Nicholes Waite a bedde of eloyse. And the residue of my beddinge to be devided emongest my children not maried. And all my puther vessell to be devided emongest my thre doughters. And I bequeith to Willm Waitę my sonne my best hat and my, best dublet. The Residue of my goodę, my body honestlie broughte fourthe and my dettę paid, I gyve them to Nicholes Waythe my sonne, whome I maike my sole executor. In wittnes whereof, Mr. Henry Ardington, John Elles, Willm Waddington, w^t^ other moo.—[*Proved* 13 *Aug.*, 1554.]

Christopher Allan, of Wakefield.

(xiv. 272 a.)

In the name of God Amen: the seconde daie of Aprill in the yere of our Lorde god a thousande fyve hundreth fiftie thre. I Chr̄ofer Alayne, of Waikefelde, seeke in body but hole in mynde, makes this my testament and last will in maner and forme followinge. Firste I bequeith my soule vnto the father of heaven, and my body to be buried w^th^in the churche or Churche yerde of Waikefeld, &c. Also I maike my wief and my two sonnes myn Executorę, and my wief to haue my hole takkę and she to kepe my two sonnes with there ptę. And if she chaunce to marry duringe my tackę then I will that she shall neither haue my takę nor my children. But than I will that my two bretherne Richerd Allan and Roger Allan shall haue my two sonnes wth there ptę and my takkę to the bringinge vp of them. Theis beinge witnes, that is to saie, s^r^ Thomas Turner, prest, John Myllę thelder, Edwarde Hardy, and John Jackson.—[*Proved* 3 *Sept.*, 1554, *by Eliz., the widow. Grant reserved to John, son of deceased, a minor, the other son being dead.*]

Humphrey Johnson, of Wakefield, Tanner.

(xiv. 272 b.)

In the name of God Amen: the xth daie of Julie in the yere of our Lorde god mill'imo quingen^mo^ liiij^to^. I Vmfray Johnson, of Waikefeld within the Countie of York, Tanner, of good and perfite Rememberaunce, seke in body, makith this my last will and testament as hereafter foloweth. Firste I bequeith my soule to God Almightie and to the Blessid Virgyn Sancte Mary and vnto all the Blessid Company of heaven, and my body to be buried w^th^in the parish Churche yerde of All halowes in Waikefeld. And I maike Jennet Johnson my wief and also my children my executric℮, my dett℮ and fynerall expens' paid, that they shall haue and enioye all my good℮ after my discease. It'm I will that Jennet my wief and my children shall haue the Tacke of this house after my discease duringe the yeres that are vnexpired. Item I maike Supervisor of this my last will Thomas Poplewell and Henry Johnson. Theis beinge witnes, Robert Lawe, Robert Norton, with other moo as sr George Lee, prest, with other moo. Theis be the debt℮ that I owe vnto John Boney for one Cowe hide p'ce iijs iiijd. And theis be the dett℮ wch thies men followinge owe vnto me. In primis, Chr̃ofer Wollayne oweth vnto me iiijs vjd. It'm Leonerde Parker oweth vnto me xvd. It'm Richard Smorthwaite oweth vnto me iiijs viijd.—[*Proved 3 Sept., 1554, by the widow. Grant reserved to the children.*]

HENRY ROAME, OF METHLEY.

(xiv. 275 a.)

In the name of God Amen: the xxx daie of Octobre in the yere of our Lorde God a thousande fyve hundreth fyftie and thre. I Henry Roame, of the ꝑish of Methley, seke in body and hole in mynde, mak℮ this my testament and Last will in maner and forme followinge. Firste I bequeith my soule to God almightie, and my body to be buried within the Churche yerde of Metheley. In primis I bequeith to the newe brige, to the buyldinge of the same, ijs. Item I bequeith to Mathewe my sonne all my raiment. Also vnto the said Mathue one calf. It' to Jenet Reme my s'unte another calf. Item I bequeith to my sonne Mathue children v yerd℮ of clothe to maike them coot℮ of. Item to my doughter Eliz. one Qwye stirke. Also to Esabell Oswold another whie stirke. Item to Effame Oswold a litle brasse potte. The Residue of all my good℮, my dett℮ paid and I honestlie broughte furthe, I gyve and bequeith to Alice my doughter, whome I maike my executrixe. Thes wittnes, Johne Dikonson, Robert Warde, Rob̃te Chamer, with other mo.—[*Proved 4 Oct.,* 1554.]

GEORGE BYWATER, OF SWILLINGTON.

(xiv. 280 b.)

In the name of God Amen: the xxiiijth daie of August in the yeare of oure lord Godd a thousand fyve hundrethe fyftye and foure. I George Bywater, of the ꝑishe of Swillington, of good and p'fyte remembr'unce, maiketh this my testament and last will in man' and fourme following, viz. Fyrst I gyve and frely betaike my soule to Godd almightie, the blissed virgyn oure ladye St Marie, and to all the Celestiall Companye of heaven, and my bodye to be buryed in the Churche yard of Swyllington. Also I bequythe to the hye altare viijd. It' I bequythe to the Churche nedes ijs. Also I bequythe to Thom's Bywaiter my brother my best jackytt. Also I bequythe to Wiłłm Bywater, sonne of the said Thom's, one whyte Rygged quye. Also I assign my farmeholde to Annes my wyfe to bring vpp my small children so long as she dothe not marye, and if she do mary then my eldest sonne, Arthure, to have yt. Also I bequythe to Mr. Arthur Dyneley to be good m[r] to my wyfe and poore children one angell noble. The rest of all my gooddes, my dettę and fun'allę paid and discharged, I gyve to Agnes my wyfe and Arthure my sonne, Jenett, Michaell, Margret, Isabell, Thom's, Wiłłm, and Rychard Bywater, my eight children, whom I make my executors to do for me as I have put theym in trust. Theise being wytnesses, John Dawson, curate, Arthure Dyneley, gentlemen, S[r] Stephen Hemsworthe, Thom's Myteley, and Richerd Peise, wth other mo.—[*Proved* 30 *Oct.*, 1554, *by Agnes the widow. Grant reserved to the children.*]

MARY HARDCASTLE, OF WOMERSLEY.

(xiv. 293 a.)

In the name of God Amen: the iiij[th] day of December in the yere of o[r] Lord God a thowsande five hundrethe fiftye and two. I Marye Hardcastell, of Wom'slaye, wedowe, hole of mynde and of good memorye, loved be god, do ordeine and make my laste will and testament in manner and forme following. First I give and witte my soule to allmightie god, to our Ladie sanct marie, and to all the celestiall company of heaven, and my bodie to be buried w[t]hin the ꝑishe church of Saxton. It' I bequeath to Wedderbe brigge xxvj[s] viij[d]. It' to Walsheworthe brigge xxvj[s] viij[d]. It' to Tadcaster brigge xxvj[s] viij[d]. It' to Castleforth brigge xxvj[s] viij[d]. It' to Ferybrigge xxvj[s] viij[d], and to mending of Feribrigge causaye xiij[s] iiij[d]. It' I bequeath to Anne Skergell my god daughter my lease of my farmolde at Wom'slaye wth all my oxen, plughe and wayn, and all other thingę ꝑteyning to husbandrie, and the croppe of corne growing vpon the grownde. It' I bequeath to my brother Thomas children iij[li] vj[s] viij[d] in monney, two gownes, two kirtellę, the one of russels and thother of clothe wth straite sleves. It' I bequeath to Wiłłm Bransbie xl[s]. It'm to Myles P'ston xx[s] and a pare of Hemptere shetę. It' I bequeath to my cosin Waren Skergell a maire, a follower, and her foole. It' to my cosyn Wiłłm Skergell a meare, a follower, and her fole, the one is baye and the other is graye. It' I bequeath to my cosyn Dorothie Skergell two kie, one wth a tagged taile and the other garded, being wth Thom's Cowꝑ, a nawmbling meare and hir foole. It' I bequeathe to eu'y one of my god childer in Wom'slaye p'ishe xij[d]. It' I bequeath to s[r] Wiłłm Gon̄t an aungell noble. It' I bequeath to my Ladie Layton a golde ring. It' to Elizabeth Hudeswell a blacke gowne. It' s[r] George Lister a blacke cloke and an aungell noble. It' I bequeath to Margaret Burdsall a hatte, a cappe, a fine kerchew, and vj[s] viij[d]. It' to Elizabeth Richardson, Alice Palden, Jennet Burdsall, and Dyonesse Grene, eu'y. one of them a kerchew, a smocke, and xij[d] of monney. It' I bequeath to Margaret Weddrell a lite white cappe, a kerchew, a hempe beire smocke, and xij[d]. It' I bequeath to Agnes Wodde xij[d]. It' to upper Crostwhaite vj[s] viij[d]. It' to Katheron Cowꝑ xij[d]. It' to Alice Lyn̄e xij[d]. It' to Margaret Brigge xij[d]. It' to Richard Thornton xij[d]. It' to Thomas Briggę xij[d]. It' to Maistres Leadę a chamblet gowne and a veluet bonet. It' to my godson her son vj[s] viij[d]. It' I bequeath to my cosyn Dorothie Skergell a cupborde, a cowntor, and two greate chestę. The residew of all my goodę vnbequest, my dettę paid and all other my legacies and bequestꝭ well and trewlie p'formed according to the true entent of this my last will and testament, I give to Warren Skergell, whom I make my full executor for to bring me forth honestlye and to dispose for the health of my soule after his discrec̃on. In witnesses wherof, Wiłłm Cowꝑ, clarke, Bryan Ottꝭ, Thomas Yoille, Xpofer Danyell, with others.—[*Proved 6 Nov.*, 1554.]

RICHARD SHARP, OF METHLEY.

(xiv. 294 b.)

In the name of God Amen: the vjth day of August in the yere of our Lorde God a thowsande five hundreth fyftee and foure, I Richard Sharpe, of the ꝑishe of Metheleye, of good wit and remembraunce, thanckꝭ be to God, make this my will and testament in manner and forme following. Furst I bequeath my soule in to the handꝭ of Allmightie God my creator and redemer, and that it may accompany wth his mother our ladye sancte Marye the Virgyn and wth all the sanctꝭ that is in the kingdom of heaven, also I bequeath my bodye to be buryed wthin the ꝑishe church yarde of the said Metheley. Also I bequeath to the blessed sacrament iiij^{d}. Also I bequeath to the most nedꝭ of the churche xij^{d}. Also I bequeath to Anne Sharpe xij^{d}. Also I bequeath to Jennet Sharpe, my eldest doughter, x shepe. Also I bequeath to Agnes my doughter on quhye. Also I will that Margaret Lowkꝭ my syster haue one yeres howse rente. Also I bequeath vnto Effam Dicconson, Anne and Jennet her systers, and vnto every one of them one ewe lambe. The residew of all my goodꝭ not bewitte, my dettꝭ paid and funerall expns's taken therof, I bequeath and geve vnto Elizabeth my wife and to John, Jennet, and Agnes, my children, whom I ordene and make my lawfull executors to the entent that they shall execute and mynister my said goodꝭ according to the teno^{r} and intent of this my said will and testament. Witnesses therupon, Robert Ward, Richard Webster, Wiłłm Shanne, and Sr Lawrence Ottꝭ, curate. It' where as I haue gyven up by surrender certayne grownde called Peillꝭ as aperyth by copys therof vnto John Dickenson for the term of x yeres, he yelding and paing yerelie for the said x yeres xx^{s} in the yere vnto Jennet Sharpe and Agnes Sharpe my children or ellꝭ to be bounde to pay to them at x yeres end xl^{s}. It' I bequeath to John my sonne one iron chymneye wch is in the handꝭ of John Dickonson, and if the said John my son dye or he come to lawfull age then I will that Jenet and Agnes my childer shall haue yt. Witnesses herof, Rychard Webstar and Edward Dobson.—[*Proved* 21 *Nov.*, 1554, *by the widow. Grant reserved to the others, minors.*]

THOMAS WILKINSON, OF WHITWOOD.

(xiv. 297 a.)

In the name of God Amen: the xxviij day of September in the year of our lord god m'cccccliiij. I Thomas Wilkinson, of Witwod within the ꝑish·of Fetherstone, knoweinge nothing more certaine then death and nothing more vncertaine than the howre of the same, makes this my last will and testamente in manner and forme followinge. The first I bequeathe my sawle to god almightie, humblie besechinge the glorious virgin Marie and all the celestiall companye in heven to pray for me, and my bodie to be buried within the church yearde of Fetherston. Item I bequeath for my mortury accordinge to the Lawe of the Realme. Item I bequeathe to the blissed sacrament at Fetherston for tiethes forgotten ij^{s}. It'm I bequeathe to Katheryn and Agnes my doughters to eyther of them one cowe. Item to Margaret my doughter an other cowe and ij yowes and ij lambes. Item I bequeathe to John and Francę my sonnes to eyther of theme a cowe or a whye at note, and to John my sonne ij yowes and ij lambes. Item I bequeathe to Robt Bloyme, yonger, a yowe and a lambe, and to Edwarde Wilkinson a yowe and a lambe. Item I will that Margaret shall haue the lease with interest of my farmeholde so longe as she leves yf she kepe hir sole and vnmaried, and yf she marrye or depte owte of this worlde then I assigne, will, and gyve the lease and the interreste of my said farmeholde to Stephen Wilkinson and Gilbert Wilkinson my sonnes, and yf Stephen be able to occupie my said farmeholde hime self then I will that the said Stephen shall gyve v^{li} of his owne propper gooddes vnto Gilbte my sonne to get hime a farmeholde withall. Also I will that my goodę not bequeathed be devided in thre p'tes, one to my children vnmaried, the second parte to my wif, and the third vnto all my children vnmaried and my wif. I brought furthe therof and my will proved therof, The Residew of my goodę, my dettę paid, I gyve and bequeathe vnto Margaret my wif, Stephen and Gilbte my sonnes, whome I make myne executors. Thes witnes, Edwarde Wormall, clerke and vicar of Fetherstone, Henrye Smyth, Willm Balge, Nicoles Everingh'm, with other.—[*Proved* 31 *Jan.*, 1554-5.]

ELIZABETH TURPIN, OF TOWTON.

(xiv. 298 b.)

In Dei nõie Amen: the xxth day of Auguste in the yeare of our Lorde God a thousande fyve hundreth lj. I Eliz' Turpin, of Towton, layte wif of Robte Turpyn, decessed, hole of mynd and of good memorie, loved be God, maketh my last will and testament in mann' and forme followinge. Fyrst I gyve and wit my soul to almightie god, to our Lady sancte Marie, and to all the Celestyall company of heven, and my bodie to be buried within the pishe cherche or churche yearde of Saxton. Also I gyve and bequeath all my gooddes, my dettes paid, to George Turpin, Alexander Turpin, and Francis Turpyn, my children, whome I ordayne and make my full executors of this my laste will and testament, and I will that they be at thorder and governynge of Alexander Laycocke my father and Margaret Turpyn my mother in lawe vnto such tyme they be of lawfull aige, and to bringe me furthe honestlie and dispose for the health of my saull after ther discressions. In witnes hereof, George Parker and Alexander Laycocke, with other.—[*Proved* 9 *Feb.*, 1554-5, *by Alexander Laicoke, guardian of George, Alexander, and Francis Turpin during minority.*]

HENRY THAURTON, OF HOLBECK.

(xiv. 301 a.)

In the name of God Amen: the vj day of October in the yere of our lorde God in m^{l}ccccclliij. I Henry Thaurton, of Hollocke [*sic*], clothier, in the pishinge of Leedes, of hole mynde and good remembrance, maketh my will and testamente in manner and forme followinge. Firste I bequeath my soull vnto almightie god my redemer and maker, and my bodie to be buried within my pishe churche yerde of Sancte *P*eter at Ledes, and also I will that dettę shalbe paid of my hole goodę. Also I giue and bequeath vnto Eliz' my wif all my farmeholde and house that I dwell in withall the appurtenance ther vnto belonginge yf the lorde therof wilbe contented and pleased, and the tactę and yeres of two closes called little Riddingę, a gray cowe, a cobborde, a flanders chiste, hir nappe ware and the sylver spones shall she haue duringe hire naturall lif and then to dispose theme emongę hir childern as she thinke the beste. Also I give and bequeath to Wiłłm, Roger, and George, my sonnes, my leade emongę theme besides ther parte and porc̃on, and to Thomas my sonne a paire of my beste chaires Schayres [*sic*]. Also I will that my goodes shalbe devided into thre p'ties, one p'tie to my wif, on other p'tie to be devided emongę my children, Thomas, Agnes, Wiłłm, John, Henry, Roger, and George, and the thridde parte to bringe me furthe withall, and I will that Agnes my doughter shall haue xx^s^ of my parte to mende hir withall, and John my sonne shall haue vj^s^ viij^d^ and Henry my sonne vj^s^ viij^d^, and I bequeathe to Alison Popellwell my s'unte vj^s^ viij^d^ and to Thomas my sonne a gray cowe or xx^s^ and to Sr Richerde Beckwith vj^s^ viij^d^. And I make Eliz' my wif and George my sonne my full executorę of this my laste will and testamente to dispose and order for the healthe of my soull as they judge beste to be done, and Richerde Haighe to be supvisor hereof this will and he shall haue my beste jackett. Recordes of this will and testamente, Richerde Leigh, Roger Leigh, George Hargraue, Wiłłm Hargraue, with other. Thomas Laythley, in the foreste of Gawteresse, oweth vnto Henry Thaurton, of Holbecke, a quarter of rye and x^s^ of money that he lente hime.—[*Proved 2 March,* 1554-5.]

NICHOLAS RODES, OF HAWKSWORTH.

(xiv. 301 a.)

In Dei nõie Amen: the xx^th^ day of Julie in the yere of our lorde God a thowsande five hundreth fiftie and thre. I Nicholas Rodes of Hawkisworth, in the p'ishinge of Otley, beinge of whole mynde and good memorie, make this my laste will and testament in manner and forme followinge. Firste I bequyethe my soull to Allmightie God my maker and redemer, and my bodie to be buried in the churche yearde of Otley my pishe churche. Item I bequeath my lease of my farmehold to Margaret my wif duringe hir lif naturall to the bringeinge vp of my children and hirs, and after hir decease I will that the same lease remayne to Thomas my sonne, he painge to every of my fower children, that is to say, Xpofer, Henry, John, and Janet, x^s^, provided alwayes that yf my sonne Thomas shalbe provided of a farmeholde by marrage or by any other meanes then I will that my said lease shalbe at the order of Wiłłm Roodes, John Roodes, and Chr̃ofer Roodes, to one of my fower childeren affore named at ther discression, then my sone Thomas (yf that forton) shall haue x^s^ of theme that shall haue the farmeholde. The Reste of my goodę I honestlie broughte furthe I giue and bequeath to Margaret my wif, Xpofer, Henry, John, and Janet, my childerin, whome I make my executors of this my last will and testament. Thes witnessinge the same, Wiłłm Roodes, John Rodes, and Xpofer Roodes, with other mo, desyringe them to se this my will fulfilled in all pointes.—[*Proved 2 March,* 1553-4.]

ROBERT GAYLE, OF BEESTON.

(xiv. 301 b.)

In the name of God Amen: the laste of December in the yere of our lord god a thowsand fyve hundreth fiftie and fower. I Robt Gayle, of Beiston in the Countie of Yorke, yoman, beinge of hole mynde and pfite remembrance, doith make this my laste will and testamente in manner and forme followinge. Fyrste I gyve and bequeathe my soull to God Allmightie, to our ladie sancte Marie, and to all the Celestiall company of heven, and my bodie to be buried within the churche or churche yearde of Ledes, also I bequeath to the hie alter xij^{d}. Also I give and bequeath to Willm my sonne iiij yewes and also to Roberte my sonn iiij yewes; also I give and bequeath to Margerye and Katheren my doughters to eyther of theme iiij yewes. Also I giuc to eu'ye one of my god chylderin xij^{d}. Also I give to Wyllm my sonn children v yewes and to Robte my sonne child one yewe. Also I will that Willm Smyth my sonn in lawe be well and truelie paid vj^{li} xiij^{s} iiij^{d}. Also I give and bequeathe to Margerye my doughter to her mariage vj^{li} xiij^{s} iiij^{d} and she to be honestlie apparelled at hir said mariage in the name of hir childes porcon. Also I will that my farmeholde be occupied as heareafter followeth, that is, to witt, that Alice my wif haue two kye gate in somer in a close called lacton leys and also one ynge called the nether end of hagg ynge and also in eu'y feilde an acre of earable ground, and also I will that Robte my sonne shall haue ij kye gayte in the dede Roodes and iij acres of Earable grounde and also the end of the close that the colepitte was in, to haue thes parcells abovesaid to suche tyme as the said Robte can better provide for himeself, and the said Robte to pay to Willm his brother for the said peels as the said Willm paid to his father. Also I give to the said Roberte my sonne one cowe, also I give to John Gayll my brother my best Jackett salvinge one. Also I will that Willm my sonne shall haue and occupie my hole farmeholde after my decease saving suche pcels as is afforesaid to Alice my wif and Robte my sonne, also the Reste of all my goode vnbequeathed, my dette paid and my funerall expenses laid downe and paid, I give to Alice my wif to bestow for my soull healthe, whome I make my treue and lawfull executrix to se that this my laste will be trulie pformed. Thes being witnes, Robte Erle, Rawff Moxon, Wordeworthe Clerke, with other mo.—[*Proved 2 March, 1554-5.*]

ROBERT CHALONER, OF STANLEY.[1]

(xiv. 311 a.)

In the name of God Amen: vij^{o} July Anno D'ni MDlv^{o}. I Robte Chalono^{r}, of Stanleye, of hole mynde and pfite memorye, make this my last wille and testamente in man' and forme followinge, that is to saye. First I bequeath my soule vnto the mercye of Almightye god my maker and Redemer, and my bodye to be buried where it shall please Almightye God to p'vide for me and to call me to his mercye. Also I bequethe to the vycar of Waikefeilde that tyme being x^{s} for my mortuarye according

(1) Mr. Walker, in the notes on the Chaloner family in the "Cathedral Church of Wakefield," does not refer to the testator and his interesting bequests to the church and the chapel on the bridge. The family were long connected with Wakefield, and the bequest to Sir Thomas Chaloner, knight, points to a probable connexion with the Guisborough family.

to the statute and other x^s^ for my tythes forgotten and not fullye paid. Also I wille that at the daie of my buriall xiij poore men bearinge xiij tapers whereof xij to be of ij^li^ wax and the xiij^t^ to be of iiij^li^ wax, and shall haue euery one of them a white gowne after the discretion of my executours. And the same tapers to be burned aboute my bodye vnto the eight daye after my decease and dep̃tinge oute of this worlde, And then all the said tapers to be offred to the most blessed sacramente of the altare. Also I will that at the said daye of my buryall cu'ye ꝑson that will aske any Almes haue j^d^ or more at the discrec̃on of my executours as theic were at my wyfes buryall. Also I will that at the said daie of my buryall dirige and messe be said for my soule and everye priest of the said ꝑishe to have viij^d^ and the vicar and Curate either of them xij^d^ and eu'ye straunge priest vj^d^. Also I wilbe gladde to haue so many trentallꝭ as can be conuententlye said that weke for my soule. And eu'ye preist that will saye masse for the same to haue iiij^d^ for eu'ye messe. Also I gyue to my brother John Sheffelde my beste gowne and xl^s^ of moneye. Also to Rob̃te Ryshworthe my ij gowne to be taken at his election. Also to Willm̃ Hobson my iij gowne to be taken at his election. Also to Michel cure my iiij^t^ gowne. Also to Bryane Sharpe my fifte gowne. Also to Rob̃te Lawsonne my sixte gowne or cote. Also to John Precharde my vij^t^ gowne, the Resydue of my gownes and also dublettꝭ of fusteane and other of myne apparell excepte silke to be bestowed amonges my s'uantꝭ and poore people at the discretion of my said executours. Also I will that eu'y one of my s'uantꝭ whiche at the tyme of my deathe shall take wages of me shall haue one hole yeare wage in Recompence of their wages for their s'uice done before that tyme. And also that eu'y one that shall not haue one my gownes as is before said shall haue one cote or leu'aye at the discretion of my said executours. Also I bequethe all my hose to be distributed amonges my maidens to make them hose of. And suche as ar not mete for them, to be gyuē to the poore folkes by the discretion of my said executors. And as for all my sylke I gyue to make ornamentꝭ of the churche or other godlye disposition by my executors. Also I gyue to s^r^ Thomas Gargrave knighte one gilted syluer spone. It'm to s^r^ Leonard Bekewithe knighte another gilted siluer spone, to Mr Franke Rookesbye one other gilted spone, desiringe them to helpe my executors in their good and Rightfull causes. Also I beqwethe to Doctor Robertson, Vicar of Wakefeilde, one of the ij ale cuppes of siluer gilted. Also I will that Edward Guye, Francꝭ Graunte, and Alland Jepson have cu'ye one of them one newe cote at the discretion of myne executours. Also I gyue to Thomas Denton, Mr Doctor Rob̃tson s'uante one newe p^a^, to Willm̃ Barmbye my best bowe and one spone. It'm to John Tyndaile the clocke whiche he gaue me and one spone. It'm to s^r^ Henrye Sayuell knight his white mare whiche he gaue me. It'm I will that all my bookes of Lawe aswell those whiche ar at Yorke as at my house, Also all those whiche be at London yf there can be conueied, hadde, or caryed by any meane to grauisin to my cosin Rob̃t Nowell. And then xl^s^ in moneye to be delyuered vnto the said Rob̃te Nowell to·thentent that he maie by cheines therew^th^ and fasten so manye of them in the Librarye at gravisin as he shall thinke conuenyente, and all the Residue whiche are not necessarye for the said Librarye my said cosin Nowell to take or gyue at his pleasure. It'm I beqwethe to cu'ye of my godchildren ij^{s} whiche will aske it wthin one yeare. Also to eu'ye of George Kente children whiche he had wth his first wyfe x^{s}. It'm to s^{r} George Lee, preist, x^{s}, and he to saie a trentall of masses for me at conueniente Laisure. Also to s^{r} Edwarde Wood, to s^{r} Xpofer Steede, to s^{r} Richard Sele, and s^{r} Williā Ball cu'ye one of them to haue x^{s} for like pu'pose. Also I will then when soeu' my Cosin Fleminge is minded and also do putt any of his children forthe of the ꝑishe of Wakefeilde to s'uice or to be prentice that eu'y of the said children putte from him as is beforesaid shall haue xx^{s} toward their apparell and settinge forthe. Also I giue to the commons of grauison xx^{s} for suche wrongꝭ as I did to the house when I contynued there. Also to Robt Hobson thelder x^{s}. It'm as conc'ninge my Landꝭ where before this tyme John Chalonar my father whose soule God p'don and *P*eares Couꝑ and others then of the substanciall tailoures of Wakefeilde were agreed that there shulde be a common aultar in the ꝑishe cherche of Wakefeilde for cu'ye preist to saie masse at that woulde and my said father appointed viij^{s} in a yere to suche a poore man as shuldbe appointed by the said occupac̄on to attend of the said aultar and also my said father willed one obett to be yerelie done in Wakefeilde churche for his soule, his auncytors, and all christen soules which was neu' executed. Nowe it is my will that Rychard Browne, William Browmehead, [*blank*] Adcocke, and other tailiors for the tyme beinge of the said ocenpac̄on of the tailiours of Wakefeilde shall haue to them their heires and assignes for eu' those ij houses in Kirkegate which Rauf Babotte and Willm Cookson holdithe to thentent that the said tailiors shall firste of all see them yearelye sufficiently Reparelled and wth parcell of the Residue of the said ij houses to giue x^{s} to thafforesaid poore man attendinge of the said common aultar accordinge to them ordiñnces and deuise and then wth the Residue of the Rentes of the said houses to make yearelye one obett for my soule, myne auncitors, and the soules of all the men of thafforesaid occupac̄on and all christen soules. Also I gyue to John Precherd for the terme of his life the house wth th'appurteñnces wherin his mother dwellethe. It'm ij Leacys of the backe syde of the same. It'm one litle close whiche was tydingꝭ and one other whiche was Roger Nowells and half an acre in the North feilde whiche his said mother nowe holdithe and so muche of the p'misses as be copie holde. I purpas God willinge to surrender accordinglee. Also I wille that Willm Hobson haue my tacke and Lease of Rothwell he painge furthe of the same yearelie so longe as the said yeares do endure the Kinges Rentes, and xiij^{s} iiij^{d} to Thomas Sheiffeilde, xx^{s} to the Reparac̄on of the bridges and causeis of Swillinton bridge and aboute Rothwell, and xx^{s} to hie wayes aboute Stanleye and xx^{s} to the poore folkes of Stanleye and hamlettꝭ belonging to the same. Also I wille that Robt Ryshworthe haue my lease and tacke of the holmes at Selbye and all the Residue of the yeares whiche I haue in the same, he painge yearlye the lordꝭ Rente and xx^{s} yerelye to the poore people of Stanleie and the hambelettꝭ belonginge to the same. Also I wille that all my ymages in my chapell the doers for the chapell of oure ladie of Wakefeilde bridge to haue so many of them for the anornmente of the said chapell as theie shall thinke and conueniente, and the Residue of them to be taken by the preistes of Wakefeilde churche for the ornament of cu'ye of their Closettꝭ yf thei will. Also I will giue to the common aultar my best vestmente, the seconde to the chapell of the bridge, and the Residue of my vestmentꝭ to the aultar of the ꝑishe churche of Wakefeilde which bathe most nede of them. Also I gyue to s^{r} John Neuell, knight, one siluer spone one of the xij Apostles. It'm to Francys Frobysher one other of the same. It'm to Frauncis Noderos' one other of the same, And to Wiłłm Hamonde one other of the same. It'm to Henry Gryce one other of the same. It'm to Nicholas Farnell, of Darton, one other of the same. It'm to Steven Paslowe one other of the same. Item I giue to Henry Witham my blacke satin cote. It'm to my brother John Sheiffeilde my tawneye damaske Jackit. It'm I giue to the comynaltie of Stanleae that whiche is called Stanleie onelye ij plate cotes or Jackes at the discretion of myne executors, ij bowes, ij shaiffes of arowes, and ij paire of splentꝭ to s'ue for them when thei shalbe called vpon by the Kinge and the queue. It'm to Michaell Eure the nagge whiche was his mothers. It'm I gyue to Richard Fornes x^{s}. I gyue to Mychaell Cheriholme ij ewes and ij Lambes. It'm I will that Bryan Sharpe and Rob̄te Lawson that either of them shall haue for their paines takinge xx^{s}. It'm I giue to Richard Fleminge one newe x^{s} of golde. It'm to John Laike one other x^{s} of golde. It'm I gyue to Brya' Bradforthe one syluer spone one of the xij Apostles. It'm one other to Christofer Feilde of the same. It'm I will that the syde table in my hall stand and be vntaken awaye. It'm I will that eu'ye of my vncle Thomas Chaloner dought' children haue xx^{s}. It'm I will that s^{r} Robert Thornton prest shall sing and saie masse at Waykfeilde church for my soule by the space of one yeare next after my deathe and he to haue for his Labor v^{li}. It'm I will that Rob̄t Smithe and Margaret *P*rechet haue one honest bedde wth all other thinges therto belonginge and all my s'uantꝭ to haue their beddꝭ which theie do lye in. It'm I giue to s^{r} Thomas Chalonar, knighte, my vnicorne horne. It'm by this my last will and testamente I make Rob̄te Rysworthe and Wiłłm Hobson my sole executors of this my last Wille & testamente. And then to dispose the Residue of all my goodes and catals not hereto fore beqwithed in the works of charitie for the welthe of my soule and that Doctor Rob̄tson shall call vpon them wth diligence to bestowe the said gooddes as is afforsaid, And theie to do all thinges that he shall reasonablye commaunde them to do. In wytnes whereof to this my last will and testamente I haue subscribed my name and sette my Seall the daie and yeare abouewritten.—[*Proved* 10 *Oct.*, 1555.]

ROGER PERESON, OF MONK FRYSTON.

(xv. j. 8 b.)

In the name of God Amen: the xxiiij daye of Januarie in the yere of oure lorde God 1555. I Roger Pereson, of Monkefriston, being hool of mynde and good of rememberaunce, makꝭ this my last will and testament in maner and forme followinge. First I bequeathe my soull to God allmightie, to oure blessid ladie, and to all the celestiall companye of heven, and my bodie to be buried in my ꝑishe churche yerde of Monkefrystone. Also I bequeathe to the holie sacrament ij^{d}. Also I giue to Jennett my wiff ij of my best sheepe and one cowe. Also I giue to Alice my doughter one yowe hogge. Also I giue to Richarde Jennynge my curate to praye for my soull xij[d]. The Residewe of my goodę, I honestlie brought furthe and my dettę paid, I giue to Jennett my wiff, William my sone, Katheryn, Agnes, Esabell, and Alice, my doughters, whom I maike myne executors. Thes beinge wytnes, Sir Richarde Jennynge, Richarde Fuyster, Thomas Richardsone, Arthure Pereson, with other moo.—[*Proved 2 March,* 1555, *by Jenet, the widow. Grant reserved to the children, minors.*]

Richard Webster, of Fairburn.

(xv. j. 17 b.)

In the name of God Amen: the last day of December in the yere of o[r] Lord god m[l]ccccc[th]Lv[th]. I Richard Webster, of Farbarne, hooll of mynde and of good and ꝑfite remembrance, ordeinne and maike my testamente and last will in maner and forme folowinge. Firste I gyve and comende my soull unto god almightie with all the blessed sanctę in heaven, and my bodie to be buried within the churche yerde of All sanctę at Ledsh'm. Also I bequeathe vnto the vicar there for tithes and oblac̃ons forgotten viij[d]. Item I gyve and bequeathe vnto Richarde my sonne one yocke of my oxen at his owne election and one iron bounde wayne, the waynhead yocke, shakkell and bolte, Also one quarter of wheate, a quarter of barlie, a quarter of pees, and a quarter of haver. Item to Thomas my sonne too quarters of barlie. Item to Alicie Talior my doughter one blacke amlinge meare. Item to William Talior and Alexander his brother to either of theme one shepe. Item to Elsabethe Talior one blacke hawkid whie. Item to Elinge Talior a yewe shepe. Item to Margarete my wif one fillie and also I will that Margarete my said wif haue one holme gaite and also vj acars of arabley land belonginge to my fermehold in the seu'all feildes of Ferborne And also one litle howse at the Laithende for her corne to lye in, And my sonne Richarde to plowe the said land, And the said Margarete to pay for plewing of the same, the saide Margarete to haue the said holme gate And vj acars of land duringe her wedowehead and no longer bot as the custome of the Countrie requirethe, and then the saide holm gate and lande to remayne vnto Richard my sonne to whome I gyve all the Residewe of my hooll Fermehold with all comodities and proffettę belonginge to the same. Also I bequeathe vnto John Talior my sonne in lawe one oxe and half a quarter of barlie. The Residewe of all my goodes not bequeathed, my dettę paid, fun'all costes maid, and my will fulfilled, I gyve vnto Margarete my wif, Richard and Thomas my sonnes, whome I orden and maike my executors of this my last will and testamente. Witnesses, John Smythe, Thomas Illingworthe, and John Bywater.—[*Proved 7 April,* 1556.]

Robert Roger, of Featherstone.

(xv. j. 18 a.)

In the name of God Amen: the xiij[th] day of Marche in the yere of o[r] Lord god m[l]ccccc[th]lv[th]. I Robert Roger, of the ꝑishe and towne of Fetherston, makithe this my last will and testamente in maner and forme folowinge. The furste I gyve and bequeathe my soull to god almightie, to our ladie sancte Marie, besechinge hir and all the celestiall companye in heaven to pray for me, and my bodie to be buried within the churche yerde of Fetherstone. As for my goodes, cattels, and dettę, I honestlie brought furthe and my dettę paid (if any be), I gyve theme to Isabell my wif the whome I maike my executrix. Thes witnes, Edward Wormall my curate, Robert Abbot, William Everingh'm, and Stephen Vsher, wth other.—[*Proved 22 April, 1556.*]

THOMAS POLLARD, OF OKENSHAW.

(xv. j. 21 a.)

In the name of God Amen: the xxvij^th^ day of December in the yere of o^r^ lord God m^l^ccccclv^th^. I Thomas Pollard, of Okynshay in the pish-enge of Byrstall, of hooll mynd, maikethe my last will in forme folow-inge. First I bequeathe my soull to god almightie and to the company of o^r^ blessed ladie sancte mary and to all the sanctę in heaven, and my bodie to be buried in the churche yerd of Byrstall of the holie Apostellę Peter and Paule. Firste at the tyme of my buriall I wilbe browght furthe of my hooll goodes, and all my dettę and dewties shalbe contentid and paid of the hooll goodes, And then the Rest that remayneth of all my goodes I gyve theme bolie to Margarete my wif and my children savinge that I gyve to Jane my doughter iij^li^ over and above her childę porc̃on. Also I gyve the taike of my Fermeholde to Thomas Pollerd my sonne, and he to stand tenand to the lord. And Margaret my wyf and he shall occupie the fermehold togethers. And my wif to be chief thereof duringe her lif with the Licence of the Lord. Item I maike Thomas and Roger Pollard my sonnes my full executors to fulfill this my laste will. Thes men berynge witnes, Willm Pereson, Lawrence Pollard, Willm Pereson yonger, and Roger Pereson, William Talior.—[*Proved 22 April, 1556.*]

THOMAS GARLICKE, OF WOODHOUSE, NORMANTON.

(xv. j. 21 b.)

In the name of God Amen: this thre and twentie day of Marche in the second and third yere of the Reigne of Philippe and Marie, &c. Wit-nessithe that I Thomas Garlicke, of Wodhowse within the pishinge of Normanton, husbandman, of good memorie and hooll mynde, maikethe this my last will and testamente in maner and forme hereafter followinge. Firste I bequeathe my soull to almightie god the father and maiker of heaven and earthe and of all thingę that is in heaven and earthe, and the onelie Savio^r^ of all mankynde, and to o^r^ blessed Ladie sancte Marie the mother of oure Savio^r^ Jesu Christe, the quene of heaven, And finallie to all the blessed company of heaven bothe Angellę and Archangellę, Apos-tellę, Evangelistę, patriarches, prophettę, confessors, m'ters and virgyns, And my bodie to be buried within the churche porche of Alhallowes in the pishinge of Normanton. Firste I gyve to the said pishe of Normanton to be praid for xij^d^. I gyve to my sister Emote xij^d^. Item I gyve to Jenet Lounde an ewe and a lambe. Item I gyve to Richard Wodd children cu'ye one of theme xij^d^ to pray for me. I gyve to John Garlicke dowghter xij^d^. I gyve to my god children en'ye one of theme iiij^d^. I gyve to the mendinge of the heighe way in Wodehowse Lone to be prayed for xij^d^. The Reste of goodes, my dettes paid, my bequestes and legacies fulfilled and funerall expenses maid aboute me to bring me honestlie furthe, I gyve to Elsabethe my wif, Nicholas Garlicke, Thomas Garlicke, Agnes

Garlicke, and Dorothe Garlicke, my children, whome I make my lawfull executors joynetlie all togeyther, and my wif to haue her thyrdę accordinge to the custome of the countie. And the Reste of my goodes to be delte emonge my children. And finallie I will that my wif haue the occupacion of my Fermehold after my decesse and to vse yt as she shall thinke beste, and my wif and my childrén joynetlie alltogether to fulfill this my will and testamente as my faithfull truste is in theme all. Thes bearynge witnes of the same, Richard Wod, John Barowghe, and John Towneend and Richard Johnson, the curate off the said churche of Normanton, with others.—[*Proved* 22 *June*, 1556.]

Agnes Waide, of Wakefield, widow.

(xv. j. 23 a.)

In the name of God Amen: the xvth day of October in the yere of oure Lorde god m^{l}cccccthlvth. I Agnes Waide, of Wakefeld, wyddowe, late wif of Costyn Waide, of Whitkirk, in the countie of Yorke, deceased, beinge of good and ꝑficte memorie, lawde and prayse be vnto Almightie god, maikę this my last will and testamente in maner and forme followinge, that is to say. Firste and princippalie I comende my soull to almightie god my maker and Redemer, and to o^{r} blessed ladie sancte Marie and to all the holie company of heaven. Also I cōmytte my bodie to be buried in the ꝑishe churche yerde of Alhallowes in Wakefeld afforesaid. Also I will and my full mynde ys that myne executor hereafter vnder namede and wrytten shall cause me to be well and honestlie browght furthe and buried and after a decent maner accordinge as my trust ys he will. Also I gyve and bequeathe vuto my sonne Henry Waide the som̄e of thre poundes. Also I gyve and bequeathe vnto my half suster Alice Casson in full recompence of all her costes and chardges and expenses whiche she haythe bestowed vpon me heretofore when I was with her husband and her in there howse And for the paynes she hadd with me the same tyme, Fourttie shillingę of lawfull money of England. The Rest of all my goodes moveable and vnmoveable and also all my cattalę, dettę, dewties, some and somes of money and other thinges whatsoeu' thei be and where and in whose handes soeu' thei be, I gyve and bequeathe vnto my nephewe Nicholas Bramley, whome I maike, ordayne, and constitute my hool and full executor of this my presente last will and testamente. Thes beinge witnesses of the same, John Burrowe, John Hargrave, Thomas Musgrave, Alexander Dicson, John Stones, with others.—[*Proved* 22 *April*, 1556.]

Ellen Dawson, of Eccup.

(xv. j. 28 b.)

In the name of God Amen: the xvj day of Januarie in the yeare of oure lorde god a thowsande fyve hunderithe fyftie and fyve. I Elyne Dawsone, of Ecope within the ꝑishe of Addle, wydowe, hooll of mynde and ꝑfytt of mem̄orie, maikethe this my testament and last will in maner followinge. First I giue my soull to God Allmightie, and my bodie to be buried within the churche yearde of sanct John Baptist at Addill. Also I bequeathe to eu'y one of William Wyke children one lambe. Also I giue to the churche of Addill on Alter clothe price xij^{d}. Also I giue to

Jane my doughter my best gowne and my best kyrtle and a chist. Also I giue to Mawde Dawsone one gowne. Also I giue to Richarde Dawson my sone one Almerie. Also I giue to Byrkynshaye wyff my workdaye coytt. Also I giue to Isabell Byrkynshay my best petticott. Also I giue to Threshe wyf my olde petycott, a pare of sleves and a smocke. Also I assyne my farmhold to Richard Dawsone and William Dawson my sonnes to occupie it together or severallie as it shalbe thought best for them. Also I will that Richarde and Wiɫɫm Dawson my sonnes shall gyve to my doughter Jane at the daye of her mariedge eyther of them xx^s^ in full recompence of all her hooll interest and tytill in that farmhold. The Residewe of all my good afore not bequeathed, my fun'all expenses maid and my dette paid, I giue to Richarde Dawson and William Dawson my sonnes and Jane my doughter to be devided emongę them by even porc̃ons. Also I ordayn and maike Richarde Dawson and Wiɫɫm Dawson my sonnes and Jane my doughter my full and lawfull executors of this my last will to se it trewlie executed and fulfilled. Recordę of my will, William Wyke, Leonarde Carlell, Wiɫɫm Jackeson, with other mo as Cuthbert With'm, clerke, person of Addill.—[*Proved* 26 *April*, 1556, *by Richard and William. Grant reserved to Jane, a minor.*]

John Studderd, of Biggin.

(xv. j. 32 b.)

In Dei nõie Amen: in the yeare of oure lorde god a thowsand fyve hundrith fiftie and sex. I John Studderd, of Bigginge within the parishe of Fenton, seike in bodie and hooll in mynde, makith and ordenith this my last will and testament in maner and forme followinge. First I bequeathe my soull to Allmightie god and to oure ladie sancte Marie and to all the holl celestiall and blessed companye of heaven, and I will that my bodie be buried in Fentone churche yearde. Also I giue unto Jennet Andrewe one yowe and one lambe, and to Anne Andrewe one hogg lambe, And to William Andrewe one hogge lambe, to John Tasker my god sone one hogge lambe. Also I giue to John Poulle one hoggę lambe. Also I giue to John Studderde and William Studderde and to eyther of them a lambe at mydsomer next. Also I giue to Thomas Studderde my sone my house with a Kylne beylded of Biginge more syde within the perishe of Fentone with toft and croft with appurteñnce therto belonginge and fower acres of lande lyinge of the South east of the said toft and croft ^wth^ appurteñnce therto belonginge. I the said John Studderde doith giue the said house, kylne, toft and croft, fowre acres of lande with appurteñnce to my son Thomas Studderde, his heirs, executors, or assignes for ever more. Also I giue to Roberte Studderde my sone one baye maire beinge with foylle, one cowe colore blacke called Sylke, and one qwye colore blacke with browne eares, and one spanynge calf colore blacke with a whitt head. Also I giue to John Studderde my yongest sone towe acres of lande lyinge in the townshippe of Bigginge within the lordeshipe of Fentone in a place called Hollicke to hym and to his heires of his bodie lawfullie begotten for ever, And for lacke of heires of his bodie lawfullie begotten then I giue it to Roberte Studderde and his beires of his bodie lawfullie begotten for ever, And for lacke of heires of his bodie lawfullie begotten then I giue yt to Thomas Studderde and his heires for ever.

Also I giue to John Studderde my sone one Cowe. Also I giue to Anne my doughter one Cowe called Flourtell, one Sowkyne calf, one cobborde, one great Brasse pott, one litle pott, one kettle, one pare of sheittꝭ, too cou'lettꝭ of the best, a mattres of the best, one charger of pewther, one dubler of pewther, one chist with a locke and one wooll whele. Also I giue to Anne Studderde my doughter ij yowes and ij lambes, And to Thomas my sone a cou'lett lome with Implementꝭ. The Residue of all my goodꝭ, my dettꝭ paid, legacies performed, my fun'alles discharged and I honestlie brought furthe, I giue frelie vnto Thomas Studderde, Roberte Studderde, John Studderde, and Anne Studderde, my children, whome I maike my full executors of this my last will and testament. Roberte Herrisone, Xpofer Herrisone, Thomas Studderde, and Frauncꝭ Toode, wytnesses hereof.—[*Proved* 8 *May*, 1556, *by Thomas. Grant reserved to Robert, John, and Anne, minors.*]

THOMAS RILEY, OF HELTHWAITE.

(xv. j. 35 b.)

In the name of God Amen: the xxvj^{ti} day of May in the yere of our lord God m^{l}ccccccliij. I Thomas Riley, of Helthawayte within the parish of Harwood, of good & p'fecte remembrance, makithe and ordyneth this my last will and testament in this maner and forme followinge. First I bequeath my soull to god almightie, and my bodie to be buried within the parishe churche yerde of Alhallos at Harwood. Also all my gooddes moveable and vnmoueable, my dettes dispatched and paid and my funerall charges accomplisshed, I giue and bequeath vnto Cicile Ryley my wif whom I ordayn and make my sole executrix. Thes being witnesses, Edmunde Mawde, John Fuller, with other moo.—[*Proved* 31 *July*, 1556.]

ELIZABETH LAKE, OF METHLEY, WIDOW.

(xv. j. 36 b.)

In the name of god Amen: the xvj day of Januarie in the yere of o^{r} lorde god m^{l}cccccthlv. I Elisabethe Laeke, of Meathlay, wedowe, of good wit and memorie, thankꝭ be to god, maikꝭ this my will and testamente of this maner and forme folowinge: the firste I bequeathe and comende my soull to god almightie my creator and Redemer, and I beseche him for his tender passione and his infinite m'cie that he will receyve my soull vnto his holie handꝭ, and yt may accompanye withe his blessed mother o^{r} ladie sancte Marie the virgyne, And wth all the holie sanctꝭ in heaven there to se his glorious face and there to haue the fruition of his godhead. Item I bequeathe my bodie to be buried within the sanctuarie of the ꝑishe churche of the said Meathley, there to Ryse in a stedfast hoope of a blissed resurrection emonge his just and electe p'sons in the last day of Judgemente. Item I bequeath to the nedes of the church iij^{s} iiij^{d}. Item I bequeathe to Isabell Webster one mattres, one cou'lett, one pare of blankettꝭ, and one pare of sheittꝭ. Itm. to Richard Lake my sonne eldest sonne one cuphord, one chymnethe, a pare of briggꝭ, and all other thingꝭ thereto belonginge and one siluer spone. And vnto his brother Robert a wayne and plowghe and all thingꝭ that to theme ꝑteyneth whiche myne ys. The Residewe of all my goodes not gyven nor bequeste I gyve vnto the said Richard Lake and to Robert, Thomas, and Agnes, his bretheren and suster. Also I desier and will that my cosyn Sr Richard Shanne and Sr Laurence Ootte shalhaue the tuytion and gou'nnce of the said Richard and Robert and also to mynyster there ptes and porcons of the said goodes as they shall thinke the best to the vse and proffet of the said Richard and Robert, and to deliu' or cause to be deliu'ed the same or the price therof vnto the said Richard and Roberte when they shall be or come to the aige and yeres of discretion, And if if shall happen, as god forbid, the said Sir Richard or Sir Lawrence to dye before the tyme that the said Richard and Robert shall come to aige of discretion then I will that the said Sir Richard and Sr Laurence shall comitte and ordenne some other frende in there steid for the intente beforesaid. Item I will that Agnes my doughter, mother of the same children, shall haue the gou'nance of the ptes and porcon of the said goode pteynge to the said Thomas and Agnes accordinge to the intente aforesaid. Moreover I will that if it shall happen any of the said children to die before thei shall come to yeres of discretion that the said porcons of goodes shall remayne vnto the survivors or survivor ove'livers or ou'liuer of theme. Witnes hereof is Robert Nalson, Thomas Shanne, and Thomas Lake.—[*Proved 22 April, 1556, by Richard Shanne, Rector of High Holland, Lawrence Oott*e, *priest, and Thomas Burton, layman, guardians of Rich., Robt., Thos., and Agnes Lake, minors.*]

HENRY FUNTANCE, OF GARFORTH.

(xv. j. 38 b.)

In the name of God Amen: the xxixth day of Auguste in the yere of o^{r} lord god m^{l}cccccthlv. I Henry Funtance, of the pishe of Garfourthe, of good and pfite reme'braunce, maikithe this my testamente and last will in maner and forme folowinge. Firste I gyve and frelie betaike my saull to God Almightie, the blissed virgyne oure ladie sancte Marye, And to all the blessed company of heaven, and my bodie to be buried in the churche yerde of Garforthe. Also I bequeathe to Jenet my wif one gared cowe. Itm. I bequeathe to Jenet Vevers my god doughter a lambe. Also I bequeathe to the pson to pray for me xij^{d}. The Residue of all my goodes, my dette and fun'alle paid and discharged, I gyve to Jenet my wif, Robert my son, Jenet my doughter, and Isabell Funtance, whome I maike my executors to do for me as I haue put theme in thuse. Thes beinge witnesses, John Dawson, curate, William Rawson, and John Dawson, withe other moo, the day and yere above said.—[*Proved* 29 *May*, 1556.]

THOMAS THORNTON, OF KIRKSTALL.

(xv. j. 40 a.)

In Dei nōie Amen: I Thomas Thorneton, of Christall, the xx^{tie} day of Maie, the yeare of oure lorde God m^{l}cccccthlvjth, maikethe this my last will and testamente in maner and forme followinge. Firste I bequeathe my soull to Almightie God, to oure ladie sancte Marie, And to all the holie company of heaven, and my bodie to be buried in the churche yeard of sancte Peter at Ledes. In p'mis I gyve to Jane Wymmersley a yewe and a lambe. Item I will that my goodes be devidede into thre partes, one parte to my wif, one parte to my children, and the thred parte to my self, and I to be brought furthe, my dettꝭ paide, and my fun'all expenses discharged. And the Residewe that leavithe I gyve to my wiff and to my yongest childe. Item I gyve to the ornamente of the blessed sacramente xij^{d}. Item I gyve to my wif my farmehold at Bramley so moche as I haue in custodie at this day. Also I maike my wif Jennet and my yongest childe William my executors of this my last will and testamente. In witnes hereof, Thomas Rauson, William Musgrave, Thomas Green, Laurence Rauson, John Thorneton.—[*Proved* 3 *June*, 1556, *by the widow. Grant reserved to William the son, a minor.*]

ROBERT HERDY, OF METHLEY, YEOMAN.

(xv. j. 42 a.)

In the name of God Amen: the xvjth day of September in the yere of o^{r} Lorde god m^{l}cccccthlvth. I Robert Herdey, of Medley in the Countie of Yorke, yoman, beynge of good and ꝑfite memorie, laude and prayse be vnto Almightie god, therefore maike and ordenne this my present laste will and testamente in maner and forme folowinge, that ys to say. Firste and principallie I comende, gyve, and bequeathe my soull vnto Almightie god my maiker and redemer, to oure blissede ladey saynete Marie, and to all the bolie company of heaven, and my bodie to be buried in the ꝑishe churche or churche yerde of Medley afforesaid. Also I gyve and bequeathe vnto Luce nowe my wif ten shepe. Also I gyve and bequeathe vnto Roberte, Edwarde, and Alicie, my children, to eu'y one of theme, tenne shepe. Also I gyve and bequeathe vnto John Hirste my s'ꝩnte one whie stirke and too shepe. Also I gyve and bequeathe vnto the reparynge and amendinge of Medley brydge vj^{s} viij^{d}. Also I gyve and bequeathe vnto Xpofer Herde my brother foure markes in money. Also I will and my full mynde and entente is that the reste of all my goodes, corne, and cattallꝭ be equallie devidede into thre ꝑtes and porc̃ons, wherof I gyve and bequeathe one ꝑte thereof vnto Luce my wif for and in the nayme of her thirde parte and porc̃on. Also I gyve and bequeathe one other ꝑte thereof to the afforesaide Edwarde, Roberte, and Alice, my children. Also I will that the thyrde ꝑte thereof be bestowede and employede towardes my fun'all expenses and the payinge of my dettꝭ, And the reste and residewe thereof I gyve and bequeathe vnto the forsaid Luce my wif. Also I constitute, orden, and maike the said Luce my wif my hooll and full executrixe of this my presente last will and testamente vnto whome I putt and assigne the order and governement and rule of my said three children withe there legacies and porc̃ons here in this presente testamente menc̃onede durynge there none ages and infancye if she kepe her wedowe so longe, yf not I will that my saide three children withe there legacies and porc̃ons as ys afforesaid be at the appoynmente of the supervisors of this my presente testamente hereafter naymede, to be orderrede accordinge to ther descrec̃ons, And if yt shall fortune anye of my saide children to deceasse before they accomplishe there said aiges and before that tyme be not maried that then I gyve and bequeathe her ꝑte or his ꝑte of them so deceassinge to the other of theyme they survyvinge. And if it shall fortune all my said children to deceasse (as god defende) before thei come and accomplishe there said Aiges and before that tyme be not maried, then I bequeath the one half of all there ꝑtes and legacies afforesaid to the said Luce my wif and the other half to be devidede emongꝰ the nexte of the kynne of my said children at the discrẽcone of my said suꝑvisorꝰ. And I ordeyne, constitute, and maike John Herde and Chr̃ofer Herde my brethern, Thomas Hymsworthe of the gaynrie, Roberte Hymsworthe his sonne, and John Burrowe of Wakefeld, the Suꝑvisors of this my said presente testamente, whome I desier to se the same trewlie executed, p'formed, and fulfillede as my truste ys in theme fynyshede and endede in maner and forme the thyrde day of Marche nexte after the daite above wrytten. Thes witnesses, Thomas Hymsworthe, Xpofer Herde, William Adamson, John Burrow, Thomas Laburn.—[*Proved* 5 *June*, 1556.]

WIILIAM BARKER, OF NEWTON KYME.

(xv. j 43 a.)

In the name of God Amen: I William Barker, of the ꝑishe of Newton Kyme, of ꝑfite mynde and good remembrance, xixth day of Maie in the yere of o^{r} Lorde god m^{l}cccccth fiftie and sex, maike my testamente and last will in maner and forme followinge. First I bequeath my soull to Almightie god my maker and to his onelie sonne Jesu Christ my Redemer and Savio^{r}, in whome I put my hooll hope and trust of saluac̃one through the merities of his blessed passion, to his blessed mother and virgyne sancte Marie, and to all the holie company of heaven, to pray for me, havinge great nede thereof, and my bodie to be buried in the churche yerde of the forsaid ꝑishe. Also I bequeathe to the churche xij^{d}. Also I bequeathe the hole intreste of my farmeholdꝰ to Jenet my wif for terme of her lif, And afterwarde to George my sonne. Also I bequeathe to Thomas my sonne vli. Also I bequeathe to Jenett my doughter xx^{s}, to John my sonne xx^{s}, so that he troble not my wif nor any of my childrene. If he doo I will then that he haue not a penny. Also I bequeathe to Roberte my sonne xx^{s}. Also I bequeathe to Anne my doughter x^{s}, to Elisabethe my doughter x^{s}, to George my son a wayne with the heade oxen after my wifꝰ tyme. Item I bequeathe to eu'ye god childe I haue of myne owne children one ewe and a lambe. And to eu'y other god childe iiij^{d}, and to Xpofer Barker an ewe. Also I bequeathe all myne other goodes, bothe moveable and vnmoveable, to Jenet my wif whome I maike full executrix of this my last will. Witnes hereof, Richard Shiplay, Xpofer Cawod, and George Wyley.—[*Proved* 9 *June*, 1556.]

WILLIAM HARDWICK, OF OTLEY.

(xv. j. 46 a.)

In the name of God Amen: I William Hardwicke, of Ottley in the Countie of Yorke, Joner, makithe this my last will and testamente in maner and forme folowinge the fift day of Maie Anno d'ni millimo qui'gen^{mo} lvj^{to}. First I bequeath my soull to the mercie of my Redemer Jesus Christe, And my bodie to be buried in the churche molde of Ottley. Also I bequeath to my brother Brian all my best apparell and raymente, that ys to say, my best shertte, my best dublett, my best hoose, my best shoos, my best jackit, my best jyrken, my best cloke, my best hatt, and my best swerde. Also I bequeathe to Margaret Hardwicke so moche tymber as shall maike her one cobborde. Also I bequeathe to eu'ye one of my brother Siluester children iiij^d, And to John his son my gray jackett. Also I bequeathe to my wif my best syluer spoyne and to my brother Brian an other, And to Richard Brathwaite wif of Askwithe my third spoyne. Also I gyve vnto my father in lawe Anstey Threplande iiij^s and vnto Brian my brother iiij^s, whome I maike Supvisors of this my last will and testamente, and Jayne my wif my sole executrix of this my last will and testament, and vnto her also I gyve all my goodes and dettes vnbequested (as for dettę I owe none bot one stroke of Rye to Richarde Hogge), she to bringe my bodie furthe honestlie and accordinge to neyburhead. Thes beynge witnes, Richard Dunwell and Myles Flessher, with other moo, the day and yere above rehersed.—[*Proved 2 July*, 1556.]

THOMAS RIDIALL, OF SPITTLE HARWICK, YEOMAN.

(xv. j. 46 b.)

In the name of God Amen: I Thomas Ridyall, of Spitle Harwicke of the pishe of Pontefract within the Countie of Yorke, yoman, hooll of mynd and pfite remembrance, the tente day of Februarie in the yere of o^r lorde God m^lccccc^th lv, dothe maike this my last will and testamente in this maner and forme folowinge. First I bequeathe my soull to almightie god my Redemer and maiker, and my bodie to be buried in my pishe churche of Pontefract. Also I bequeathe to Elsabeth Darley xv^s and to her children, that ys to say, Isabell, Richard, and Jenet, to eu'y one of theme ten shillinges and a shepe, and to Elsabethe Darley her doughter vj^li xiij^s iiij^d to be paid by the handes of John Ridiall the day of her marriage or when she ys able to occupie yt herself, withe a chiste and a gyrdle. Also I bequeathe to my brother Robert Ridiall my brother [*sic*] xvj^s viij^d, and to his thre children xiij^s iiij^d a peice. Also I bequethe to Robert Turner xxx^s, and to Margarete his wif xv^s, and to his fyve children that ys at home to eu'ye one of theme a yewe and a lambe. Item I bequeathe to John Ridiall wif xv^s, and to Elsabethe Savage her dowghter xv^s, and to eu'ye one of there children a yewe and a lambe, and to Thomas Ridiall a syluer spone, to Agnes a spone, and to Barbaray a siluer spone and a chymney. Also I bequeathe to Elsabethe Shillito xv^s, a counter, and a panne, and to cu'ye one of her childeren a sheipe, and to Robert Shillito a siluer spoyne and v^li to be gyven emongest theme which ys in the handes of John Flemynge of Sharleston. Also I bequeathe to Jenet Fuyster a sheipe. Also I bequeathe to Katheryne Wilkinson xv^s, and to eu'y one of her children a sheipe, and to Thomas her sonne a syluer spoyne. Also I bequeath to Buckle wif xiij^s iiij^d, and to either of her childer a sheippe. Also I bequeathe to Robert Adam vj^s viij^d, and to Isabell his wif vj^s viij^d. Also I bequeathe to Allane Androo wif xv^s and a siluer spone. Item to eu'y one of my god childer viij^d a pcice. Item to eu'ye one of John Ridiall s'untę vj^d a pcice. Also I bequeathe to Sr William Chamber iij^s iiij^d. Also I bequeathe to Agnes Horner xij^d. Also I bequeathe to Robert Farnell iij^s iiij^d. Item to Lawrence Wile ij^s, and to Agnes Fischer xij^d. Item to John Androo iij^s iiij^d, and to Agnes Clowghe iij^s iiij^d. The Residewe of all other my goodes nott bequeste nor gyven, all fun'all expenses discharged, I will thei be at the order of John Ridiall and Sir Richard Ridiall his brother, whome I maike myne boill and full executors to haue to there owne vse. Provided alwayes that John Darley shall not meddle with suche money as ys bequeathed his children bot thei to receyve yt themselfę at the executors bandes at suche tyme and tymes as the frendę of the saide children shall thinke it convenient whe' thei ar able to occupie it to theire most proffet and advantage. In witnes whereof John Barcar, vicar, Sr Thomas Mettringh'm, Robert Farnell, Sr Anthony Flemynge, Sr Alexander Carver, wth other moo.—[*Proved* 28 *July*, 1556, *by John Ridiall, Sir Richard Ridiall renouncing.*]

JOHN CUTLER, OF THORNER, LABOURER.

(xv. j. 48 a.)

In the name of God Amen: the last daye of December in the yere of o^r lorde God m^{l}ccccclv. I John Cutler, dwellinge in Thornar within the countie of Yorke, laborer, seike in bodye and wholl in soull, of good and quieke remembrance, make this my last will and testament in maner and forme followinge. First I bequest my soull to Almyghtie god and to his blessed mother our ladye saint Marie and to all the faire companye of heven, and my bodie to be buried within sancte Peter churche yerd of Thornar. Also I bequest to the Churche of Thorman [*sic*] xij^s. Item I bequest to Peter Beregs one shepe. Also I bequest to Wiłłm Beregs one shepe. Also I make Jenet Reame my full executrix to haue all my gooddes vnbequest, moveable and vnmoueable, to pay my dettes and to brynge me honestlie forth at the day of my buriall and to pay my funerall expenses. Thes be the witnesses, Wiłłm Leves, Henry Writhe, Richarde Hube, with other mo.—[*Proved* 17 *June*, 1556.]

WILLIAM WALKER, OF ADEL.

(xv. j. 48 a.)

In the name of God Amen: the thirde daye of Nouember in the yeare of our lorde god m^{l}dlv. I Wiłłm Walker, of Athill, hoole of mynde and perfyte of memorie, makithe this my testament and last will in maner followinge. First I bequeath my soull to God almightie, and my bodie to be buried within the churche yerde of sancte John Baptist at Addill. Also I bequeathe to Richerd Walker, Thomas Walker, Wiłłm Walker, Henrie Walker, iiij of my sonnes, all my working toles. The residew of all my gooddes not bequeathed, my funerall expens' made and my dettę paide, I give to Isabell Walker my wif, to Richard W., Thomas W., Wiłłm W., Henrye W., Elisabeth W., Isabell W., Alison W., Dorothe W., my wif and children, to be divided emonge them by even porc̃ons, whom I make my full and lawfull executors of this my last will to se it trulye executed and fulfilled. Recordes of my will, Thomas Browne, Henrie Tomlynson, Richerde Wood, Thomas Tayt, withe other mo.—[*Proved* 17 *June*, 1556, *by Isabel the widow. Grant reserved to the eight children, minors.*]

JAMES DENTON, OF WAKEFIELD.

(xv. j. 50 b.)

In Dei nõie Amen: the xxvijti day of Maye in the yere of our lord God m^{l}dlvj. I James Denton, of the ꝑishe of Wakefelde, seike of bodie and hooll of mynde & good of remembrance, makith this my last will & testament in man' & forme following. First I giue & bequeath my soull to almightie God my savyore & redemer, to o^r^ blessed ladie sancte Marie Virgyn, to all the celestiall companye in heaven, & my body to be buried within the churche of Wakefelde aforsayd nye to my stall ende. It' I giue to Robert Denton son of Amere Denton my Brother one tenement w^t^ appurtenancę called Kirkhouse lyeing & beyng in Cōmerworthe to him & to his beires for eu'. It' I giue to the said Roberte Denton one howse with app^r^tēncę in Wakefeld no[w] in the tenure & occupacōn of Roger Slater in Kirkgate to him & to his heirs for eu'. It' I giue to Margaret & Jane Denton either of them xx^s^. It' I giuc to George Lee, Sybell, Anne, & to Elizabeth Lee, eu'y of them xx^s^. It' I giue to Amere Dyckonson, Richard and John Dyckonson, eu'y of them xx^s^. It' I giue to Richard Dawson viij children viij^li^ equallie emong them. It' I giue to Wiłłm Denton vij children vij^li^ equally emong them. It' I giue to Elisabeth Denton vj^li^ xiij^s^ iiij^d^. It' I giue to Jenett Robert vj^li^ xiij^s^ iiij^d^. It' I giuc to John Denton xx^s^ & a payre of sherę. It' I giue to Wiłłm Denton & Richard Denton either of them xx^s^. It' I giue to Robert Gamell xx^s^. It' I giue to the wif of Robert Hemysley of Pontfrett xx^s^. It' I giuc to the amending of the ways about Wakefelde v^s^. The residew of all my goodę vnbequest, my dettę & legacies payd, I giue & bequeth them to Amere Denton my brother, whom I make & ordayne to be my full & onely executor, he to dispose for my soull as my trust is in him. Thes being witness', John Boothelder, Wiłłm Denton, Miles Talyer & Edward Myddope, the whom also I make the sup̄visors of this my last will to se it is fulfilled & done. Witnes also of this my last will, Sr James Brodbent & John Syddall. Item I giue to Jenett Doley vj^s^ viij^d^.—[*Proved* 19 *June*, 1556.]

Richard Hollings, of Horsforth.

(xv. j. 50 b.)

In the name of God Amen: the last day of Julye the yere of our lord god m^l^ccccclj. I Richard Hollyngę, of Horseforth within the p̄ishe of Gyseley, being of hooll mynde & p'fecte remembraunce, thankę be to God, do constitute, ordayne & declare this my last will in man' & forme followinge. First I bequeath my soull to the mercy of almightie God, & my bodie to [be] buried w^t^in the churche yerd of Gyseley aforesayd & my funerall chargę to be done & my legacies to be payd by myne owne brother Wiłłm Hollingę & my syster his wif & ther children, whom I do make myne executors ioinctlie & seu'allye. It' I will that my brother Wiłłm Hollynge haue the leace of my fermholde imediatlie after my deathe to the vse of one of his sonnes whom I or he shall nomynate. Thes being witnes, Mr John Grene, gentleman, s^r^ Olyu' Ashe, curate, Peter Chouler, with other mo.—[*Proved* 22 *June*, 1556, *by William Hollings and his wife.*]

Thomas Riding, of Woodhall.

(xv. j. 51 a.)

In the name of God Amen: the xj^th^ day of February in the yere of our lord God 1555. I Thomas Rydyng, of Woodhall w'in the p̄ishe of Caluerley, seke of bodye & hooll & p'fecte of mynd & remembrance, thankę be to God, doth ordayne & make this my last will & testament in man' & forme folowing: first & principally I yeld & comend my soull vnto Almightie God my creater & Jesu Christe my redemer & to o[r] blessed ladye sancte Marie & to all the holy & blessed co'pany of heven, & my body to be buried w[t]in the ꝑishe churche yerd of Calu'ley before said. Also I giue vnto Isabell my wif my holl ten'nt during her naturall lif & after her death it to remayne vnto Thomas Rydyng my son during all suche termes & 'yeres as I haue in the same. Also I will that all my goodꝭ shalbe dyuyded in thre seu'all p'tes, wherof I giue one part vnto Isabell my wif, the second p'te I giue vnto Thomas, James, Richard, Nicholas, Willm & Alice Ryding, my children, the thirde part I will be res'ved to myself and to bring me forth. Also I giue & bequeath for tithes & oblac̃ons negligentlye forgotten to the hye alter at Calu'ley xij[d]. Also I gyve vnto Xpofer Pollerd my son in law vj[s] viij[d]. Also I giue and bequeath vnto Agnes Ambler my doughter vj[s] viij[d]. Also I giue & bequeath vnto John Sclater my son in law iij[s] iiij[d]. Also I giue & bequeath vnto Willm Ambler yonger xij[d]. Also I giue & bequeth vnto John *P*ollerd xij[d]. The residew & remanent of my sayd goodꝭ not bequest nor gyuen I honestly brought furth, thes my legacꝭ fulfilled & dettꝭ paid, I gyve holly vnto Isabell my wyfe, whom w[t] Thomas & James Rydyng my sonnes I make my lawfull executors. Thes being witness', *P*eter Kytson, Vicar of Calu'ley, Thomas Taylyor, and John Kytchyne.—[*Proved 26 June, 1556, by Isabel and Thomas. Grant reserved to James, a minor.*]

THOMAS YEDALL OTHERWISE CHASTERTON, OF KIRKSTALL.

(xv. j. 51 a.)

In the name of God Amen: the vij day of the moneth of August in the yere of our lord God 1555. I Thomas Yedall called otherwise Chasterton, of Kyrkestall w[th]in the ꝑishe of Ledꝭ, beinge of good memory, p'fecte & hooll mynde, makith this my last will & testament in maner & forme followynge, neu' to be altered or changed hereafter. First I gyf & bequeath my soull to almighti God my creator & redemer & to our blessed ladye & to all the sanctꝭ in heven, & my bodie to be buried in the ꝑishe church yerd of sanct *P*eter at Ledꝭ. Also I gine & bequeath all my goodꝭ vnto Dowsabell my wif & to my thre sonnes, that is to say, Hughe, John & Thomas, in forme & effecte hereafter following, that is to saye, I do giue & bequeath vnto Dowsabell my wif the wholl third part of all m̃y goodꝭ, moueable & vnmoueable, to her awne proper vse & behof. The seconde part I giue to my thre sonnes, Hughe, Yedall, John Yedall, and Thomas Yedall. The third part of my goodꝭ to be taken in the bringynge furthe of my bodye & to the payment of my dettꝭ, my funerall chargꝭ mayd & done, & my bodye brought forth of my p'te. The rest lefte I gyue to my wif & my thre sonnes. I gine to Hughe Yedall my sword & buckler & my best dager. It' I giue to the blessed sacrament for the anornamente xx[d], and where as I haue lent to my brother Richard Yedall iiij markꝭ of money at seu'all tymes & aboue that som, I give hym it freelye condic̃onallie that wher as I haue lent my brother Richard one bay geldyng, saddle & brydle, for a tyme & space at my pleasure & no other ways & now I gyue the sayd geldyng & all other gere to my wif & my thre sonnes frelye. And if the said Richard my brother will not delyn' the sayde money & gelding, to ther proper vse for ever. It' I gyve to Marie my syster xiij[s] in money wherof she hath had vij[s] syns she came to me for to pay for the cariage of her rayment from London. Also I giuc to Dowsabell my wif my takke to the fynding & keping of my children. It' I will that Dowsabell my wif haue all my children p'tes in her custodie & keping to they com to lawfull age by the law, & if Dowsabell my wif marie & take a husband that [then] I will that the said Dowsabell and he that marieth her shall fynd sufficient sureties before he or she mary to be boundon by obligačon to Mr Gilbert Leghe for my children partę & porčons to be delyu'ed vnto them or suche as they shall or will appoincte it to when they com to lawfull yeres & to be bounden to the supvisors of this my last will & testament, whom I make my supvisors my Mr Gilbert Leighe, of Myddleton, Esquier, and if it fortune any of my sayd sonnes to dye before they come to lawfull yeres of aige in the law that then I will that the other at ar lyving shall have the deade p'te emongest them dyuyded, And if that two of my sonnes dye then I will at the third at is lyving shall have all the other p'tes, ānd if at all dye than I will at Dowsabell my wif shall haue all ther p'tę to her awne proper vse and behofe, And I make my full & hooll executor my yongest son Thomas Yedall. Thes men being witness', Mr Gilbert Leighe, esquier, Thomas Rawson, Roberte Judson, Lawrence Rawson, Willm Taylyer, Robert Schothrope, Henry Walker, Willm Archedallue, Thomas Thornton, John Bromhed, and before thes men I haue putte my hand & seal the day & yere aboue wrytten. Also I giuc to Mr Gilbert Leighe my crosbowe & racke & all at belongę to it for terme of his lif, & after his deathe to remayne to my yong mr Thomas Leighe.—[*Proved* 1 *July*, 1556, *on the certificate of Dom' Paul Mason and John Mathew, of Leeds, priests, by Dulsabell, the widow, and guardian of Thomas Yedall, the executor, a minor.*]

John Smith, of Sherburn, husbandman.

(xv. j. 51 b.)

In the name of God Amen: the xiij day of May in the yere of our lord God 1556. I John Smythe, of Sherburne, husbandman, hooll of mynd & of p'fecte remembrance, makę this my testament & laste will. First I giuc & bequeath my soull to Almighti God & to or lady sancte Marie & to all the holye company of heven, & my bodie to be buried in my pishe churche yerd of Sherburne. It' I giue to my curate for tythes forgotten vjs. It' I giuc to the churche workę vjd. It' I giuc to Elisabeth my wif on amblinge gray mare called throstell. It' I giuc to Francę my doughter on sylu' spone. It' I giue to John Lofte my bukskyn dublett & to eu'y of his thre childer xijd. It' I giue to my doughter Anne Lofte one yowe and a lambe. It' I giuc to John Hynd iiijd. It' I giue to Robert Hutchinson iiijd. It' I giue to Robert Smyth and to Nycholas Toode to either of them iijs iiijd, whom I make supvisors of this my testament & last will to se that it be pformed. The residue of all my goodę, my dettę & legacę payd & my body honestlie brought furthe, I giuc to Elisabeth my wif & to Margaret & Francę my doughters, whom I make my executrices. Thes being present at the declaračon of this my last will & testament & witness' of the same, Mathew Smythson, my curate, John Taylyer, chaplayne & Henrye Nelsthrope, with others.—[*Proved* 1 *July*, 1556.]

Richard Gieges, of Knottingley, husbandman.

(xv. j. 56 a.)

In Dei nōie Amen: the xvj day of Marche in the yere of our lord God 1555. I Richard Giegꝭ, of Knottyngley, husbandman, in the ꝑishing of Pontefrett, hooll of mynd & of ꝑfecte memorye, makithe this my last will & testament in maner & forme following. First I bequeathe my soull to Almightie God my Redemer & maker & to the blessed virgin Mary & to all the holy company in heven, & my body to be buried in the churche yerd of Alhallowes in Pontefret. It' inprimis I bequeath for my mortuary according to the Institution of the law & to haue a diryge at the day of my buriall song w^{t} all the p'istꝭ that belongethe to the churche & ij ꝑish clarkꝭ & eu'y prest to haue iiij^{d} & clarkꝭ ij^{d}. It' I bequeath to the hye altare of *P*ont' ornourne it w^{t} & my tithes & oblacōns forgotten vj^{d}. It' I bequeath to cu'ye one of my godꝭ children ij^{d}. It' I bequeath to the poore people of Knottingley iij mettꝭ of barly to be diuided emonges them to pray for me. It' I bequeath to Thomas Hamshay wif xij^{d} & to euery one of her children iiij^{d}. It' I bequeath to Hughe Atkinson & to Margaret my doughter for her childꝭ porcōn iiij^{li} xiij^{s} iiij^{d}. It' I bequeath to Richard Gicgꝭ my son to helpe him to his lernyng xx^{s}. It' I bequeath to John Bakker one quye stirke of ij yeres old & vpward & the said John to haue his findyng at the house till he come to lawfull aige. It' I bequeath to Mathew Hemson my graye jacket & my lether doblet. It' I bequeath to Agnes my doughter the best beast that falleth in my p'te & she to chuse horse or beast that falleth therin & one quarter of barlye fayre dight & durst. It' I bequeath to the said Agnes iij quarters of malte & to be delyuered imediatly after my death. It' I bequeath vnto Jenet Hawmond xij^{d} & to euery one of her children iiij^{d}. It' I bequeath to Wiłłm Hawmond iij^{s} iiij^{d} & to be suꝑvisor of my will & to haue costs borne for that at I haue given the said Wiłłm w^{t} my doughter Jenet of my goodꝭ I gaue to him for his childꝭ porcōn & that I will take of my charge ant that the said Wiłłm Hawmond shall not medle w^{t} no ꝑte of my goodꝭ if he be aboutward to let or interrupte my will no otherwise but to medle as suꝑvisor. It' I bequeath vnto Alice Bayker xij^{d} & to eu'y one of her children iiij^{d}. It' I bequeathe to Wiłłm Bayker iij^{s} iiij^{d} & to be suꝑviso^{r} of my will & to haue his costꝭ borne for that at I haue given the said Wiłłm Baker w^{t} my doughter Alice of my goodꝭ I gaue it him for his childꝭ porcōn & that I will of my charge & that the said Wiłłm Baker shall not medle w^{t} no ꝑte of my goodꝭ if he be aboutward to let or interrupt my will no otherwise but to medle as a suꝑviso^{r}. It' I bequeath vnto Wiłłm Giegꝭ my son one bounden wayne. It' I bequeath vnto Richard Giegꝭ my son ij quarters of malt. It' I bequeath to Agnes my wif ij of the best kyen that she will chuse that goith in Credylling parke. Also I giue and assigne my fermhold in Knottingley to Agnes my wif, Wiłłm Giegꝭ & Richard Giegꝭ my sonnes to occupie during all my yeres. It' I bequeath to Agnes my wif, Wiłłm Giegꝭ & Richard Giegꝭ my sonnes, all mucke & maner [manure] that is at the house. It' I will that all my goodꝭ moueable & vnmoueable, to be set in thre p'tes & Agnes my wif to haue one p'te, Wiłłm Giegꝭ, Richard Giegꝭ & Agnes Giegꝭ, my children, to have a nother p'te, my dettꝭ paid & I to be broughte furthe honestly & my fun'all expens' made & my will fulfilled, I giue frely vnto Wiłłm Giegꝭ & Richard Giegꝭ my sonnes, whom I make my full executors both as one of this my last will & testament & to do in workę of m'cy for my soull as they thinke best. Thes witness', Thomas Haull, Willm Abbott.—[*Proved* 17 *July*, 1556.]

JOHN OLREDE, OF BRAMHOPE, HUSBANDMAN.

(xv. j. 59 a.)

In the name of God Amen: the xvj[th] day of Marche in the yere of our lord god m[l]cccccl v. I John Olrede, of Bramope in the ꝑishe of Otley, husbandman, seike of bodye but hooll of mynde & good remembrance, do make my last will & testament in man' & forme following. First I bequeathe my saull to almighty god my maker & redemer & to our lady sancte Mary & to all the holy company of heven, & my body to be buried in the churche earthe at Otley & all other dewtyes to be done as the law requirethe. Also my mynde & will is that Grace my wif, Willm, Richard, & John my sonnes, & Johan my doughter shalbe my wholl executors & possesse, vse & enioye my goodę, moueable & vnmoueable, my dettę paid & my funerall expens' discharged according to the lawe. Witness' of this my last will, S[r] John Baynes, prest, Robert Oldred, John Cawdray, Thomas Sykes, with other mo.—[*Proved* 2 *July*, 1556, *by the widow. Grant reserved to the children, minors.*]

HENRY BROOM, OF WRENTHORPE, GENTN.

(xv. j. 59 a.)

In the name of God Amen: in the yere of our lord God m[l]d fiftie & sex, the xxvij day of M'ehe, in the secu'de & thyrde yeres of the reignes of our sou'aigne lord & lady Philippe & Mary, by the grace of god King & quene of England, France, Naples, Jerusalem & Yreland, defenders of the faithe, Princes of Spaine & Cicile, Archedukę of Austre, Dukę of Millaine, Burgon & Brabant, Countes of Haspurge, Flanders & Tyroll. I Henry Brome, of Wrenthorp in the county of Yorke, gent., being of hooll, good & ꝑfecte mynde & remembrance, makith & declarith this my last will & testament in man' & forme following, that is to say. First I bequeath my soull vnto almighty god my saveyo[r] & redemer desiring him of his infinite m'eye & graciose goodness to accepte and take the same emongest the holy company ther to his m'cy & grace, & my body to be buried w[t]in the ꝑishe churche of Wakefeld nygh vnto my stall at the queare dore & w[t] such obsequies & ceremonyes as the churche dothe nowe vse w[t] a dirige & soull masse w[t]in the said churche to be songe or said & as the law will suffer, ev'y prest hauyng therfore iiij[d] & eu'y clerke & scoler w[t] surples ij[d], & that myne execut' se this done or otherwise as they shall thinke conuenyent to be done for the helth & welthe of my saull & all christen saulls. And I giue & bequeath vnto the blessed sacrament of the high alter for my tithes forgotten if any suche be iij[s]. And further I will that myne execut' cause a trentall of mass' to be said w[t]in the said churche by some honest preist or preistę hauyng for eu'y masse iiij[d] & j[d] besidę to say *de ꝓfundę* w[t] this collet *Inclina d'ne*, &c., for my soull & all christen soulles at the first lauatorye & at that tyme or whan masse is done to receyve v[d] & so lykewise for eu'y masse during the whole trentall. Also I will that myne exec' shall pay & bestow towardę & vpon mending of the high ways about Wakefeld vj[s] viij[d]. Further I giue &

bequeathe to s^{r} Ric' Wortley, clerke, my faithfull brother in law, & Elisabeth now my wif, the third p'te of all myn owne landꝭ & tentꝭ w^{t} ther app^{r}tẽñcꝭ to haue & to holde to them & ther assignes vntill suche tyme as they haue receyved & taken therof the sōm of lxiij^{li} vj^{s} viij^{d} of lawfull Englishe money whiche said som I will the said Sr Ric' Wortley and Eliz' my wif & ther assignes shall giue & bestow emongest my children as hereafter shalbe declared, that is to say, to Beatrix Brome my doughter now lady Nevile a gelding or ^{v} markꝭ in redy money to by her a gelding therw^{t}, trusting that Sr John Nevile knight, wilbe eu' freyndly to my said wif & children for his cōnsell who I wolde if I durst be so bolde w^{t} his assistence, &c. Also I giue & bequeath to Eliz' Brome my doughter now maried to Edward Kellet vj^{li} xiij^{s} iiij^{d} & a cow for thė rest of her childꝭ ꝑte. Also I giue & bequeathe to Ric' Brome my son x^{li} & the lande late purchased by my late father Sr John Brome if he be deide as appeareth by evidence therof. Also I giue & bequeath lykewise to Henry Brome x^{li} & that land late purchased as afore is said by lyke evidence, if John Brome be deide. Also I giue & bequeath to Francys Brome if she be vnmaried at the day of my death xx^{li}. Also I giue & bequeath to Brian Brome my yongest son x m'kꝭ & to be founden of my goodꝭ vnto he come to the aige of xxj yeres & then to haue his childes ꝑte delyvered. And further I giue & bequeath to Sr Edward my ghostly father ij^{s}. Also to s^{r} William Ball for his peynes taken w^{t} me xx^{d} at all tymes, furthermore I gif & bequeath to Eliz' my wif her lawfull ioynter & feoffement made by me heretofore. And the residew of all my goodꝭ & landꝭ in Yorkeshire & Darbyshire I giuc & bequeath to Stephen Brome now my eldest son who I make my full beire. And if the said Eliz' my wif dye before the abouesaid som of lxviij^{li} vj^{s} viij^{d} be levied & receyved of the abouesaid third ꝑte of my landꝭ & teñtꝭ then I will & bequeathe the reu'c̃on of the abouesaid third ꝑte assigned to my wif & s^{r} Ric' Wortley p'ste to haue & to holde to him & his assignes vntill suche tyme as the abouesaid som of lxiij^{li} vj^{s} viij^{d} be fully receyved of the said third ꝑte of landꝭ abouesaid. And further I will & bequeath that the abouesaid som̃es shalbe delyvered to my said children at the dayes of ther mariages or at ther aiges of xxj yeres if they do not mary before the said aige, prouyded always that if any of my abouesaid children do dye before ther mariage & before ther abouesaid aiges of xxj^{ti} yeres then I will that the porc̃on & parte of those children or that childe so dyeng shalbe equallye dyuyded the other of my aforesaid children being maried or at the aforsaid aige. And further I will that if any of my said children do refuse to be ordred by my abouesaid wif & Sr Ric' Wortley, clerke, or on of them then I will that suche childe so refusinge shall loose v^{li} of his or her bequest & shall only haue by this my last will but v^{li} for his or ther porc̃on so refusing, & the residow to be bestowed emongest the other of my abouesaid children being ordred as is abouesaid by myne exec' or one of them. Item I give & bequeath to eu'y on of my s'untꝭ hauynge wages a quarter wages more than ther wages cometh to if they or so many of them as dothe s'ue my wif a quarter of a yere after my death if she so lyke them, & all those that takethe no wages I giue & bequeathe to them if any suche be iij^{s}. It' I giue & bequeath to my suster Agnes a cowe or a quye & a met of Rye. It' I giue & bequeath to Eliz' my suster all such dettꝭ as she dothe ow me at this daye whiche is xxvj^s viij^d, if it be vnpaid at the day of my buriall & if it be payd then I giue her a quye of iij yeres olde or suche lyke. Further I constitute, ordeyn & make the aforesaid Eliz' my wif & my brother pson Wortley myn execut', and do gine & bequeath to the said s^r Richard Wortley, clerke, my brother in law, xl^s for his paynꝭ to be taken ou' & besidꝭ his charges to be spent for or aboute this my will or any thing thervnto perteynyng. And I do giue & bequeath to Elisabeth my wif, my dettꝭ, fun'alls & bequestꝭ paid, all my goodꝭ & cattalls reall & p'sonall, for the vpholding & mayntenance of my said chilren being then vnmaried. In witnes whereof vnto this my will I haue written it w^t myn awne hande the forsaid xvij day of M'che . . . Thes beyng witnes, Thom's Westing, John Oliuer, Edward Wood, preist, Willm Baull, preist, Willm Sproxton, preist.—[*Proved* 28 *July*, 1556.]

RALPH FIELD, OF BEESTON.

(xv. j. 60 b.)

In the name of God Amen: I Raufe Feilde, of Beiston w^tin the parishe of Leidꝭ and countye of Yorke, Corvessore, in hooll mynd and perfecte remembrance, the first day of February and the yere of o^r lorde god 1556, makythe this my last will and testament in man' and forme followinge: first I bequeath my soull vnto almighty god my maker and redemer, to our lady sancte Marye, and to all the holy company of heven, and my bodie to be buried w^tin my parishe churche yerde of sancte Peter at Leides. Secondly I will my gooddes be dyuyded in thre partes, the first is my owne, the seconde parte I giue and bequeathe to Margret my wif w^t all that remaynethe of my forsaid parte, my funeralls and all other my necessary expensis discharged. Also I will that out of the third parte being hooll and vndyuyded iij^li vj^s viij^d to be taken and giuen to John Feilde my yongest son, and that done the rest to be equally devyded emongest my three children, that is to say, Rauf Feild, John Feilde, my sonnes, and Elisabeth Gaile my doughter. Also I giuc to euery one of my god children viij^d, to the blessed sacrament of thaltar at Leides viij^d, and to the blessed sacrament of thaltar at Ballay viij^d. Moreouer I giuc Margaret my wif too kye pastorage in on closse called coperclosse lyeng and belonging to the towneshipe of Holbecke as doth appeare in one payre of Indentures made betwixte Willm Shafton of Holbeck and me the said Rauf feilde of beiston. Furthermore I giue Rauf feilde my son on cowe gate in the same closse and that the forsaide Rauf Feilde shall fynd his naturall mother, Margret my wif, two kye in edisheing fogge and also to winter the same kye w^t hay and straw so well as he dothe his owne his mother lif induring, and for that shall she pay no rent nor rentꝭ to him or any person or persons. Also if it fortune that god shall call Margret my wif to his great mercye before thend of the yeres that we haue in the same closse, that then the said thre kye gates shalbe equally dyuyded betwixte Rauf Feilde my son and Elisabethe Gaile my doughter. Also I will vj^s viij^d to be delte to poore people. Also I giue Margret my wif from the middle dore inward all the rōmthes called thopper parte of the house holly to herself. Also I giuc her in euery feilde one half acre of lande of the best without any rent. Also I giue Thomas Feilde son of Rauf Feilde on brasse pot. Also to my son Rauf Feilde iij children euery of them on ewe and on lambe. Also I giuc to Elisabeth Gaile my doughter and Alyson Gaile her doughter either of them on ewe and on lambe. Finally I will and bequeath that if it fortune my son Rauf to dye before my wif his mother that then my wif shall haue, holde, occupie and enioye thalfe parte of the farmholde or any with her or for her. And thus Margaret my wif and Rauf my son my full executors of this my last will and testament. Thes beynge witnes, John Waterworthe, Willm Gaylle, Edward Becroft, and John West, with other mo.—[*Proved* 31 *July*, 1556.]

ROBERT ADMERGILL, OF BARDSEY.

(xv. j. 60 b.)

In the name of God: in the xxvj day of July in the yere of our lord god a thousand five hundred and sex and fiftye. I Robert Admargill, hooll of mynde and of good memory, makith my last will and testament in maner and forme following. First I bequeath my soull to Almighty god and to the celestiall company in heven, and my body to be buried in the churche earthe of sancte Oswolde at Collingham. Item I bequeath to my son Oswolde Admargill vilj oxen and two horse or mares with all my plowes, waynes, harrowes, and all other thinges belonging to my draught. It' I bequeath my takke and full interest of my farmeholde that I dwell vpon at Collingham to my said son Oswolde. It' I bequeathe all my interest and takke of my fermholde at Bardsaye hill called the intakke vnto Oswolde my son and Rauf Ward my son in lawe equallye betwixte them. It' I bequeath to the Vicar of Collingham ij^{s}. It' I bequeath to my doughter Marye Crofte a gymmer hogge, and to euery one of her iiij childrene, Robert, Anne, Oswolde, and Jenet, a gim̃er lambe. It' I bequeath to Willm Crofte my son in lawe vj^{s} viij^{d}. It' I bequeath to my foure doughters, Elisabeth, Agnes, Isabell, and Jane the halfe of all my gooddes not bequest for ther childes porc̃ons. The residewe of my gooddes I giue Oswolde my son, whom I make my executor. And I make Thomas Browne my brother in lawe my executor for to be his coadiutor to se that the fermholdes and gooddes bequest and giuen by me the forsaid Robert vnto Oswolde Admargill my son be clerely occupied and employd to the onely vse of the said Oswolde. And I bequeathe to the said Thomas Browne iij^{s} iiij^{d}. Furthermore I make Mr Browne and Auerey Rauson supervisors of this my last will, thes beyng witness', Christopher Chamber, of Compton, and Alexander Richardson, of Collingham.—[*Proved* 14 *August*, 1556, *by Thomas Browne, guardian of Oswold Admargill, sole executor, a minor.*]

JOHN FAWKES, OF FARNLEY, GENTN.[1]

(xv. j 63 a.)

In Dei nõie Amen: the fourte day of August in the yere of our lord god a thousand five hundrethe fifty and sex. I John Faukes, of Ferneley in the county of Yorke, gent', wholl of mynde and of good and perfecte remembrance, ordeyn and make this my last will and testament in maner and forme folowing. First I bequeathe my soull to almighty God my creator and to Jesus Christe my redemer, desiring our blessed ladye sancte

---

(1) See pedig^{r}ee in *Dugdale's Visitation*, ed. J. W. Clay, vol. ii, p. 204.

Mary and all the celestiall companye in heven to praye for me that my soull may take place emongest the electe people of god, and my body to be buried in the churche or churche yerde of Otley. And I will that my mortuary be paid as the law will admit. Also I will that my goodes shalbe dyuyded in thre partes, that is to say, the first parte to my self, the second parte to my wif, and the third parte to my two doughters, that is to say, Jane and Elisabeth. Item I giue and bequeathe to the said Jane one hundred markes and to the said Elisabethe fourtye markes to be paid, levied, and receyved of my landes and tenementes in Fernley aforesade, that is to say, of one tenement in Ferneley aforsaid in the holdyng of John Garnyte of the yerely valew of xliiij^{s}, one other tenement in Ferneley aforsaid in the holdyng of John Teale of the yerly valew of xxxix^{s}, one other tenement in Ferneley aforesaid in the holdyng of Elisabeth Pawson, widow, of the yerely valew of xl^{s}, wherof x^{s} is yerly to be payd other ways, one other tenement in Ferneley aforsade in the holdynge of Thomas Cave of the yerely valew of xx^{s}, and one other tenement in Ferneley aforsaid in the holding of Thomas Faukes of the yerely valew of xx^{s}, to the full sōm of seven score markes be well and truly contented and paid to the said Jane and Elisabeth my doughters by the fermers, tenantes, and occupiers of the fermes and tenementes in Ferneley aforsaid together withe ther childes porc̃ons of my gooddes to them appertaynynge after my decesse, whiche sōm of ther severall porc̃ons to the full valew shalbe always accepted and taken seu'ally as part and percell of the said som̃ of vij score markes, and the landes and tenementes aforsaid to be discharged of so moche rent of the said som̃ of vij score marks as ther seu'all porc̃ons of my goodes amountethe vnto. It' I giue and bequeath to Mr Henry Arthington, Esquier, my bay stagge w^{t} a long Rache. It' I giue and bequeath to my brother Marmaduke one other bay stagge of ij yeres old. It' I will that my said doughter Jane shall haue her owne sex kye well delyvered. And I will that my son Richard shall haue all my gere perteynyng to husbandry. It' I giue & bequeth vj^{s} viij^{d} to the churche of Otley to be bestowed at the discretion of the churche wardens, and iij^{s} iiij^{d} to the quere to be bestowed where most need is. I giue and bequeath vj^{s} viij^{d} to the poore people of Otley, iij^{s} iiij^{d} to the poore people in Ferneley, and other iij^{s} iiij^{d} to the poore people in Letheley, to be giuen and dyuyded w^{t}in on fortenight after my deathe at the order of Thomas Dunwell and Thomas Cave. It' I giue and bequeath iij^{s} iiij^{d} to the high waye in Ferneley to be bestowed betwene the pynfelde grene and the west ende of the towne. It' I giuc and bequeath to Sr Chr̃opher Waid, preist, to pray for me ten poundes, that is to say, xx^{s} to be paid yerely of the rentes, yssues, and profittes of one tenement in Ferneley aforsaid in the tenure and holding of Nicholas Pawson for the terme and space of ten yeres if the said Sr Chr̃ophor so long do lyve, and the same to be in discharge of all dettes whiche the said Sr Chr̃ophor shall or may hereafter demande of me or myne Executors. And also I will that my gooddes whiche shall not be delyvered before my deathe remaynyng of my parte shalbe to the vse of Anne Wharton my doughter vpon condic̃on that neither her husband nor she shall make any more title or clayme to any parte or porc̃on of my gooddes, and the same to be in full contentac̃on of her childes porc̃on.

And I desire of charity the said Mr Henry Arthington and my said brother Marmaduke to be supvisors of this my last will and testament, praying them to se the same fulfilled in all caises. And I make my said two doughters Jane and Elisabeth my full executrices of this my last will and testament. Thes be witnesses, Sr Anthony Jackeson, my curate, Christophor Swallow, Thomas Dunwell & Thomas Cave.—[*Proved 29 August, 1556, by Jane. Grant reserved to Elisabeth.*]

ROBERT WRAY, OF CLIFFORD, HUSBANDMAN.

(xv. j. 65 a.)

In the name of God Amen: the fourth day of Septembre in the yere of our lorde god m[l]v[c]lvj. I Roberte Wray, of Cliffurthe in the county of Yorke, husbandman, of good and perfecte remembrance, do make this my last will and testament in maner and forme following. First I bequeath my soull to almighty god and to our blessed lady and to all the holy company of heven, and my body to be buried w[t]in the churche yerde of Alhallowes in Bramham. Item I giue and bequeath to my youngest son John all my interest of my fermholde whiche I haue by lease of s[r] Robert Stapleton, and my yron bound wayne and on yoke of my oxen of the best that he will chuse, and all my husbandry gere whiche I haue redy made, and two horses or ij mares ou' and besides his portion and barn parte. Item I giue and bequeath to my two sonnes Peter & Sandere to either of them xx[s] in full contentacon and payment of ther portions and barne partes. The residew of all my goodes, moveable and vnmoveable, vnbequest nor giuen, I giuc them freely to my foure children, Stephen, John, Custance, and Katheryn, whom I make my holl and full executors and executrices of this my last will and testament, to pay my dettes and to bringe me furthe honestlye at the day of my buriall according to my liability. Witnesses herof, George Robynson, Robert Stoote, and John Richardson.—[*Proved 12 September, 1556.*]

NICHOLAS HODGSON, OF GARFORTH.

(xv. j. 65 b.)

In the name of God Amen: the xvj day of August in the yere of o[r] lord god m[l]v[c]lvj. I Nycholas Hodgeson, of Garforth, of good & p'fecte remembrance, makith this my testament & last will in maner & forme following, that is to say. First I giue & frely betake my saull to god almighty, the blessed virgin o[r] lady sancte Mary, & to all the celestiall company of heven, & my body to be buryed in the parishe churche yerd of Garforthe. Also I bequeathe to the churche wardens on ew shepe. It' I bequeath to Robt Hodgson on ew sheipe & somthinge to make him a cote of, & to Elen Hodgson on ew lambe. It' I bequeth to Willm Hodgson my son my red Jaket. Also I will that Katheryn Haryson shall haue as moche new clothe as will make her a cote. Also I will that Anne my wif shall haue my cowe & Elisabethe my doughter shall haue my quye. The residew of all my goodes, my dettes & fun'alls payd and discharged, I gine to Anne my wif & Elisabeth my doughter, whom I make my executrices to do for me as I haue put them in truste. Thes being witnesses, John Dawson, curate, Robt Rawson, Vmfray Dawson, John Holdell, Willm Westerman, w[t] other.—[*Proved 7 September, 1556.*]

MARGARET MIDGLEY, OF MOORGRANGE, WIDOW.

(xv. j. 69 a.)

In the name of God Amen: the xviij day of September in the yere of oure lord god m'ccccclvj. I Margaret Migeley, of Moregrange in the parishe of Ledes within the county of Yorke, widowe, being of hooll mynd and god remembrance, makith this my last will and testament in maner and forme hereafter followyng. The first I giuc my soull to Almightye god my maker and redemer, beseching oure blessed ladye sancte Marye and all the gloriose company of heven to pray for me that I trusting in the merits of Christes passion may be partaker of the celestiall Joye of his Kingdom, and my body to be buried within the pishe churche of sancte Peter in ledes. And also I gine to my son Willm my best beades withe one ryng and ij of my best yron temes. Also I giue to Richard my son iij^li^ vj^s^ viij^d^ and half a quarter of Rye. Also I gine to Alexander my son iij^li^ vj^s^ viij^d^. Also I giue to Anne my doughter iij markes of lawfull money and on girdle and on paire of awmer bedę and on gowne clothe. Also I gine to Jane my doughter iij^li^ vj^s^ viij^d^ ouer and besides iiij^li^ being her childes portion left to her by her father, and also my best gowne and my best kirtle and my best girdle and on paire of siluer crokes. Also I giue to the wif of Richard Megeley my son my best scarlet hat. Also I giue to Willm Megeley my godson one wedder of the best. Also I giue to Margaret Megeley my god doughter one why of the best. Also I giue to the blessed sacrament iij^s^ iiij^d^. Also I make my executors of this my last will and testament, Michaell Haull, Alexander Megeley my son, and Jane Megeley my doughter, to whom I giue, after my dettes paid and funerall expens's discharged, the residew of all my goodes, moveable and vnmoveable, vnbequest. Thes being witnes, Thomas Rauson, Robert Judson, Lawrence Rauson, Chrofer Megeley, preist, with other mo.—[*Proved 2 Oct.*, 1556.]

ANNE BARKESTON, OF BARKSTON, WIDOW.

(xv. j. 70 b.)

In the name of God Amen: the xxviij day of August in the yere of our lorde god a thousand five hundred fifty and sex. I Anne Barkeston, of Barkeston within the pishe of Shereborne, widowe, late wif vnto Edward Barkeston thelder latly decessed, holl of mynd and perfite of remembrance, stedfastlye beleving in the faithe and lawes of Christ, thankes be gyven vnto Almighty god, do ordayne, cōstitute, and make this my last will and testament in maner as hereafter doth appeare. First I giuc and bequeathe my soull vnto almighty god, to his mother the blessed virgin oure lady sancte Marye, and to all the holy celestiall company of heaven, and my body to be buried whithin the queare where my sayde husband dothe lye within the sayd parishe churche of Shereborne, and as nere him as can be possible. Also I giue and bequeathe to the blessed sacrament within the sayd church xij^d^. Also I giue and bequeath vnto syr John Taylyer xij^d^. Also I giue and bequeathe to Nicholas Barkeston two busshells of wheate. Also I giue and bequeath to Peter Barkeston, Jane Barkston, and Anne Barkeston, my son Edwardes children, euery on of them xiij^s^ iiij^d^. Also I giue and bequeathe vnto the churches workę at Sherborne xij^d^. Item I giuc and bequeath vnto euery one of my servantes iiij^{d}. Also I giue and bequeath vnto my suster Alice my mournyng gowne withe the hode or worsted kyrtle and kerchief. Also I giue and bequeathe to my suster Elizabethe Harcoytes my best gowne. Also I giue and bequeath vnto my cosyn Margerye Nevell on pisculate of vj^{s} ij^{d}. Also I giue and bequeath to Jane and Anne Barkeston my son Edwardes doughters one gowne and one chamlet kyrtle. Also I giue and bequeath to Nicholas Barkeston wif my best silken hatt and my best white cappe. Also I giue and bequeathe to Edward Barkeston my son on payre of greate sheites. Also I gine and bequeath to Francis Barkeston my son one payre of greate sheites. And also the residew of all my goodes and chattells not bequested, my dettes and legacies paid and fun'alls discharged, I giue and bequeath vnto Frances Barkeston my son, whom I do ordeyne, cōstitute, and make my sole executor of this my last will and testament to distribute and dispose for my soulls helthe as he shall thinke most co'venyent and meyte. Also I do ordayn, constitute, and make my brother Mr Nicholas Hall the sup'viso^{r} of this my last will and testament, to whom for his paynes taking in this behalf I giue and bequeath one Riall of gold. In witnes herof, sir Richard Hemsley, vicar there, s^{r} Robert Blanche, curate, Thomas Morret, Thomas Longley, John Hillom, and Roberte Man, with others. Also I will that my said husband Edward Barkeston will shalbe p'formed before this my last will, and it so done than I will that this my last will be p'formed and my full strengthe of my executrixshippe of my sayd husband's will, I giuc and bequeath to Frances my son accordinge to the meanynge of this my last will. Also I will that one preist shalbe foundon one half yere to pray for my soull and my husband soull and all christen soulles, and he to haue for his salary v^{li} vj^{s} viij^{d}. Witnesses herof, Sr Richard Hemsley, Sr Robert Blanche, Robert Mā, Thom's Longley, w^{t} other.—[*Proved* 10 *Oct.*, 1556.]

William Barker, of Scarcroft.

(xv. j. 71 a.)

In the name of God amen: the xijth daye of Septembre in the yere of our lord god m'ccccl and sex. I Willm Barker, of Scarcrof in the parishe of Thornar in the countie of Yorke, beyng hooll in mynde and of pfecte remembrance, do make this my last will and testament in maner and forme foloing. First I bequeath my soull to almighty god my creator and redemer, to o^{r} blessed lady sancte Mary, & to all the holy company of sanctes in heven, & my body to be buried within the church of sancte peter of Thornor aforsayd. Also I gine & bequeath to the sayd churche of sancte peter ij^{s} yerely to be paid for eu' wherof xij^{d} is for the discharging of the last will & testament of John Barker my father, decessed, and the whiche said xij^{d} was giuen by my said late father to the fyndynge & kepynge of a lampe & oyle burnyng therin in the said churche of sancte peter and the other xij^{d} I will to be at the ordryng & disposing of the churche wardens of the said churche of sancte peter & ther successors yerely to & for the most advantage & comoditye of the said churche of sancte Peter. And also I will that the said ij^{s} shall yerely be paid as rent goyng out of a closse called nonedoers lyeing in Thornor aforsaid at the feastes of sancte Martyn in Winter & pentecost by even porčons so long as the said churche of Thornor shall contynew & remayne in the same estate as it is at this instant tyme, if not, then I will & from thensforthe the said ij^{s} shall remayne to my right heires for eu'. Also I giue & bequeath to bye ornamentes & necessaries for the highe altare in the ꝑishe churche of sancte Peter aforsaid iij^{s} iiij^{d}. Also I gine & bequeath to bye ornamentes and necessaries for the highe altare at Bardsay other iij^{s} iiij^{d}. Also I giuc & bequeath to Andrew Barker my son to kepe him at schole withall on annuyty of iiij^{li} of lawfull money of England to be paid yerly to the said Andrew & to his assignes from the feiste of sancte Martyn in winter whiche shalbe in the yere from the incarnacõn of o^{r} lord Jħs Christ m.ccccc.l & seven vnto th'end & terme of vij yeres then next & imediatly folowing as hereafter folowith, first I will & bequeath xl^{s} p'eell of the said iiij^{li} to be paid to the sayd Andrewe or to his assignes out of my farmhold at Rigton by thandes of John Barker my son or by his assignes at the feastes of sancte Martyn in winter & pentecost by even porcõns. And if it shall fortune the sayd annuytie of xl^{s} to be behind vnpaid in ꝑte or in all by the space of xl dayes next after either of the said feastꝭ at whiche it ought to be paid, that then I will it shalbe lawfull to the said Andrew & to his assignes to enter into ij closses at Rigton aforsaid, the one called Mylne hill & the other called mylnhil feilde, to haue & to hold the said ij closses to the said Andrew & to his assignes during so many yeres of the said vij yeres as shall then fortune to be behind & not spent.. Also I will that the other xl^{s} residew of the said iiij^{li} be paid at the feastꝭ aforesaid to the said Andrew & to his assignes yerly during the said vij yeres out of my landes, messuagꝭ & tentꝭ situate, lyeing & being in Kirkby and Shadwell in the said ꝑishe of Thornor. [Power of entry in case of non payment for 40 days.] Item I will & bequeath to Xpofer Barker my son all suche interest & terme of yeres as I haue of & in to on messuage & certen land of Willm Poule set lyeing & being in Skarcroft aforsaid, whiche said interest & terme of yeres of late I had & bought of John Afeild. Item I will & bequeath to the said Xpofer Barker my son all suche interest & terme of yeres as I haue of, in & to on water mylne sett in Skarcrofte aforsaid to the bringing vp & fynding of my thre doughters, Elisabeth Barker, Agnes Barker, & Francys Barker. Item I giue & bequeath to the said Xpofer Barker my son my vilj oxen, my yron bound wayn, my bare wayu, my ploughes & all other necessaries belonging to same as harrowes, yockes, teams & suche other husbandry gere, paing therfore to myn executors xj^{li} vj^{s} viij^{d} of lawful money of England. It' I giue & bequeath to the said Xpofer my son on presse, on almery & on gret chiste standing in the firehouse at Skarcroft aforesaid, paing y'for to myn execut' xxxv^{s} of lawfull money of England. It' I giue & bequeth to Thom's Chamber the occupacõn of on close lyeing nigh the water mylne during my lease, paing therfore yerly to ye said Xpofer my son xiij^{s} iiij^{d} at ij vsuall termes in ye yere accustomed. It' I gine vnto the said Thom's one cow whiche he hath alredye by note. It' I give to my brother in law Willm Shan my blak Jacket. It' I give to Xpofer Barker son of Willm Barker my son on silu' maser. It' I give to Eliz' Barker doughter of John Barker my son iij^{li} vj^{s} viij^{d}. It' I giuc to Willm Barker son of the said John Barker on cow wch the said John hath now by note. I giuc and bequ'ath to Katherin Barker & to Mary Barker doughters of the said John Barker either of the' iiij gym' lam̃es. It' I giuc to my doughter Jenet Stevinson iij^{li} vj^{s} viij^{d} in full cõtentac̃on & payme't of childꝭ porc̃on & barne p'te. It' I giue to my ij doughters Agnes & Francys either of the' on gold ring. It' I giuc to my dought' Eliz' Barker on girdle of silu' & gold. It' I giue to Wiƚƚm Harrison on old riall of gold. It' I giue & bequeth to John Barker my son xx yowshepe in full conte'tac̃on & paime't of his childꝭ p'te & porc̃on. It' I giue and bequeth to Wiƚƚm Barker my son vj^{li} xiij^{s} iiij^{d} in full contẽtac̃on, satisfacc̃on & paime't of his porc̃on and childes p'te. It' I giue to my son P'civall Barker vj^{li} xiij^{s} iiij^{d} ou' & besides his porc̃on & childꝭ p'te. It' I giuc to John Fairchild on whye w^{t} a calf. It' I giue to Wiƚƚm Wright on yow. It' I giuc to Miles Watson ij^{s}. It' I giuc to John Long xij^{d}. It' I giue to John Wilkinson on red cote. It' I giue to eu'y of my s'untes, y^{t} is to saye, John Jakson, John Beamont, John M'shall & Agnes Lawson, to eu'y of them xij^{d}. It' I giue to eu'y on of my god children xij^{d}. It' I will & bequeth to Wiƚƚm Barker my son the moietie of the manor of Skarcroft w^{t} thapp'tin'cꝭ during suche interest & terme of yeres as I haue of & in the said mano^{r} excepted the water mylne before willed & bequethed to the said Xpofer. It' I will & bequeth to the said Xpofer Barkar the other moiety of the said manor of Skarcroft w^{t} thapp'tñncꝭ during suche int'est & terme of yeres as I haue of, in & to ye said manor. It' I giue to John Barker my son my lease, int'est & terme of yeres wch I haue of, in & to my fermhold at Rigton, paing yerely during vij yeres as is aboue written to the said Andrew & to his assigns xl^{s} of lawfull money of England excepted before willed & beq'thed as is aforsaid. It' I giue & bequeth to the said Xpofer all my messuagꝭ, landꝭ, ten'tes sett, lyeng & being in Thornor aforsaid to haue & to hold to the said Xpofer & to his heires males of his body lawfull begotten & for defalte of suche heire male of his body lawfully begotten I will the same messuagꝭ, landꝭ & ten'tꝭ shall remayne to P'civall Barker & to his heires males. [In default to Andrew Barker my son & his heirs male. In default to William Barker my son & his heirs male. In default to John Barker my son & his heirs male. In default to the right heirs of him the said Wm. Barker for ever.] It' if Wiƚƚm Barker my son do not p'mit & suffer the said Xpofer my son quietly & peacefully to occupie & enioye the said water mylne & the said moietye of the said manor of Skarcrof according to this my last will [*P*ower to enter the said lands in Kirkby & Shadwell to hold to him & his heirs male]. It' I will that Wiƚƚm Harrison shall haue the ordring & keping of my son Andrew Barker during the above specified vij yeres & I will that the said Wiƚƚm Harrison shall haue the abouesaid iiij^{li} yerely during the said vij yeres for the sustentac̃on, finding and keping the said Andrewe at schole, if the said Andrewe fortune to dye before thende of the said vij yeres y^{t} then and from thensforthe the said Annuytie of iiij^{li} shall cease and determine anye thing herin to the cõtrary notwithstanding. It' I will and bequeath all my gooddꝭ, moveable and i͛movable, before not bequeathed nor given, I giue them frely to my sex children, that is to say, Xpofer Barker, P'civall Barker, Andrewe Barker, my sonnes, Elisabeth Barker, Agnes Barker, and Frauncys Barker, my doughters, whom I make my holl and full executors and executrixes of this my last will and testament, and they to pay my dettes and to bring me forthe honestly the day of my buriall as shalbe thought seamyng by my freyndes, and according to my degre. Moreouer I giue and bequeath to Wiłłm Levet and Wiłłm Harrison and to either of them [*sic*], whom I make supvisors of this my last will and testament, desiring them to se all thinges executed herin according to the true meanyng & interest herof as my trust and confidence is in them to do. Witnesses herof, Wiłłm Clughe, Thomas Allyn, Robert Clughe son of John Clughe, of Rigton, and Wiłłm Harrison.—[*Proved* 27 *Oct.*, 1556, *by Christopher and Percival. Grant reserved to the other four children co-executors, minors.*]

RICHARD VEVERS, OF *PUDSEY*.

(xv. j. 87 b.)

In the name of God Amen: the xxviij day of Marche in the yere of oure lord god m.ccccc.lv. I Ric' Vevers, of Pudsaye w^t^in the pishe of Calu'lay in the coũtye of Yorke, seike of body & holl & p'fecte of mynde & remembrance (thanks be to god), doth ordeyn & make this my last will & testament in mañer & forme following. First & principaly I coññend my soull vnto almighty god my maker & to Jesu christ my redemer, to our lady sancte Mary & to all the holy & blessed company of heven, and my body to be buried w^t^in the pishe churche yerd of Caluerley beforsaid. Also I will that Agnes my wif shall haue & inhabite the fermhold & tenement in Pudsay beforsaid w^t^ all the lands and tentᵱ to it pteynynge whiche I now dwell in vnto suche tyme as Richard Vevers my son accōplishe thaige of xxj yeres, paing the rent that is dewe to be paid for the same during the said tyme, and whan my said son Richard Vevers comes to thaige of xxj yeres or at any tyme before if my said wif his mother fortune to dye or he come to the said aige, I will, assigne, bequeath, & set ouer from thensforth to the said Ric' Vevers my son, his executors & assignes, all my said teñte & fermhold in the said towneshippe & feildᵱ of Pudsay w^t^ all the landᵱ, closses, medowes, pasturᵱ & tentᵱ w^t^ ther apptñncᵱ to the said fermhold or teñte pteynyng or belonging in as large maner as Thomas Rothelay granted the same by his lease or grante to Richarde Vevers father of me the said Ric' Vevers for terme of foure score & xviij yeres and in as large maner as the said Richard Vevers my father gaue, granted, assigned & set ouer the said fermhold, landᵱ, medowes & teñte to me the said Richard for his terme he had granted of the said Thomas Rothelay by such yerely rent as he held the same premiss' to haue & to hold all the said teñte, fermhold & the said landᵱ to the said Ric' son of the said Ric' Vevers, of Pudsay, his executours & assignes imediatly after he come to thaige of xxj yeres or to enter at any tyme afore if his mother dye or he come to thaige of xxj yeres . . . Also I will that whan my said Ric' Vevers [*sic*] comes to aige of xxj yers that then he shall kepe & fynd honestly Agnes my wif his mother meate, drynke & clothing & other necessarys vnto such tyme as it shall please god to call her to his mercy. Also I will & bequeath vnto John Vevers my yonger son & his assigns the house w^t^ all such closes & landᵱ as is nowe in the occupac̃on of Rauf Hill in Pudsay, paing to Ric' my son & his assigns the rent therof accustomed during the said terme. The residewe of all my goodᵱ, cattalls & dettᵱ not bequeathed nor giuen, my dettᵱ & legacies paid & fulfilled & my funerall expens' discharged, I giue and bequeathe all the same to the said Agnes my wif, John & Agnes my children. Also I will and make the said Agnes my wif & Ric' Vevers my son myne executors of this my last will and testament. Thes being witnesses, Richard Lepton, Robert Dawson, Thomas Grave & other.—[*Proved* 18 *Jan.*, 1556-7, *by Richard, Agnes, the widow, being dead.*]

AGNES SKIPTON, OF PONTEFRACT, WIDOW.

(xv. j. 87 b.)

In Dei nōie Amen: the viij day of Aprile in the yere of our lord God m.ccccc.lvj. I Agnes Skipton, of Pontfraite, wedowe, w^t^in the conty of Yorke, holl of mynd & good remembrance, makith this my last will & testament in manner & forme following: first I giue and bequeath my soull vnto almighty god my maker & redemer & to the blessed virgyn mary and to all the holy cōpany in heven, & my body to be buried in my ꝑishe church of Pontfrett nigh vnto my husband as may conveniently be. It' I giue to Jenet Hirst & to Isabel Hirst my workday gowne & my violet kirtle & Jenet Hirst to chose. It' I giue to be heirelomes in this house thes ꝑeells following, the yron chymney in the hall w^t^ the bawke & foure crokꝭ hanging of the same, a standing bed in the ꝑloure & a long chiste standing by the same bed & a bed of bordꝭ in the chamber & a laver hanging at the garthe dore & a paire of yron rackꝭ. It' I giue to Wiłłm my son a coūter & the carpet lyeing on it. It' I giue to the same a landyron w^t^ a payre of rakkꝭ & a brason morter. It' I giue to Wiłłm my son my best Spytt, and I giue the second spitt to my son John. It' I giue to Agnes Skipton doughter of my son John a brasse pott & iiij pewther doblers. It' I will haue dirige & masse the day of my buriall, and I will that my executors shall make a dyner vnto my poore neighbores to the valewe of xx^s^. It' I will that all suche goodꝭ and houses that my late husband haith giuen in his will to stande firme & stable. It' I giue vnto my son John Skipton the house that Tatam wif dwellithe in bycause I was ioyned purches w^t^ my late husband for avoydinge troble hereafter. It' I make my son Wiłłm & my son John myne executors ioyntly together. It' I will that my soñes shall lovingly devide all suche goodꝭ as I leave them & to cary & recary at all tymes from tyme to tyme. The residewe of all my goodꝭ not bequest I giue vnto my said executors to dispose for the helthe of my soull & my husband soull & all christen soulles. Thes being witnesses, Thomas Wakefelde, gent., John Mylner thelder, Thomas Stable, and Richard Tatam, with other mo.—[*Proved* 18 *Jan.*, 1556-7.]

HENRY THOMSON, OF WAKEFIELD.

(xv. j. 88 a.)

In the name of god Amen: the xxiij day of August in the yere of oure lord god m.ccccc.lvj. I Henrye Thomson, of Wakefeld, seike in body & holl of mynd & of good & ꝑfecte remembrance, makithe this my last will & testament in maner and forme followinge. First I giue & bequeath my soull to god almighty my saueyo^r^ & redemer, to our blessed lady sancte Mary the vyrgin, & to all the celestiall company of heven, & my body to be buried in the ꝑishe churche yerde of Wakefeld aforsaid. It' I giue to John Thomson my son my house in Wakefeld with thapptñncꝭ wherin I nowe inhabite & dwell imediatly after the decesse of my wif to him and to his beires for eu'. It' I giue to Thomas Thomson my son one closse called John Meyr buttyng vpon Jack ynge to him & to his heires for eu'. And if it fortune the said John & Thomas to dye wᵗoute heires I will that the said house & close remayne to Xpofer Thomson & for lacke of heyres of his body lawfully begotten I will it remayne to Henry & Richard Thomson my soñes & to ther heires for eu'. It' I giue to Ric' my son on sworde, on gyrdle dagger, ij yron ha'mers & iiij yron wedges. It' I giue to Henry my son my bowe & shafe of arrowes & half of my shop geare if he wilbe a shomaker. It' I giue to Wiłłm Hartlay on blake jaket. It' I giue to Henry Thomson my son on gray jaket & a lether doblet. It' I giuc to John Goldsmythe a paire of gray hose & a paire of newe shois. It' I giue to Robert Thomson my brother a paire of blewe hose & my best sherte. The residewe of all my goodę vnbequest, my dettes & legacies paid, I giue & bequeath to Jenet my wif, whom I make & ordeyn to be my full & only Executrix, she to dispose for my soull as my trust is in her. Also I will that John Mylnes, Geffray Rycherdson & Robert Thomson be the supvisors of this my last will & testament to se it fulfilled & done & eu'y of them to haue for ther paynes & labore xijᵈ. Thes being witness', James Brodbent, my curate, & John Roo.—[*Proved* 17 *Jan.*, 1556-7.]

JOHN SALE, OF TONG.

(xv. j. 38 a.)

In the name of God Amen: the vj day of October in the yere of our lord god m.ccccc.lvj. I John Sale, of Tonge in the pishe of Birstall, of holl mynd & good reme'brance, maketh my last will & testament in maner & forme followinge. First & principall I giue & bequeath my soull to God Almighty, to oure lady sancte Mary, & to all the holy company of heven, and my body to be buried in the churche yerd of Birstall. Also I will that Elisabethe my wif shall haue the gou'nance & bringing up of my ij soñes at & by the discreċon & order of Henry Batte, of Birstall, & Richard Jenkinson, of Pudsey. Also I will that my holl goodę shalbe dyvided into thre egall partę, the first part therof to be to my said wif according to the lawes of this Rialme, and the second parte therof to Ric' Sale my yonger son & the last third part therof to be bestowed for & toward the bringing of my ij sones vnto they coñe to thaige of discreċon at & by the aduyse, order & discreċon of the said Henry Batte & Ric: Jenkynson. And if any pte of the said last third of my said goodę shall remayne vnbestowed of the bringing vp of my said ij sones as is said, then I will that the remaynder of that parte shalbe giuen & paid to the said Ric: my yongest son at suche tymes as my supvisors shall thinke conven-yent. Also I giue & bequeath unto the said Eliz' my wif all my landę & teñtę vnto such tyme as my son & heire James Sale be & come to thaige of xxj yeres to thintent that my said wif shall bestowe all thissues & profittę of the same landę & teñtę excepte only her owne dower or third toward thexhibition & fynding at scbole of my said ij sones and toward ther lernyng of soñ honest crafte or otherwise for & towardę ther profett as shalbe thought requisite & meite by the discreċon, consell & advise of the said Henry Batte & Ric' Jenkynson. Item I giue vnto the said Ric' my son a greate arke & a chiste. Also I will that the said James my son shall pay vnto the said Ric' my yonger son furth of my said landę five m'kę evenly in v yeres nexte after the said James shall come to thaige of xxj yeres. Also I ordeyn & make the said Eliz' my wif & Ric' my son my executors so that my said wif shall not order then [*sic*] dispose any thinge otherwise or co'trary to this my said will as is afore declared. Also I ordeyn & make the said Henry Batte & Ric' Jenkinson supvisors of this my said will & testament desiring them to se & helpe the same executed & pformed accordingly. Thes witnes, Richard Goodall, Robte Sale, the sayde Henry Batte, Richard Jenkynson, and other mo.—[*Proved* 18 *Jan.*, 1556–7.]

NICHOLAS LOCKAY, OF BOLTON, JUNIOR.

(xv. j. 90 a.)

In the name of God Amen: the xxj day of Septembre in the yere of oure lord god m'cccclvj. I Nicholas Lockay, of Bolton, iunior, within the pishe of Calu'ley, seike of body & holl & p'fecte of mynd & remembrance (thankę be to God), doth ordeyne & make this my last will and testament in manner & forme following. First & principally I comend my soull to Almighty god my maker & to Jesu christ my redemer & to all the holye & blessed company of heven, and my body to be buried wtin the pishe churche yerd of Calu'ley aforsaid. Also if it please god that the child nowe being in the wombe of Eliz' my wif to be a son that than I will giue & bequeath vnto the same son the preferment of my lease & tente in Bolton to haue, occupie and convert the same lease and tente to him, his executors & assignes at suche tyme as he shall accomplishe thaige & yeres of discrecion during all suche termes & yeres as then shall or may be to come & vnspent in the same. Also I will that Eliz' my wif during the nonage of my said son shall haue the occupacon & preferment of my said tente & lease for the keping and bringing vp of my said child & children & for defalte of suche issue I will & bequeth the preferment of my said tente & lease vnto Eliz' my wif during all suche termes and yeres as is yet to come & vnspent in the same. Always prouyded that after the daye of the death of my said wif the yeres than to come & vnspent shall remayne equallye vnto my doughters than lyvinge. Also I bequeath vnto the high altare at Calu'ley for tythes & oblacons necligently forgotten xij^{d}. The residewe & remanent of all my goodę, cattells & dettes not bequest or gyven, I honestly brought furthe, my dettę paid and thes my legacies fulfilled, I giue to Eliz' my wif, Jenet & Katheryn my doughters & to the child now being in the wombe of my said wif, whom I make fully & hollye myne executors of this my present testament. Thes being witnesses, Ric' Hodgeson, preist, John Wilkynson, John Walker, yonger, Hughe Cowper, Thomas Balye & other.—[*Proved* 21 *Jan.*, 1556–7, *by widow. Grant reserved to children.*]

EDWARD BARKSTON, OF SHERBURN-IN-ELMET.

(xv. j. 96 a.)

In Dei nōie Amen: the vth daye of August Anno D'ni millmo qui'genmo qui'quagesimo sexto. I Edwarde Barkestone, in the pishe of Shereburne in Elmett, of holl memorie and pfytt of Remembrance, laude and praise be vnto Allmightie God, doo ordeyn, constytute, and maike this my last will and testament in man' and forme followinge. First I gyue and bequeathe my soull vnto Allmightie God, to our ladie sancte Marie, and to the holie celestiall companye of heven, and my bodie to be sepulted and buried at the southe ende of the aulter in sanct Thomas quere within the said ꝑishe churche of Shereburn. Item I will to be geven for my mortuarie after my decease suche sōmes of moneye as is or hereafter shalbe lymytted by the Law and custome of the churche. Item I gyve and bequeathe to the highe aulter of the said ꝑishe churche of Shereburne for my tythes forgotten v^s^. Also I gyve to the repacons of the said churche v^s^. Item I gyve to the churche workes at Fentone v^s^. Item I will that at the daye of my buriall for my fun'allꝭ and exequies to be doyne for me to be gyven to the vicar xij^d^. Item to eu'y prest vj^d^, eu'y ꝑishe clerke iij^d^, and eu'y scoler j^d^, and for other thingꝭ necessarie & requisite the said daye about the bryngynge furthe of my bodie into the growne, I will it be doyne at the discretion and sight of myne executors. Also I will that myne said executors imediatlie after my deceasse shall conduct and hier one prest for the tearme of one hole yeare to singe and saye the devyne services at the alter in the said quere of sanct Thomas where as my bodie lyethe buried for my soull and all christen soules. And that my executors shall gyve and paye for the said prest for his Salarye and waiges the sōme of v^li^ vj^s^ viij^d^, the same to be leuyded and paid out of my hooll goodꝭ accordinge to the trewe intent and meaninge of this my last will and testament. Also I give and bequeath to my brother Thomas Barkestone one cowe. Also I give and bequeathe vnto my suster Alice Silles one cowe. Also I gyve and bequeathe to Willm Barkestone one whie. Also I gyve and bequeath to Edwarde Barkestone my Secounde sone one silver salt withe a cover p'teyninge to the same percell gylt And also one silver spoyne. Also I bequeathe to eu'y one of my servantꝭ nowe dwellinge withe me over and aboue ther waigeꝭ xij^d^. Also I bequeathe to Anne my wiff all the hool interest & terme of yeares in all my farmes, to haue, holde, occupie, and inyoie to her duringe the yeares then remainge not ended nor expyred after my deceasse yf she so longe lyve. *P*rovided that if any of the same terme of yeares be not fullye ended nor exspired at the daye of her deathe then I will the Residewe of the said yeares not beynge so ended nor expired to remayne to Fraunces Barkestone my sone.

And where as Brian Bales and others by ther ded obligatorie berynge date the ix^th^ of Septembre in the first yeare of the late Kynge Edwarde the sext, standethe boundone & in the sōme of one hundreth m'kꝭ to me the said Edwarde Barkestone, Edward and Fraunceꝭ my sonnes for the performaunce of certayne covenutꝭ contyened in one paire of Indentures maid betwixt me the said Edward, Edwarde and Fraunces my sonnes of the one ꝑtie, and the said Brian Bales one the other ꝑtie, beryng date the daye and yeare of the said obligacon, that is to saie, that Elsabeth Bales doughter of the said Brian Bales when she accomplysshe and come to the full aige of xxj yeares or anye heire or heires of the said Elsabethe when tyme shalbe shall maike or cause to be maid one sure sufficyent estate by surrender or other wise accordinge to the custome of the maner of Shereburne of one pennye place, buylded, sett, lyinge and beynge in Shereburn afforsaid: And also fyve rodes of pennye lande lyinge in Barkestone Feildꝭ to me the said Edwarde, Edwarde and Franceꝭ my sonnes and to our heires or to theires of one of vs as by the said Indentures more playnlie apperithe. And for the better declaringe of this my last will and testament to be p'formed, obserued, fulfilled, and kepte in maner and forme followinge, that is to saye, I will by this my said will that the said Surrender by the said Elsabethe Bales or by anye heire or beires of her hereafter to be maid of the said pennye place and fyve rodes of lande shall passe and be executed to Fraunceꝭ Barkestone my sone and to his heires for ever. And where as Nicholas Barkestone my sone and beire apparent by his dede obligatorie beryngc date the viijth daye of Julie in the first yeare of the late Kynge Edwarde the Sext, standethe bounden in the so͞me of Foortie poundꝭ to me the said Edwarde Barkestone the Elder and to myne Executors [Condition for repayment of £20 by instalments]. P'vided that yf the said Nicholas do not content and paye vnto thandꝭ of my said Executors the said some of twentie poundꝭ at the said feastꝭ as before is declared, then I will that my said Executors shall enter to one tenement or messuage withe all the arrable lande, medowes, and pastures with the appurte͞nnces to the same belonginge, sett, lyinge and beynge within the towne and Feildꝭ of Barkestone nowe in tenure and occupac͞on of Robert Hidsone [power to receive the revenues until fully satisfied]. And that my said executors shall dispose of the said xx^{li} in maner and forme followinge. First I gyve and bequeathe to George Bucke vj^{li} xiij^{s} iiij^{d}. Item I gyve and bequeathe to Jane Barkestone Fyve poundꝭ. Item to Anne Barkestone fyve poundꝭ. Item I gyve and bequeathe to Richarde Barkestone iij^{li} vj^{s} viij^{d}. Also I will further that the said Nicholas Barkestone my sone and heyre apparaunte after my deceasse shall suffer myne Executors peaceablie and quyatlie to occupie and enioye the Mansyone house which I nowe dwell in called Barkeston Hall with all arrable lande, medowe, and pasture withe all other thappurte͞nnces to the same belonginge frome the feast of sanct Martyne in Wynter after my deceasse vnto thend and terme of one hooll yeare then next followinge the said Feast, yeldinge and paynge therfore to the said Nicholas and his beires v^{li} vj^{s} viij^{d} at towe vsuall termes equallie to be devided, and that the said Executors shall paye all suche rentes as ar dewe to the cheif lord or lordꝭ of the fee over and above the said rent of vj^{li} vj^{s} viij^{d}. Also I will that the towe tables in the haull withe the formes belonginge to the same shall remayne for eu' and hereafter be taken for heyre-lomes remanynge w^{t}hin the same haull. The Residewe of all my goodꝭ moveable and vnmoveable vnbequeathed, my dettꝭ paid, my legacies fulfilled and all the poyntes & articles in this my said last will and testament fulfilled and kept, I gyve and bequeath to Anne my wiff, Edwarde and Fraunceꝭ my sonnes, whome I doo orden, constitute and maike myne executors of this my last will and testament, and there to dispose the same for the benyfytt of my soull accordinge as theye thinke most requysite. Also I doo orden, constytute, and make the sup̲visor of this my last will and testament maister Nicholas Hall, clerke, whome I gyve for his paynes takinge in this behalf one olde riall. In wytenes, sir Robert Blanche, curate of Shereburn, Thomas Crosthwait, Thomas Morret, Thomas Steadmã, John Hillome, Robert Man, with others.—[*Proved 12 October, 1556, by Edward and Francis,*[1] *Ann, the widow, being dead.*]

(1) Probably she may be identified with Alice, daughter of Thomas Leeds, of Milford. See 'Ellis of Barnborough' in *Glover's Visitation of Yorkshire* (Foster), p. 135.

ANNE JENKINSON, OF BIRSTALL.

(xv. j. 97 b.)

In the name of God Amen: the xiiij[th] daye of Maye in the yeare of o[r] lord god a thowsande fyve hunderithe fiftie and sex. I Anne Jenkynsone in the pishinge of Byrstall, of hooll mynde, makethe my last will in forme followinge. First I bequeathe my soull to god Almightie and to the cōpanye of o[r] blissed ladie sancte Marie and to all the sanctę in heaven, and my bodie to be buried in the hye quere of Bristall of the holie apostles Peter and Paull. In primis at the daye of my buriall I wilbe brought furthe of my hooll goodę honestlie after the mynde of Robert Poplay and other of my frendę. Item I gyve to Jane Smythe my serunte a cofer, a mattres, a blankett, a sheitt, ij couerlettę, x[s] of money, and her hooll yeare wayge past ix[s]. Item I give to Alicie Westwro x[s] of moneye, a blankett, a sheytt, and a gowne purfeld. And I give to Jane Smythe and Alicie Westwro an olde goose and v yonge geysse. Item I give to my daughter in law, Elsabethe Poplaye, and to Dorothe Kyllingbecke the rest of all my other rayment. Item I gyve to Peter Myrfeld, gentilmā, a mattres, a paire of lynynge sheittę, and sex pece of pewther seu'allie. The Rest of all my other goodę nother gyven nor bequeathed I gyve them hoollie to Robert Rayner and Dorothie Kyllingbecke betwixte them, that is to saye, this parte of goodę thus devyded to Robert Rayner a fether bed, a mattres, ij paire of sheyttę, xij peis of pewther, iij candilstickę, a basynge, half my brasse pottę, ij sylver spoynes, and a cowe. Item as moche I gyve to Dorothee Kyllingbecke a fether bed, a mattres, ij pare of sheyttę, xij pece of pewther, iij candilstickę, a basenge, half of my brasse pottes, ij siluer spoynes, and a cowe. And al my other goodę to be devided yonctelie betwixt them. Item I maike and ordayne the said Robert Rayner and Dorothee Kyllingbecke my full executors after my deathe, desyringe my sone Robert Poplaye to be supvisor of this my last will that it be fūlled after my mynde as my speciall trust is in hym to helpe my said executors in ther right. Thes men beringe wytnes, Willm Tailyor, William Stead, chaplayne.—[*Proved 22 Oct., 1556, by Robert Raynor. Grant reserved to Dorothy Killingbeck.*]

RICHARD DENISON, OF HECKMONDWIKE.

(xv. j. 98 b.)

In the name of God Amen: the xviij daye of August in the yeare of oure lorde god a thowsand fyve hunderithe fyftie and sex. I Richard Denysone of hekmūdwyke in this pishe of Byrstall, of hooll mynde, maketh my last will in forme followinge. First I bequeathe my soull to God Allmightie and to the companye of our blissed ladie sanct Marie & to all the sanctę in heaven, and my bodie to be buried in the churche yeard of Bristall of the bolie apostles Peter and Paull. In primis the good will of my farmhold as far as in me lyethe and withe the lycence of my lorde I gyve yt to John Denysone my sone after my wiff deceasse. Item all my goodę that I haue after my deceasse, all maner of dettes and dewties content and paid, I gyve them holie to Jennet my wiff, John and Thomas my sonnes, according to the lawe, savinge that my wiff shall haue all moveables within my house as pottes, pannes, bedinge and suche others duringe her lif except she go any where to dwell frome this house, And if she so do then she shall haue the thyrd parte therof, And my too sones John and Thomas shall haue the rest. And all my other maner of goodę shall be devided to my wiff and my too sones after my deceasse as is aforsaid. Also I gyve to litle John Denyson a yowe and a lambe and to Jane Clerkeson a lambe and to litle Richard Denysone a nother lambe. Also Jennett Clerkeson my doughter shall haue my half or parte of hyues whiche is mean [? mine] at Nicholas Brokeę. Fenallie I maike John Denysone my sone my full executor after my deceasse, and to dispose for my soull as he thynkest best. Thes men beinge wytnes, Nicholas Broke, Thomas Kyghlay, James Roydhous, and Willm Walker. Item I bequeathe to the children of Thomas Denysone a cowe to be put to pfytt by the sight of freyndę, and that the said Thomas Denysone ther father shall haue nothinge to do withe her.—[*Proved* 17 *October*, 1556.]

JOHN WALKER, OF HECKMONDWIKE.

(xv. j. 100 b.)

In the name of God Amen: the third daye of Aprill in the yeare of or lord god a thowsand fyve hunderithe fyftie and sex. I John Walker, of Hecmūdwyke in the pishinge of Bristall, of hoole mynde, maikethe my last will in forme followinge. First I bequeathe my saull to god Allmightie and the companye of or blissed ladie sanct Marie and to all the sanctę in heaven, and my bodie to be buried in the churche of Bristall of the holic apostles *P*eter and *P*aull. First at the tyme of my buriall I wilbe brought furthe of my hooll goodę, And at my dettę and dewytes shalbe content and paid of the hooll. Item furthermore I gyve to John Walker my sone the yonger, and to Alicie my doughter to ayther of them iiijli ou' and aboue ther childę porcons, and also my wiff to haue her thyrdę accordinge to the lawe. And fenallie the Rest of all my goodę nether gyven nor bequeathed I gyve them hollie to all my iiij children equallie to be devided emonge them, and I maike Willm my sone and John Walker my sone, the yonger, my full and lawfull executors after my deceasse to fulfill this my last will after my mynd. Thes men beynge wytnes, John Strenger, Thomas Kyghlay, Nicholas Broke, and John Denysone.—[*Proved* 22 *Oct.*, 1556.]

BRIAN TAYLOR, OF HEATON.

(xv. j. 101 a.)

In the name of God Amen: the first daye of September in the yeare of our lorde god a thowsand fyve hunderithe fyftie and sex. I Brian Talyor, of Heatone in the pishinge of Bristall, of hooll mynde, maikethe my last will and testament in forme followinge. First I bequeathe my soull to God Allmightie, to the companye of or blissed ladie sanct Marie, and to all the sanctę in heven, and my bodie to be buried in the churche yeard of Bristall of the holie apostles peter and paull. First I will that all my dettę and dewytes be content and paid of my hooll goodę. Also the good will of my farmehold after my wiff decease as fare as in me liethe and by the lycence and favor of my lord I gyve it to James my sone. Item I gyve to John my sone a pane after my wiff deceasse, and wtn that and suche thingę as he haithe and haithe gotten vnder me he shalbe content. Also Willm my sone haith had of me wooll a certayne and gressinge and fodderinge of a quye till she was sold for xxs, and also bordinge at certayne tymes for space of manye yeares, and I haue parte money of hym agayne for whiche mattors I haue poynted iiij men, and he shalbe ordered by them and wtn that he shalbe content for his childę parte. Fenallie the Rest of all my other goodę, all dettę & dewites discharged, I gyve thē hollie to Jennett my wiff & James my sone. And the said Jennet and James shalbe my executors after my deceasse to dispoose for my soull as they thinke best. Thes men beynge wytnes, Randall Brere, Joħn Broke, and Thomas Talyor.—[*Proved* 22 *Oct.*, 1556.]

WILLIAM BURGH, OF WOODKIRK.
(xv. j. 101 b.)

In the name of God Amen: the yeare of or lord god a thowsand fyve hunderithe fiftie sex, the xxvj daye of Maye. I Wiħm Burghe, of the perishe of Woodkyrke, holl of mynde and ꝑfytt of remembrance, maiketh this my last will and testament in maner and forme followinge. First I gyve my soull to allmightie god, and my bodie to be buried in the churche yeard of Woodkyrke. Item I gyve to the churche of Woodkyrke towarde the byinge of a chalice xijd. Item I will that at the daye of my buriall that my bodie be brought furthe of my wholl goodę, my dettę paid and fun'all expens' maid at my buriall. The Residewe of my goodę I gyve vnto Alicie my wiff & my children, that is, Thomas Burghe, Xpofer, Dorothe, Alice, M'garet, Agnes, Elsabethe & Clare, whiche I maike my lawfull executors. Thes beinge witnes, sir Richarde Robert, John Foss'd, Thomas Bradley, John Burghe, Robert Fournes, with other.—[*Proved* 22 *Oct.*, 1556, *by the widow. Grant reserved to the children.*]

JOHN DAWSON, OF LOFTHOUSE.
(xv. j. 111 a.)

In the name of God Amen: the sext daye of August in the yeare of oure lord god a thowsande fyve hunderithe fyftie and sex. I John Dawson, of Lofthouse wthin the ꝑishe of Rothewell, hooll of wytt and mynde and of good and perfytt remembraunce, makith this my last will and testament in this forme followinge. First I bequeathe my soull vnto Allmightie God and to or blissed ladie sanct Marie and to all the celestiall companye in heven, and my bodie to be buried wthin the churche yearde of Rothewell of the holie trinitie. I bequeathe to the blissed sacrament of the Alter iiijd. Item I bequeathe to the repacons of the churche xijd. I bequeathe my hooll farmhold wherin I do dwell to my wiff durynge her lif and after her deceasse to turne holie to John my sone. The rest of all my goodę, my dettę paid and my fun'all expencę maid, I gyve and bequeathe to Jennett my wiff, whome I maike my lawfull executrix. Wytnesses hereof, Robert Haull, Wiħm Veuers, Brian Mylns, Thomas Walker, Alinus Maner, with other moo.—[*Proved* 12 *Nov.*, 1556.]

JOHN CLAUGHTON, OF BRAMLEY.
(xv. j. 112 b.)

In Dei nōie Amen: the xxvjth daye of Maye in the yeare of or lorde God a thowsand fyve hunderithe fyftie and sex. I John Claghton, of Bramley within the ꝑish of Leedę, beinge of good and ꝑfyte memorie, makithe this my last will and testament in man' and forme heareafter followinge. The first I bequeathe my soull to allmightie God my maker and redemer and to or blessed ladie sancte Marie and to all the blissed companye of heven, and my bodie to be buried within the churche yearde of Leiddę yf it shall please Allmightie god that I shall dye wthin the said pishe. Also I gyve to Isabell Whytley vjs viijd. Also I gyve to Isabell Whitley and to Alisone Seele one hyve betwyxt them. Also I gyve to Thomas my sone my best jacket. Also I gyve to John my sone my pressinge yrone and my tailyer sheres. Also I gyve to Nicholas my sone my best dublett. Also I gyve to Alison, Nicholas my sone wiff, my hatt. Also I gyve to Agnes my wiff all my corne and all the huslement in my house as chaires, scoles, wod boilles, woddishes, cardes, whelę. Also I gyve to the said Agnes my wiff my farmhold and tenement wher-vpon I nowe dwell duringe her naturall lif and after her deceasse to re-mayne to Thomas my sone. Also I will that my goodę be devided into thre ptes, one parte to my self and one to my wiff, and the thirde parte to my fyve children, Nicholas, Thomas, Robert, John and Margaret for ther childes porcons. Also I will that my dettę be paid and I brought furthe of my owne parte, and the Rest of my parte, fun'all expencę discharged, I give to Agnes my wiff and Thomas my sone my executors of this my will and testament. Also I maike Sir Thomas Gybson the supvisor of this my last will and testament desiringe hym faithfullie to se that this my will be fulfilled accordinge to the premisses. Thes beynge wytnesses, Richarde Gybsone, Willm Mvsgrave, John Thornetone, John Slater, with other.—[*Proved* 12 *Nov.*, 1556.]

JOHN BYWATER, OF LITTLE PRESTON.

(xv. j. 112b.)

In dei nōie amen: the xxvijth daye of September, the yeare of oure lord god a thowsande fyve hunderithe fiftie and sex. I John Bywater, of litle prestone within the parishe of Kyppax, seke of bodie and of pfytt remembrance, do make my last will and testament in maner and forme followinge. That is to saye, First I bequeath my soull to god allmightie, to or blissed ladie sanct Marie, and to all the holie companye of heven, and my bodie to be buried in the churche yearde of Kippax aforsaid. Item I bequeathe to the churche warkę of Kippax xvjd. Item I bequeathe to my eight god children eu'y one of them iiijd. Item I bequeathe one hive of bees to maister Dyneley. Item I bequeathe my best jackett to Thomas my brother and a pare of hose clothe. Item I bequeathe to Anne Evers a coytt clothe. Item I bequeathe to Robert Evers a hogge shepe. The Rest of all my goodę not bequeathed, my dettę paid, my fun'all expencies discharged, I gyve to Margarett my wiff and to Anne my doughter, whome I maik my hooll executors of this my last will to distribute my said goodę at ther will for my soulles healthe. Thes witnesses, Richard Bywater and Thomas Beall, wth other mo.—[*Proved* 12 *Nov.*, 1556, *by the widow. Grant reserved to the daughter.*]

THOMAS ROBERT, OF SWILLINGTON.

(xv. j. 113a.)

In the name of God Amen: the xxviijth daie of September in the yeare of or lorde god a thowsand fyve hunderithe fyftie and sex. I Thomas Robert, of Swyllington in the countie of Yorke, Smythe, beynge hooll of mynde and of good and pfytt remembraunce, laude and prayse be vnto Allmightie god, maketh and ordenythe this my last will and testament in man' and forme followinge. First I com̄ende my soull vnto the handꝭ of allmightie god my maker & Redemer, and my bodie to be buried wthin the churche yearde of Swillington. And I bequeathe vnto the hie Aulter for tithes and oblac̄ons forgotten xij^{d}. Item I will my goodꝭ be devided in thre partes, that is to saye, one parte to my wiff, a nother to my childer, and the thirde parte after my fun'all expencꝭ maid I gyve vnto my wiff and my children equallie to be deuided emongest them, whome I maike myne executors of this my will and testament. Thes beinge wytnesses, Michaell Haull, Thomas Grene, curate, William Robert, Thomas Dyneley, John Thawkcore.—[*Proved* 12 *Nov.*, 1556, *by Isabel the widow, John and James, sons. Grant reserved to Thomas, William, Ursula, Francis, and Michael, sons, minors.*]

JOHN BONNER, OF OTLEY.

(xv. j. 113a.)

In the name of God Amen: the xxv^{ti} daye of the monethe of Septembre, the yeare of o^{r} lorde god a thowsande fyve hunderithe fyftie and sex. I John Bonner, hole of mynde and memorie, maikꝭ and ordayns this my last will and testament vnder this forme followinge. First I bequeathe my soull to Allmightie god, o^{r} ladie sanct Marie virgine, and to all the celestiall companye of heven, and my bodie to be buried in the p̱ishe church of Ottley. Also I bequeathe to the sacrament in Otley for forgotten tithes iij^{s} iiij^{d}. Also I bequeathe to Sir george Shawe, prest, iij^{s} iiij^{d}. Also I haue gyven to George Bonner my sone at Mydsomer last past the third part of my farmhold withe the thirde parte of my corne and iiij oxen and half of all the gere belonginge to husbandre and one quye and to sawe half of the Fawgbe and to enter at o^{r} ladie daye the admi'ciac̄on next following to the half of my farmhold, in full contentac̄on and payment of his childꝭ porc̄on, and he haith sealled me Acquitaunce. Also I haue gyven to Thomas my eldest sone all his childꝭ porc̄on and haith sealed me acquitance. Also Xpofer my sone haith his porc̄on and haithe sealed me acquitance. Also Alisone my doughter is furthe withe her childꝭ porc̄on and haithe sealed me acquitance. Also Jane my doughter haithe her childꝭ porc̄on wthout acquitance but her father rewarde and my reward was named at the daye of marage that she should haue towe oxen styrkꝭ and towe quye styrkꝭ when they enter to ther farmhold at Smawbankꝭ. Also the other half of my farmhold I gyve to Isabell my wiff and Anthony my sone, and my wiff to haue the best house as longe as she kepithe her widowe, and it is my will that Anthonye my sone shall haue all his goodꝭ that the said Anthonye haithe at my house besidꝭ his childꝭ porc̄on. Also I will that Anthonye my sonne, Isabell and Agnes my doughters haue the thirde parte of my goodꝭ equallie devided amongꝭ them for ther childꝭ porc̄ons. The Residewe of my goodꝭ not bewytt, my dettꝭ paid and fun'all expencꝭ maid, I will that my wiff Isabell Bonner and Anthonye Bonner my sone haue them, whiche I make my executors, and Constance Banton, Henrye Hardwike and Thomas Dryver to be sup̱visors of my will that they maye se my will fulfilled. Thes being wytnes, Robert Foster, Edward Wayrde, Costanne Threpland, Thomas Lyster, and s^{r} George Shawe, with other mo, as John Wayrde and James Wylley. —[*Proved* 12 *Aug.* [*Nov.*], 1556.]

George Simson, of Leeds, Clothier.

(xv. j. 114 a.)

In the name of God Amen: the sext daye of Marche in the yeare of o[r] lord god a thowsand fyve hunderithe fyftie and thre. I George Symson, of Leddę, clother, of hooll mynde and good memorie, makithe this my last will and testamente in man' and forme followinge. First I bequeathe my soull vnto allmightie god & to o[r] blissed ladie and to all the sanctę in heven, and my bodie to be buried within the ꝑishe churche of sanct Peter at Leadę. Also I gyve and bequeathe to Willm Harrysone my sone in laye one hooll yeare mylninge of his owne clothe after my deceasse. Also I will that Alicie my wiff shall haue all my goodę and taikę painge to eu'y one of my children ther childę porc̃ons accordinge to the lawe. And also I maike the said Alicie my wiff my full executrix to paye my dettę & to fulfill this my last will & testament and to dispose the rest of my goodę as she shall think best pleasenge Allmightie god. Also I gyve & bequeathe to Margaret my doughter vj[li] xiij[s] iiij[d] for her childę porc̃on. Also I gyve to Willm Symson my sone my best jacket & my buckskyn coyt. Also I gyve to Willm Harrison my sone in laye my next jacket and my best hoose and x[s] in moneye for the cowe which Elisabethe Wharton gave to Elisabethe Symson. Also I gyve to Willm Symson my sone xl[s] in money for his hooll parte of his childes porc̃on and he to sealle my wiff my executrix a quytaunce for his childę parte or els he to cast in that that he haithe had & to haue that that the lawe will gyve hym or his childę parte as yt shall come to. Thes beinge wytnes, Richard Mathewę, Nycholas Reame, and John Kyrke.—[*Proved* 12 *Nov.*, 1557[6].]

Thomas Falconer, of Hunslet.

(xv. j. 114 b.)

In the name of God Amen: the xxijth daye of September in the yeare of oure lord god a thowsand fyve hunderithe fyftie and foure. I Thomas Fawkener, of Huntslett, of hooll mynde and good memorie, makithe this my last will and testament in man' and forme followinge. First I bequeathe my soull vnto Allmightie god my creator and redemer, and my bodie to be buried w[th]in the ꝑishe churche yearde of Ledę of the sonnsyd. Also I gyve to eu'y god childe iiij[d]. Also I gyve to Richarde Fawkener, George sonne, a yowe and a lambe. Also I will that my goodę be devided in thre p'tes, one p'te to my wiff, a nother parte to be devided equallie betwixt my children, George Fawkener, Richard Fawkener, Margaret Fawkener, and Alicie Fawkener. And I gyve to Richard Fawkener my sone yoockę, teimes & plowes ou' and besidę that. And I will that George my sonne haue that goodę counted in his parte whiche he had at his mariage. Also I give to Richard my sone my goodwill of my farmhold after the deceasse of my wiff. Also I gyve to William Fawkener my sonne one whie. Also the thirde parte of my goodę, my fun'all expencę and chargę paid, I give to Elsabethe my wiff, whome I maike my full executrix of this my last will & testament. Thes beinge wytnes, George Bratwhate, Robert Wilkynson, with other.—[*Grant* 12 *Nov.*, 1556, *to William, George, and Richard, sons, the widow having renounced.*]

ROBERT BARTELOTT, OF BARKSTONE.

(xv. j. 118 a.)

In Dei nõie Amen: quarto decimo die Octobris Anno D'ni Miłłmo qui'-gen^mo qui'quagesimo sexto. I Robert Bartelott, of Barkestone w^th^in the ꝑishe of Shereburne in Elmett, hooll of mynde and ꝑfytt of Remembrance and knowleadge, lawde and praise be gyven vnto allmightie god, do ordayne, constitute, and maike this my last will and testament in maner and forme as hereafter doith ensue. Firste I gyve and bequeathe my soull vnto allmightie god yf it please hym to call me oute of this transytorie worlde at this present tyme, and to the blissed virgyne oure ladie sanct marie his mother, and to all the holie companye of heaven, and my bodie to be buried w^th^in the sanctuarie of my ꝑisshe churche yearde of Shereburn aforsaid. It'm I gyve and bequeathe to the blissed sacrament for my tithes and oblac̄ons forgotten iij^s^ iiij^d^. Item I gyve and bequeathe to the church workꝭ at Shereburne vj^s^ viij^d^. It'm I gyve and bequeathe Alicie Bartelott, my brother John doughter, xl^s^. Item I gyve and bequeathe to Henrie Holdaile xij^d^. It'm I gyve and bequeathe vnto John Burlande wiff one ewe and one lambe. Item I gyve and bequeathe to Thomas Smythe one ewe and one lambe. Item I gyve and bequeathe to Anne Marshall my s'unt one peticott clothe. Item I give and bequeathe to Leonarde Snawden my s'unte one dublett. Item I gyve and bequeathe to eu'y one of my god children iiij^d^. Item the Residewe of all my goodꝭ moveable and vnmoveable not bequeathed, my dettꝭ and legacies paid and fun'allꝭ discharged, I gyve and bequeathe to Jane my wiff, whome I do ordayne, constitute, and maike my sole executrix of this my last will and testament to distribute and dispose for my soules healthe as she shall thinke most convenient and meite. Wytnesses, Sir Robert Blanche, curate, Robert Forman, John Wharledaill, and John Polle, with others.—[*Proved* 26 *November*, 1556.]

WILLIAM HEWIT, OF LEDSTONE.

(xv. j. 135 a.)

In the name of God Amen: in the yeare of oure lorde a thowsande fyve hunderithe fyftie and sex and xxvj daye of Julie. I William Hewyt, in Ledstone, beinge of hoole mynde and good memorie, maikꝭ this my laste will and testament in maner and forme followinge. First I bequeathe my soull to Allmightie god, oure ladie sanct marie, and to all the sanctes in heaven, and my bodie to be buried in the churche yearde of oure ladie in Kypax. First I bequeathe to the blissed sacrament xij^d^. Also I bequeathe to Jennet Pole my s'unte a yowe and a lambe. Also I bequeathe to William Boltone the goodwill of my farmholde after the deceasse of my wiff. Also I bequeathe to a childe of Richarde Nycalson whiche I am godfather to, a yowe hogge. Also I bequeathe to Margaret my wiff and John Hewyt my cosing The rest of all my goodꝭ, my dettꝭ and fun'all expens' maid of holthe my buriall and then to deale boithe in towne and feilde after the deceasse of my wiff, whome I maike my full executors. Thes beinge recordes, James Dodge, Maister Vicar, Wiłłm Boltone, Richarde Nicalson, withe other moo.—[*Proved* 1 *Oct.*, 1556, *by the widow. Grant reserved to John Hewyt, a minor.*]

CHRISTOPHER HARRISON, OF LEATHLEY.

(xv j. 135 a.)

In the name of God Amen: in the yeare of oure lorde god a thowsand fyve hunderithe fyftie and sex and on the xviij daye of August. I Christofer Harrisone, of Lethelaye, beinge seike in bodie but of pfytt mynde and in good memorie, doithe ordayne and maike this my last will in maner and forme followinge. First I bequeathe my soull to Allmightie god, or ladie sanct Marie, and to all the celestial companye in heaven, And my bodie to be buried in the churche yearde of Leathelaye. Item I will that my goodę accordinge to the custome of the cuntre to be equallie devided in thre partę, one parte to my self, one other parte to Jane my wyff, and the thyrde parte to my poore children. Item I will that all my dettę and fun'all expensis be taiken hollie forthe of my parte and the remainder thereof I giue to Jaine my said wiff. Also I will and desire in the waye of charitie Willm Fenteman and Robert Moyses to haue and taike the ordre and mynistracon of all my goodę and they to see this my last will to be fulfilled, that my poore wyff and children maye haue ther right, and I putt my hool trust vnto them and they to haue ther chardges borne of the hole goodę. Thes berynge wytnes, John Watson, curate, Umfraye Hodgeson, Willm Fentymā, Roberte Moyses, and Roberte Bradbelt.—[*Proved* 1 *October*, 1556.]

GEORGE BRAMLEY, OF OTLEY.

(xv. j. 135 a)

In Dei nōie Amen: Anno Dñi millmo qui'genmo quadragesimo nono, vicesimo terc'o die Februarij. I George Bramelaye, seike of bodie but hoole of rememberaunce, maikethe this my last will and testament in maner and forme followinge. First I bequeathe my soull to Allmightie God and to all the holie companye in heaven, and my bodie to be buried in christen manes buriall. Item I bequeathe my goodę to be divided in thre accordinge to the lawe. That is to saye, one parte to my self, an other to my wiff, and the third to my chyldren. Item I will that my dettę be paid of my hole goodę. Item I will that my bodie be broughte furthe of my owne parte. Item I will that the Residue of my goodę when my bodie is brought furthe and all other costes and chargies done that then the residewe of my p'te be devided equallie emonge my wyff and children. Item I bequeathe the good will of my farmholde to Margaret my wiff and Henrye my sone as longe as my wiffe is wedowe if the lorde be content therwithe, to brynge vppe my children therwithe, and yf my wyff marie agayne I bequeathe the good will of my farmeholde to Henrye my sonne. Item I maike Margaret my wiff and Henrie my sonne my executors. Item where as Roger Mawsone haithe tolde my maister Sir William Fairfaxe that I did gyve hym the good will of my farmhold I taik yt of my chardge as I shall aunswere at the daye of Judgement that he saye falselie and vntreulie of me. Thes beinge wytnes, William Smythe the elder and Willm Smythe the yonger, Robert Wylson, William Slator, sir Thomas Lowcoke, withe other moo.—[*Proved* 1 *October*, 1556.]

MARGARET FIELD, OF BEESTON.

(xv. j. 135 b.)

In the name of God Amen: the viijth daye of August in the yeare of oure lorde god a thowsand fyve hunderithe fyftie and sex. I Margaret Feilde, of Beistone within the ꝑishe of Ledes and in the countie of Yorke, maiketh this my last will and testament in maner and forme followinge. First I bequeathe my soull vnto Allmightie god and to oure ladie sancte marie and to all the sanctes in heaven, and my bodie to be buried within the ꝑishe churche yearde of sanct Peter at Ledes, neighe vnto my husbande, secundlie I bequeathe vnto the blissed sacrament of the alter at Ledes vj^{d}, vnto the blissed sacrament of the alter at Battlay vj^{d}, vnto the poore people vj^{s} viij^{d}, vnto Rauff Felde my eldist sonne iiij sheippe, vj^{s} viij^{d}, and his owne parte of his corne, ij partes of one loid of haye, a kettle and one litle pañe; to his sonne Thomas one yowe and a beige panne, to my doughter Katheryn his wiff a kyrchef, to her ij doughters ij sheippe and one rayle, to my youngest son John Feild ij newe pannes, my pewther vessell, one brasse pott, one candilsticke, my water kyttes, one chirne, one stande, my dyshes, boylles, tubbes, and all other wood vessell, my aile pottes, ij seves, one redle, one almerie at my bedꝭ feytt, one arke in the p'lor, one cowe, one loid of haye, one half of my corne, ij cou'lettꝭ, ij blankettꝭ, ij paire of lynne sheittꝭ, one pillowe, one bolster, one mattres, one half of my sheippe, and to receve of my sonne Rauff Feild whiche he owe to me, vj^{li} xiij^{s} viij^{d}, for his owne whiche I gyve hym, wherfore he shall maike fun'alitie and other my necessarie chardgies. To my sonne Roberte Gaill one loid of haye, one half of my corne, and one half of sheipe to hym and my sonne John one swyne, paynge to my sonne Rauff xvj^{d}. To my doughter Elisabethe one arke, one almerie, one chiste, and my blacke kyrtle, to her doughter Alicie one cowe and one peticotte, to my sone John and my doughter Elisabethe all my naperie wayre, to my doughter Elisabethe Feilde and Margaret Gaille one henne with vij chekyns, to eu'y one of my god children vj^{d}, to my syster Wayde one gowne, to my brother Roberte Feilde wiff one gowne, to my syster Marie one harden sheitt, one cou'lett, one apperone, one raille, one readd coitte, and one kyrshif, to Atkynson wiff one peticotte, to her doughter Margaret one grenne coitte, to Wright wiff one kerchiff and one apperon, to Lawraunce Williams wiff one peticott, and the Rest of my goodꝭ to be equallie devided emongest my thre children, Rauff Feild, John Feild, my sonnes, and Elsabethe Gaill my doughter, and thus I maike Rauff Feild and John Feild my sones my full executors of this my last will and testament. Thes being wytnes, Wiłłm Gaille, George Mylner, and Rauffe Moxon, withe other.—[*Proved* 1 *Oct.*, 1556.]

THOMAS HALLILEY, OF SOUTH MILFORD.

(xv. j. 161 a.)

In Dei nōie Amen: the xvth daie of Decembre in the yeare of oure lord god a thowsand fyve hunderithe fyftie and sex. I Thomas Halile, of Mylforth wthin the ꝑishe of Sheyrburn, hooll of mynd and memorie, thankꝭ be to god, doith maike this my last will and testament in maner and forme followinge. First I bequeathe my soull to god Almightie and to our ladie sanct Marie and to all the celestiall companye of heven, and my bodie to be buried wthin the ꝑishe churche of Sheirburn in the myd alye before the Royd. First I bequeath to the blissed sacrament xvjd. Item I bequeathe to my sonne John the elder one oxgañ of land within the feildꝭ of Shereburn whiche he haithe surrender of, to be sowed, and my best yron bownd wayne and one yocke of oxen and one oxe of his owne called Darlinge, one garded whiche was Thomas Sledmans, and a browne which was Robert Burmans, of Newthorpe. Also I gyve hym one graye colt which was of the bald meare, and also I gyve hym one ploughe withe all that belongꝭ to yt, towe teames, towe yockes and a yron harrowe. Also I gyve hym xlvjs viijd of the whiche I will that fyve nobles of that some shall helpe to brynge me fourthe and the Rest to be paid to hym by myne executors at the daye of his mariage, I gyve hym thes porc̃ons of good in the name of his childꝭ porc̃on. Item I bequeathe to John my sone the yonger one yocke of oxen whiche is called yslima' and lyone, one yocke and a teame and a yrone bound wayne. I will that myne executors maike hym withe the olde yrone that is in the house newė whėles and a newe bodie and xls in penye or in penye worthe, thes porc̃ons of good I gyve hym in the name of his childꝭ porc̃on. And I will that my wiff or els John my sone, whiche haithe the ꝑfytt of suster house, shall paye one marke at my buryinge. Item my dettꝭ paid and my will ꝑformed, I make Jennett my wiff and Thomas my sonne and Jennett my doughter myne executors and assignes. And the Rest of my childer to stande to ther porc̃ons. Thes beynge wytnesses, Godfraye Towneraye, Rawff Burtone, William Halile, Wiłłm Burtone.—[*Proved* 18 *Febr.*, 1556–7, *by the widow. Grant reserved to the children.*]

Edward Meerbeck, of Burton Salmon.

(xv. j. 161 a.)

In the name of God Amen: the viijth daye of August in the yeare of our lord god a thowsand fyve hunderithe fyftie and sex. I Edward Merebecke, of Burton in the ꝑishe of Monkefristone, hooll of myud and good of remembraunce, maikꝭ this my last will and testament in maner and forme followinge. First I bequeathe my soull to God Allmightie and to or blissed ladie sancte Marie and to all the celestiall companye of heaven, and my bodie to be buried within my ꝑishe churche yearde, Monkefriston. Also I gyve to the blissed Sacrament xxd. Item to Sr Richard gennynge my curate xxd. And to John Mettam, clarke, viijd. Item to Edward Wilson a yowe and a lambe. Item to Agnes Wilsone a yow and a lambe and half a quarter of barlie. Item to Richard Merebecke, of Hamylton, sex poundꝭ of woll and yarne. Item to John Smythe, of Fareborne, my best jackett. Item to Thomas Homblocke one mattres, a pare of sheittꝭ, a cou'lett. Also I will that my wiff shall haue the Rule and occupac̃on of all my goodꝭ duringe her naturall lif and after her deathe I gyve it to Thomas Homblocke and George Hoppaye whome I maike my full Executors and they to bringe me honestlie furthe and paye my dettꝭ. Thes beinge wytnes, Sir Richarde Gennynge, my curate, William Halalye, yonger, and Henrye Myttone, William Myttone, with other moo.—[*Proved* 18 *Feb.*, 1556–7.]

JOHN FYXSER, OF NEWTHORPE.

(xv. j. 161 b.)

In the name of God Amen: the iiij[th] daye of June in the yeare of o[r] lord god a thowsand fyve hunderithe fyftie and fyve. I John Fyxser, of Newthorpe in the countie of Yorke, myln', hoole of mynd and ꝑfytt in remembrance but seke in bodie, doithe maike this my last will and testament in maner and forme followinge. First I give and bequeathe my soull to god allmightie, o[r] ladie sanct Marie, and all the blissed companye of heaven, and my bodie to be buried within the ꝑishe churche yearde of all sanctꝭ in Sheirburne or els where it shall please Allmightie god to call me to his great mercy and grace. Item I bequeathe to the blissed sacrament at Shirburne for my tithes forgotten xij[d]. The Resydewe of all my goodꝭ, my dettꝭ paid and my fun'allꝭ, I gyve to Anne Fyxser my wiff, John Fyxser, Wiƚƚm Fyxser, and Katheryn Fixser, my children, whome I maike jonctelie my holl executors. Wytnesses, Anthonye Nelstroppe and Robert Burnand.—[*Proved* 18 *Febr.*, 1556–7, *by the widow and son John. Grant reserved to William & Katherine, minors.*]

RALPH FIELD, OF BEESTON.

(xv. j. 161 b)

In the name of God Amen: the xxv[ti] daye of Novembre in the yeare of o[r] lord God a thowsande & fyve hunderithe fiftie and sex. I Rauff Feild, of Beistone, beinge of holl mynd and ꝑfytt remembrance, makithe this my last will and testamente in maner and forme followinge. First I gyve and bequeathe my soull vnto Allmightie god, and my bodie to be buried within the ꝑishe churche yeard of sanct Peter in Ledes. Also I giue for my mortuarie as the lawe requirethe. Also I will that my goods shalbe devided in thre ꝑties, one ꝑte to myself, the secounde ꝑte to my wiff, and the third pte to my children. And that Katheryne my wiff shall haue my farmehold to bringe vp my children w[th]all to they come to lawfull yeares of discression. And than I will that one of my children shall have my said Farmehold, the which of them as it shall best please my good maister to admitt it vnto. And I will that vpon the daye of my buriall ther shalbe v[s] delt in almes to the poore people. Also I gyve to the blissed sacrament at Ledes iiij[d]. Also I gyve to the blissed sacrament at Battelay iiij[d]. Also I gyve to eu'y one of my god children ij[d]. Also I will that if it please god to call to his marcie any one of my children before they come to lawfull aige than I will that that parte of that childe or children so deceassed shall remayne to the other. Also I gyve to Jennett Boll and my s'unte ij[s]. The Rest of all my goodꝭ not geven I gyve to Katheryne my wiff, Anne & Isabell my doughters and Thomas my sonne, whome I maike my full executors of this my last will and testament. Thes beinge wytnesses, Henrye Chanler, clarke, Wiƚƚm Gaile, Brian Bolland, Edward Bicroft, Robert Erle, and Robert Gaile, withe other.—[*Proved* 18 *Febr.*, 1556–7, *by the widow. Grant reserved to the children.*]

RICHARD PEARSON, OF LEEDS, BARBER.

(xv. j. 162 a.)

In the name of God Amen: the third daye of Decembre in the yeare of o[r] lord god a thowsand fyve hunderithe fiftie and fyve. I Richard

Peirson, of Ledę in the countie of Yorke, barber, beinge of hooll mynd and of good and ꝑfytt remembrance, thankę be to Allmightie god, maikethe this my last will and testament in maner and forme followinge. First I gyve my soull to Allmightie god my maker and Redemer, besechinge o^r^ ladie sancte Marye and all the blissed companye of heaven to praye for me, and my bodie to be buried within my ꝑishe church yeard of sanct Peter at Ledes. Also I gyve to the blissed sacrament for tithes and oblac̃ons forgotten viij^d^. Also I gyve to James my brother a case of Rasers, a pare of Sysers, a combe and a whetstone therto belonginge. Also I gyve to my godsone Lawraunce Wodd one Jackett newe dressed without lyninge. Also I gyve to Katheryn my doughter one duble counter. And the Residewe of all my goodę vnbequest, my fun'all expences discharged, my dettę paid, I gyve vuto Jennett my wiff and to Katheryne my doughter, whome I maike my full executricę of this my last will and testament. Also I maike Thomas Hardwycke, of Potter Newtone, esquier, and Richarde Boythe suꝑvisors of this my last will, desiringe them of charitie to se yt fulfilled. Thes beinge wytnesses, Sir Xpofer Bradlaye, vicar of Ledes, Richard Sympsone, Thomas Waidd, of Ledes, with others.—[*Proved* 18 *Feb.*, 1556-7, *by the widow. Grant reserved to the daughter.*]

WILLIAM HODGSON, OF PONTEFRACT, ALDERMAN.

(xv. j. 168 a.)

In the name of God Amen: the x day of Octobre in the yere of our lord God m^l^cccccIvj^th^ and the first yere of the reigne of our sou'aigne Ladye Marye by the grace of god of England, France and Ireland Quene. I Wiłłm Hodgeson, of Pomfrett, alderman, holl of mynd & perfecte remembrance, dothe make this my last will & testament in this maner & forme followynge, first, I bequeath my soull to god almighty my redemer & saueyore, and my body to be buried in the churche yerde of all sanctę at Pomfrett, nighe vnto the piller of the southe syde of the procession dore. Also I gyve vnto Thomas Moy xx^s^ if he either come or send for it. Also I giue to Effam my doughter in the name of her childę porc̃on vj^li^ xiij^s^ iiij^d^. Also I giue to the same Effam iij^li^ vj^s^ viij^d^. Also I giue to Henrye Hodgeson my son & beire iiij^li^. Also I giue to Wiłłm my son in the name of his porc̃on vj^li^ xiij^s^ iiij^d^. Also I giue to John my son in the name of his porc̃on vj^li^ xiij^s^ iiij^d^. Also I giue to Edmund my son in the name of his porc̃on vj^li^ xiij^s^ iiij^d^. Also I will that Isabell my wif shall haue a standyng cuppe during her lif and after her decesse it to remayne to my son Edmũde & his beires for euer. Also I will that John Skipton, of Pomfrett, alderman, and Antony Thornay, of heghton, shall have v^li^ to occupie for the behofe of Jenet my doughter, and she to be succored of the incresse therof, and after her decesse it to remayne to Wiłłm, John & Edmunde my sones. Also I bequeath to John Huntyngden a violet Jacket. Also I bequeath to Nicholas Carlile a fustyan doblet, to John Bawge my violet hose. Also I gine to s^r^ Wiłłm Chambre my curate a quarter of wheate. Also I giue to eu'y on of my tenantę at Kellyngton viij^d^. Also I bequeathe to my son John base begotten my better fox furred gowne. The residewe of all my goodę not bequest I will that they be all at the order of Edmonde my son, whom I make my holl executor. Also I will that Antony Thornay,

John Skepton, Ric. Wylbore, and John Hodgeson, of Pomfret, aldermen, shalbe the supvisors of this my will and eu'y on of them to haue for ther paynes takynge vj[s] viij[d]. In witnes herof, Nycolas Carlyll, John Bawge, Edward Rusby, and s[r] Willm Chamer, my curate.—[*Proved* 3 *Feb.*, 1556–7, *by Henry Ellis, guardian of Edmund the son, a minor.*]

THOMAS HARDWICK, OF NEWLAY.

(xv. j. 175 b.)

In the name of god amen: the iiij day of September in the yere of our lord god m[l]ccccclvj. I Thom's Hardwike, of the Newleythe w[t]in the towneshippe of Horsefurth, being of holl mynd & of good & p'fecte remembrance, dothe make this my last will & testament in manner & forme herafter followinge. First I gine & bequeath my soull to god almighty my maker & redemer, faithfully besechinge o[r] blessed lady sancte Mary the blessed virgyn & all the celestiall company of heven to pray for me that I faithfully trusting in the meritę of Christę passion may come to the euerlastinge joye of heven, & I will that my bodye be buried in the churche or churche yerd of sancte Oswold in Giesley. Also I giue to the blessed sacrament iij[s] iiij[d]. Also I gine to my syster Jenet Fisheburne xx[s] & one cowe gaite in the nuñe rode or coppe rodde at Yedon during the yeres of my lease in the same. Also I giue to Eliz. my wif my lease of the psonage of Whitkirke whiche I bought of John Prestman to occupie, enyoye the same onely to her during her naturall life & after her decesse I giue it to Thomas Hardwyke my son & I giue to my said wif my lease of sletis. Also I giue to my said wif the third parte of all my landę. Also I giue to my son Willm Hardwyke all that my parte of the lease of the tythe of Ledę & Wodhus. Also I giue to the said Willm my son my copye or lease whiche I had of the late Abbott of Kirkstall & the covent of the same of all the landę lyenge in the feildę of Leidę & Wodhus. Also I give to my said son Willm my lease whiche I haue of my m[r] s[r] Willm Vavaso[r], knyght, of the balywike of Addinghm, for certaync yeres yet not expired. And I will that Henry Herdwike, of Addinghm, be his depute to suche tyme as he shall come to laufull aige & to levye & receyve all rentes & duties due vnto the said Sir Willm Vavaso[r] belonging to the said baylywyke & therof to make a true accompte & paymente as I hertofore haue done & discharge my said son Willm Hardwike for & cõcernynge the same & I will that the said Henry Herdwike shall haue for his paynes taking vj[s] viij[d] yerly of the fee over and besidę all such profettę as he hath nowe yerly by me. Also I giue to my said son Willm Herdwike all my purchased landę, my wif third parte except. Also I giue Willm Herdwike my lease of Haukesworth whiche I had of Thomas Pepper. Also I gine to Thomas Herdwike my son in recompence for the said Haukesworth whiche he shold haue had one lease which I haue of Margret Jeffray then widowe of certayne landę lying w[th]in Leidę & Wodhus & also my lease whiche I haue of Edward Vavaso[r] & Alice his wif of certayne landę lyeing w[t]in the said towns of Ledę & Wodhus yet not expired. Also I giue to the said Thomas my son my lease w[ch] I haue of one ferhold in Yedon & on close called noñe rode. Also I giue to the said Thomas my son my lease which I haue of M[r] Willm Boyes pson of Gieslay, of the tythe corne of Rawdon. Provided always that the said Thomas my son shall suffer Mr Stephen Paslewe to occupie & enioye the one half of the sayd tythe & to pay the one half of the rent yerlye according as he nowe doth & if the said Stephen Paslewe dye before the said lease be ended then I will that my said son Thomas shall enioye the holl lease. Also I gine to my said son Thomas my interest in lease wch I bought of Laurence Baynes of the tythe corne & hey of Hocke, Hensall, Goldley & Baume. *P*rovided alwaye that Eliz. my wif shall receyve the holl rentę & pay the kinges rent out of the same & eu'y yere to reserve & kepe safe of the profettę of the said lease viijli to the vse & profet of the said Thomas to he cōm at laufull aige. Also I will that Eliz' my wif shall give to Myles Fisheburne yerly furthe of the profettę of the lease of the psonage of Whitkirke the some of vs during suche tyme as she shall enioye the same & after the decesse of my said wif I will that Thomas my son shall pay the said some of vs to the said Myles so longe as he shall enioye the said lease of the said psonage. Also I will that Willm my son shall pay also to the said Myles Fisheburne yerly the some of vs out of the profettę of my landę duringe the lif of the said Myles. Also I giue to Richerd Pollerde my son in lawe my best cote & one whie. Also I gine to George *P*ollerd my son in lawe my doblet of tawney satten & on whie, and I giue also to John *P*ollerd my son in lawe on yong gray amblinge nagge. Also I giue to my servant Roger Saxton my copye whiche I haue of Margret Jeffray than widowe of the third pte of my [*sic*] at Wodhus & further I gine to the said Roger my copie which I haue of Thomas Stable of thre rodę of land lyeing in on close called Newlandę. Also I gine to Jenet Candeler my servante xs. Also I glue to euery on of my servantę beyng here at the daye of my detthe on quarter wages ou' & besidę that whiche is there is then due to them. Also I gine to Isabell Fisheburne iijs iiijd. Also I giue to Gilbert Saxton iijs iiijd. Also I gine to Jenet Saxton iijs iiijd. Also I giue to Agnes Moore iijs iiijd. Also I gine to Thomas Crosbye my godson one sylu' spoyne & on crowne in gold. Also I giue to Ric' Boythe yonger on silu' spone. Also I giue to Thomas Grene my godson xijd. Also I giue to eu'y one of my god children beynge on lyve iiijd. Also I make Eliz' my wif my holl executrix of this my will & testament & I will that my holl goodę be divided in iij partes, wherof on parte therof my wif to haue & a nother parte to my ij children Willm & Thomas Hardwike equally to be diuided betwixt them according to the lawes of this Realme & the third parte to pay my legacies & to make my funerall expenses, & after I gine to my said wif the one half of the goodę of my part then not expended & the other half of the said goodę of my part I giue to my sones Willm & Thomas & I will that if either of my said sones dye before they come to lawfull aige that then the other of them beyng on lyve shall haue his part and porcon of suche goodę & other thingę as to him is giuen by this my will. Also I will that my cosyn[1] Thomas Hardwike, of Potternewton, gent', haue the custody & bringing vp of my son Willm Hardwike during his nonage wt suche porcons of goodę, landę & fermes as to him is giuen by this my will, requiryng hym to bryng my said son vp in lernyng and vertuose lyving wt suche yerely profettes as to him is giuen by this will or wt so moche therof as shall suffise for the same & the rest therof to imploye

(1) His will is printed *post*, p. 116.

to the vse of my said son Wiłłm at his discretion & also I will that Eliz' my wif shall haue the bringing vp of my son Thomas Hardwike & to have his parte & porc̃on of his good℘ & fermes to him giuen by this my will during his nonage & the said Thomas m̃y son to be guyded & ordred by the good aduyse & counsell of my said cosyn Thomas Herdwike, of Potternewton, gent'. Also I make my said cosyn Thomas Hardwyke & Mr Boyes, ꝑson of Gieslay, suꝑvisors of this my last will & testament & they to se the same executed in eu'ye behalf as my trist is in them for the same & I giue to either of them xs for ther paynes takinge therin. Also I giuc to Eliz' my wif & to Ric' Pollerd my son in lawe all my wayne geare as waynes, cowpes, plowes, yokes, temes & suche like beyng here & all maner of tymber therto belonginge. Thes beyng witnesses, Thomas Herdwike, gent., Sr Xpofer Mydgeley, clerke, and Thomas Ranson, withe others.—[*Proved* 18 *Dec.*, 1556.]

WILLIAM SOWERBY, OF EAST RIGTON, LABOURER.

(xv. j. 176 a.)

In the name of God amen: the ix daye of Octobre, anno D'ni ccccclvj. I Wiłłm Sowrby, of Estrigton in the county of Yorke, laborer, seke in body & of good remembrance, maketh this my last will & testament in maner & forme followinge. First I giue my soull vnto God Almighty, vnto our lady sancte Mary, & vnto the celestiall companye in heven, & my body to be buried in my ꝑishe churche yerd of all sanct℘ at Berdsay. Also vnto Thomas Wautr' my son in lawe & Eliz' his wif v yewes. Also I giue vnto John Atkinson & his wif ij yewes. Also I gine vuto my doughter Sibell Sourbye one cowe. Also I giue vnto Mundans my wif the lease of fermhold during her lif naturall & after her decesse that my doughter Katheryn shall haue the forsaid lease of my fermhold. The residewe of all my good℘ vnbequest, my dettes paid & funerall expens' discharged, I gine vnto Mundans my wif whom I make my full executrix of this my last will and testament. Thes beyng witnes, John Brereclif and Nicolas Rowley.—[*Proved* 18 *Dec.*, 1556.]

DAME ANNE CALVERLEY, OF MILN GREEN, LEEDS.[1]

(xv. j. 191 b.

In the name of God Amen: the last day of December in the year of our lord god m[l]ccccclvj. I Dame Anne Calu'ley, of Mylnegrene in the ꝑishe of Led℘, of holl mynd & good remembrance, makith my will & testament in maner & forme following. First I giue & bequeth my soull vnto Almighty God my maker & redemer, & my body to be buried wtin my pishe churche of sancte Peters at Led℘. And I will that my dett℘ shall be paid of my holl good℘. Also I gine vnto the blessed sacrament to anournament℘ therof iijs iiijd. Also I giue & bequeth vnto mr xpofer Hopton lx wethers vnto the helpe & mariage of his doughters. Also I giuc & bequeth vnto my sister Eliz' Vavasor xli. Also I gine vnto Sr Wiłłm Caluerley, knyght, a ring of golde wt a grene stone. Also I giue vnto Gilbert Calu'ley a crosse of gold. Also I giue vnto Mr Wiłłm Vavasor,

(1) Second wife of Sir Walter Calverley and daughter of John Vavasour, of Weston. See *Dugdale's Visitation of Yorkshire*, ed. Clay, vol. 1, p. 245.

of Weston, a girdell & a crosse of gold. Also I giue vnto Mr Xpofer Hopton a paire of beidꝭ w^t^ gold gaudyes & a silu' coppe gilted. Also I giue vnto Mr John Hopton a sylu' salt & iiij sylu' spones. Also I giue vnto Robte Vavaso^r^ my brother xl^s^. Also I giue vnto my brother Marmaduke Vavaso^r^ my weddyng ring. Also I giue vnto Edward Danby a quite goblet of sylu' & a flat ring of gold. Also I gine vnto Roger Danbye xl^s^. Also I giue vnto Marie Vavaso^r^ v^li^. Also I giue vnto Brigitt Walworth vj^li^ xiij^s^ iiij^d^. Also I giue vnto my sister Eliz' Vavaso^r^ a peice of black puke clothe. Also I giue vnto my sister Cicilie Calu'ley a gowne of blacke chamlet, a worset kirtle & a cowe & a calf. Also I gine vnto Brigitt Walworthe a gowne of worset & a kirtle of white silke w^t^ sleves & all that belongeth vnto it. Also I giue vnto thanournament of the churche vj^s^ viij^d^. Also I gine vnto the high ways xx^s^. Also I giue vnto Willm Vavaso^r^ xx^s^. Also I giue vnto John Vavaso^r^ xx^s^. Also I giue vnto Laurence Ferro vj^s^ viij^d^. Also I giue vnto Thomas Beane a cowe. Also I giue vnto James Bartlot a cowe. Also I giue vnto Thomas Atkinson a cowe. Also I gine vnto my serunte Gilbert Spence a cowe. Also I giue vnto Cicilye Fawcet a blacke quye. Also I giue vnto Alyce my servant a red quye. Also I giue vnto my s'unte the mylner a quye stirke. Also I gine vnto Margaret Adamson a quye stirke. Also I giue vnto Ric' Leigh iij^s^ iiij^d^. Also I giue vnto George Sedall iij^s^ iiij^d^. Also I gine vnto Ric' Mylner iij^s^ iiij^d^. Also I giue vnto John Thornton my godson ij^s^. Also I giue vnto John Musgrave son, of Writley, my godson, ij^s^. Also I giue vnto John Mosse iij^s^ iiij^d^. Also I gine vnto Sr Ric' Beckew^t^, clerke, vj^s^ viij^d^. The Rest of all my goodꝭ vnbequested, I honestly brought furthe & my dettꝭ paid, I gine vnto M' Xpofer Hopton my son in lawe & M' Marmaduke Vavaso^r^ my brother to order & dispose as they thinke most neidfull to my poore freyndꝭ that neideth most, whom I make my full executors of this my last will & testament. Thies being witness', Xpofer Bradley, vicar of Ledꝭ, Ric. Leigh, George Sedall, w^t^ others.—[*Proved* 6 *April*, 1557.]

ROBERT BRADFORD, OF MORLEY.

(xv. j. 193 a.)

In the name of God Amen: the xviij^th^ day of Auguste in the yere of o^r^ lord God m^l^ccccc^th^lvj. I Robert Bradforthe, of Morlay in the ꝑishe of Batley, of hooll mynd and good remēbrance, maikithe my last will and testamente in manner and forme followinge. First and principall I gyve and bequeathe my soull to God almightie, to oure ladie sancte Marie, and all the holie companye of heaven, and my bodie to be buried in the churche of Batlay or ells where in Christen man's buriall. I gyve and bequeathe to Elynor Strynger and Katheryne Strynger, doughters of Roger Strynger, to either of theme iiij^li^, and that my executors to kepe theme to the aige of xxj yeres. Item I gyve and bequeathe vnto Dorothe my basterd doughter iiij^li^ to be paid to her by myne executors at her aige of xviij yeres. Itm. I gyve vnto Alice Backhouse my sister x^s^. And also to Elisabethe Burnell my suster [*blank*]. Item I gyve vnto William Bradforthe my brother x^s^. Also I gyve and bequeathe vuto eu'ye one whiche I am godfather to beynge alive at my death vj^d^. It'm I orden & maike Dorothee my wif and Katherine my doughter nowe wif of Thomas

Clerkson my full executrixes for to dispose the Residue of my goodes whiche in this my will ys not gyven then bequeathed by there discrecõne for the health of my soull. Item I orden & maike M[r] Thomas Wentworthe my maister and Henry Batt, of Birstall, supvisors of this my last will and testamente desieringe theme to se the same perfurmyd & executed accordinglie. And I gyve and bequeathe to the said Thomas Wentworth my m[r] xiij[s] iiij[d] and a great brasse pott. And I gyve to the said Henrie Batt x[s] for there payns takinge in seynge the execucõn of the same. Item I gyve and bequeathe vnto the said Dorothe my wif my lease of the Newefeld with all other landes comprysed in the said lease durynge all suche yeres as I have in the same if she kepe her widowe & sole vnmaried, and if she happen to be maried then I will that imediatlie after her mariege the said lease to be & remayne vnto the said Katheryne my doughter. And also I gyve vnto the said Dorothe my wif my leases of the Smythe flatte and Sanderson flatte in like wise if she kepe her sole and vnmaried. And if she happen to be maried then the same leases immediatlie after her marriage I will shall remayne to the said Katheryne my doughter duringe all suche yeres as shall then be to spende in the same. Thes beinge witnesses, John Otte, William Clerkson, John Webster, Nicholas Burnell, and other. Also I giue and bequeathe vnto Isabell Ellys my sister vj[s] viij[d]. Item I gyve and bequeathe vnto Maud Otte my suster iij[s] iiij[d]. Also I gyve and bequeathe vnto Margarete Bakhowse vj[s]. Also I gyve and bequethe vnto Saunder my s'uand xij[d]. Also I gyve vnto Richard my s'uand ij[s]. Also I gyve and bequeathe vnto Richard Bakhouse iij[s] iiij[d]. Also I gyve vnto M'garete Clerkson xx[s]. I will that Thomas Clerkson shall have the custodie of the iiij[li] that I have bequeste to Elynore Strynger, And John Ottes shall have the custodie of the other iiij[li] bequeathed to Katherine Strynger her suster vnto they come to lawfull aige or redie to be maried. Thes witnes, John Ottes, William Clerksone, and Nicholas Burnell, with other moo.—[*Proved* 25 *Dec.*, 1556.]

William Loveday, of Ferrybridge.

(xv. j. 193 b.)

In the name of God Amen: the xvij[th] day of Maie in the yere of o[r] lord god m[l]ccccc[th]lvj. I William Loveday, of Ferrybrige, hooll of mynd and pfite of remembrance, maike this my last will and testamente in maner and forme as hereafter followith. First I comende my soull into the hande of God Almightie, to oure ladie sancte Marie, & to all the holie companye in heaven, and my bodie to be buried in the churcheyerde of Alhallowes in Pontefract. Item I gyve to the hye Altare for tithes forgotten xij[d]. Item I gyve to Edie my doughter towe yewes and too lambes and a quarter of barlie when it comes of the grounde. Item I gyve to Richard Snydall one yowe and one lambe and one quarter barlie. Item I gyve Nicholas Ellote one yewe lambe. Item I gyve to William Skelton one white horse that he hays nowe in his custodie. Item I giue to Rawf Lovedaye, of Ledstonne, my father, my best Russell dublett. Item I gyve to William Banke my best gray jakkett. Item I gyve to William Fox my godsonne one yewe lambe, and to eu'ye one of my god children ij[d]. Item I gyve to Agnes my wif my gray stagge. Item I gyve to Agnes Byrkynshawe my s'unte viij[d]. Item I gyve to Robert Loveday, of

Ledstonne, my saye dublett. My dettę paid, my fun'all expenses maid, not bequest I gyve [the residue] to Agnes my wif, Jenet my doughter, and Edie my doughter, whome I maike my hooll executrices for to dispose for my soull as they shall seyme beste. And vppon this my laste will I do make and ordenne to be the supvisors of this my will Richard Bubwithe, Rawfe Loveday and Richard Croft, and eu'ye of theme to haue for there payns ij^s a peice. Thes beinge witnesses, Rawffe Loveday, Chr̃ofer Coottę, Richard Bubwith, Robert Lighton & Richard Crosse.—[*Proved* 16 *Dec.*, 1556, *by the widow. Grant reserved to the daughters, minors.*]

———

MILES LONGBOTTOM, OF ROTHWELL.

(xv. j. 194 b.)

In the name of God Amen: vj^th day of October in the yere of oure lord God m^ldlvjth. I myles Longbothome, of the Roodę within the pishe of Rothewell, of hooll mynde and pfite remembrance, maikę this my last will and testament after this maner & forme folowinge. Firste I bequeathe my soull to God Almightie and to oure ladie sancte Marie and to all the celestiall companye in heaven, my bodie to be buried within the churche yerde of Rothwell. I bequeathe to the blissed sacramente xij^d, And to the mendyng of the hye way betwixt my howse and the churche xij^d. Also I bequeathe to Agnes my wif & Robert my sonne iiij oxen, iiij stottę, iiij kye, and a meare. Item I bequeathe to Wiłłm Longbothom my sonne xx^s in full contentac̃on of his pte. I bequeathe to Gilbert Longbothom my sonne xx^s in full contentac̃one of his parte. I bequeathe to Vmfray Longbothome xx^s in full contentac̃on of his pte. Item to eu'ye one of my childer children one ewe lambe. I bequeathe to Katheryne Buktrowte one whye calf. I bequeath my howse wherin I now do dwell with all the grounde therevnto belonginge as I have yt at this presente day to Agnes my wif & Robert my sonne. I bequeathe to Gilbert Longbothome, son of Vmfray Longbothome, that he shalbe founde meate, drynke, and clothe at my howse to he come to the aige of xij yeres. And I desier Robert Buktrowte my sonne in lawe to be supvisor of this my last will and testamente, and to se that my wif and children agree so moche as in him shall lie. The Rest of all my goods not bequeathed, my dettę paid & my funerall expenses maid, I give and bequeathe to Agnes my wif and Robert my sonne, whome I maike my lawfull executors. Thes beinge witnes, Joh̃n Savell, gentleman, and Thomas Byrkynshay, with other moo.—[*Proved* 16 *Dec.*, 1556.]

———

THOMAS CAVE, OF BURLEY.

(xv. j. 195 b.)

In the name of God Amen: the xvj^th day of March, Anno d'ni miłłmo qui'gen^mo lv^to secundũ computac̃onem eccłie Anglicane. I Thomas Cave, of Burley within the pishinge of Otley, beinge of hooll mynde & good memorie, maikithe this my last will and testamente in maner and forme folowinge. First I gyve and bequeathe my soull to almightie god my maker and my Redemer, and my bodie to be buried within the pishe churche yerde of Otley. Also I will that my goodes shalbe devided in thre ptę according to the lawe, the firste parte to my self, the secunde parte to my wif, the third pte to my thre childern, that ys to say, John,

Alis, and Agnes. ' Also I will that my wif and her ꝑte of my goodes shall remaine with John my sonne enduringe her lif naturall. Itm. I give and bequeath to Thomas Cave all thingꝭ ꝑteynynge bothe to husbandrie, wayne, and plowghe. Also I give and bequeathe to too children of John Shackerd's to either of theme v^s. It'm the Residewe of all my goodes I honestlie brought furthe, my dettꝭ paid and legacies fulfilled, I giue and bequeathe theme hoolie to Joħn my sonne and to Alis and Agnes my doughters, whome I orden and maike my full and lawfull executors. Thes beinge witnes, Chr̄ofer Thomson, Thomas Smythe, Richard Thackwro, George Jackson, Robert Wrase, with other moo.—[*Proved 26 Dec.,* 1556.]

ROBERT HALLILEY, OF SAXTON.

(xv. j. 195 b.)

In Dei nōie amen: the eight day of October in the yere of our lord god a thowsande fyve hundrethe fiftie and sex. I Robert Halile, hoole of myud and of good memorie, thankꝭ be given to god, ordeyns and maiketh my will and testamente in maner and forme folowing. Firste I gyve and wit my soull to God Almightie, to o^r blessed ladie sanct Marie, and to all the Celestiall companye of heaven, and my bodie to be buried within the ꝑishe churche of Saxton. It'm I giue to the hye altare xij^d. Itm. to Anthony Halile my sonne xl^s. Item to the said Anthonye my best Jacket and a dublet. It'm I bequeathe to Robert Halile my sonne a litle masser topped wth silver with the Rest of my Rayment excepte my best gowne. It'm to en'ye one of my god children iiij^d. It'm to Robert Wilton iij^s iiij^d. It'm I bequeathe to en'ye one of my sonnes and dowghters children eu'y one of theme too shepe and to thos whiche is my god children eu'y of theme thre sheipe. It'm I bequeathe to Sir William Cowper iij^s iiij^d. It'm I bequeath to John Halile my son a bownd wayne and too oxen. It'm I bequeathe to Jane my doughter a cowe. It'm I bequeathe to Robert Halile sonne of Anthonye Halile a felie foole. It'm I bequeathe to John Halile son of Thomas Halile, a quarter of barlie to be deliuered in the next yere after my deathe. It'm I bequeath vnto Agnes Burton too shepe. It'm I bequethe to Isabell Newbie, Agnes Rawson, and Alice Laicok, my doughters, cu'ye one of theme a yong stirke in the Sower close. It'm I bequethe to William Newbie xl^s wherof xx^s is in his hande, and to Isabell Newbie his wif a pare of Corall beedꝭ after the deceese of my wif. It'm I give to Robert Rawson xx^s. It'm I giue to Raycoke xx^s. It'm I bequeathe to William Halile wif and Anthonye wif either of theme a yonge stirke. It'm I giue to Isabell my wife one free messuage buylded in Southe Mylford and one acree of free land lyenge in the West feild there nowe in the tenure and occupacōn of one Edward Watsone durynge the lif naturall of the said Isabell and after her deceasse to remane to Jane Halile my doughter and to the heiers of her bodie lawfullie begotten, and for defalte of such isshue to remayne to the beires of Anthonye Halile my son for ever. It'm I gine to Isabell my wif all my frehold land lyenge within the towne feildes and territories of Lumbye late one Thomas Turpyns to have to her duringe her lif and after her decease to Andrew Halile my son and his heires for eu'. It'm I giue to Isabell my wif one free messuage in South mylford afforesaid in the tenure of one John Crawe, and one dovehowse and one garthe called the chappell garthe in the teno^r of Richard Halile laitlie purchased of William Hamond, Esquier, to have to her durynge her lif. And after her deceesse to remane to Anthony Halile my sonne and his heires for ever. And whereas I am indetted and bounde by coveñnte and dedes obligatone to content and pay or cause to be contentid and paid vnto my brother John Halile, esquier, for the purchcase of certane landes lyeng in Beswycke in the Countie of Yorke, sold and grantid by the said John vuto me the said Robert Halilee and John my sonne and his heieres for ever as by certen deidę thereof maid more playnlie apperethe the som̄e of Cxlij^li xvj^s of lawfull englishe money whereof ys paid vnto my said brother xxviij^li as by the same deidę will appere and xxx^li lente vuto Marmaduke Fawkę, gentleman, vpon one obligac̄on and so ys yet remaynynge in my handes vnpaid to my saide brother for the saide landę in Beswicke the som̄e of xxiiij^li xvj^s, Residue of the said som̄e of Cxlij^li xvj^s. Therefore I the said Robert Halile doith gine and bequethe vuto John Halile my said sonne aswell all my intreste of the said land in Beswicke as all the said som̄e of Cxlij^li xvj^s and he to pay all the Residewe of the said som̄e yet vnpaid to my said brother according to my said coveñnte and bargane yf he may have and enyoie the said landę in Beswicke to him and his heiers for eu'. And if not I gyve him frelie all the said som̄e of Cxlij^li xvj^s aswell that whiche ys alredye paid to my said brother John as also all the reste thereof yet vnpaid to be taken and maid of all my goodes moveable and vnmoveable to bye him other landę withall over and besidę his legacies whiche I have alredie gyven him by this my said will. And also I give him iiij^li to sewe furthe one Licence of Alienac̄ons withall. Itm. I gyve vnto my said sonne John Halile my wood knyf. Itm. I gyfe to Isabell my wif too acrees a rode and a half of arrable lande and medowe lyenge within iij seu'all feildę of Shereburn laitlie bought of William Barton and Isabell his wif to have to her durynge her lif. And after [her] deceese to remayne to Robert Halile my sonne and his heiers for ever. Item I giue to Isabell my wif a blake gowne and to eu'ye of my sonnes and sonnes in lawe a blake cote of vj^s the yerde to be worne the day of my buriall. Also I will there be too torches burnynge affore me to the churche the same daye, and too poore men to beere theme of the whiche Frauncę Newbye to be one and the other to be taken by the discretion of my wif and children, and either of theme to have a blake gowne. Itm. I give to John Halile, Esquier, my brother, for a remembrance, one old Ryall of gold, trustinge he wilbe contentid with the same as thowghe yt were a greater valowe, hertelie desieringe him to contynewe his goodnes and be good maister vnto my children, and one old Angell also. The Residewe of all my goodes vnbequest, my dettes and legacies paid and well & trewlie ꝑformyd, I gyve and wiłł to Isabell my wif, John and Robert Halile my sonnes and Jane my doughter, whome I orden and maike my full executors of this my last will and testamente for to bringe me furthe honestlie and dispose for the healthe of my soull at there discrec̄ons. And also I maike Suꝑvisors of this my will, William Newbye, gentleman, Robert Rawson, Anthony Halile, and Richard Laicocke, to se that althingę herein be well and trewlie ꝑformyd accordinge to the trewe intente hereof. And also I the said

Robert Halile by this my present will and testamente will make declarac̃on of what goodes and cattels my sonne William Halile haith had of my gifte aswell before mareedge at mariedge as sence in the nayme of his childꝭ porc̃on. Firste I did geve him the occupacion of one fermehold with certene landꝭ, medowe, and pasture therevnto belonginge, sett, lyeng & beynge within the towne Feildꝭ and territories of Mylford for my goodwill whereof I might have had at that tyme xx^{li}. And he had also the said fermehold well stored, that ys to saye, with sex oxen, one Iron bounde wayne with yockꝭ and teemys therevnto belonginge, harrowes, iiij horses, ij kyne, v scoore sheipe, ij swyne, croppe in the laithe and croppe in the feilde to the valowe of xl^{li}, whiche did amounte all togethers to the som̄e of lx^{li}. All whiche fermhold and goodes I did gyve hym at that tyme in the name, recompence, and satisfacc̃one of his hooll childꝭ porc̃on and therewithe I will he shall be contented. Thes beyng witnesses of this my said last will and testamente, William Cowper, curate, Robert Danyell, John Smythe, and Robert Skelton, cũ alijs.—[*Proved* 16 *Dec.*, 1556.]

William Hudson, of Knottingley.

(xv. j. 199 a.)

In Dei nõie Amen: in the yere of o^{r} lord god m^{l}cccccthlvjth, the xxjth day of October. I William Hudson, of Knottyngley, hole of mynde and of ꝑfite and of goode remembrance, doith maike this my last will and testamente in this maner & forme followinge. First I com̄end my soull vnto God Almightie my maker and Redemer, and my bodye to be buried in the churche yerd in Pontefract. It'm I giue and bequeathe to Richard my son a plowghe wth a yron shakkill and a newe coulter and a share and ij ewes and ij lambes and a paire of harrowes. Itm. I gyve to Agnes my doughter a blake whie wth a bald head. Itm. I gyve to Thomas Pynder wif of Norton in Campsall ꝑishe one wyndle of barlie. Itm. I gyve vj^{d} to maister Vicar. Itm. I gyve to the chappell in Knottinglay vj^{d}. Itm. I gyve and bequeath to Elsabethe my wif and to Richard my son and to Agnes my doughter all my leaces and landꝭ durynge the terme & termes of my yeres. The rest of all my goodꝭ not legate nor bequethed I give frelie to Elisabeth my wif and to Richard my son & Agnes my dowghter, whome I maike my full executors to have to there owne vses. Itm. I will that Wiłłm Eu'imgh'm shalbe the Suꝑvisor of this my last will and testamente for to se that yt be fulfilled. Witnesses hereof, John Scolay, John Bolton, John Hunttyngton, w^{t} other moo.—[*Proved* 22 *March*, 1556–7, *by the widow. Grant reserved to the children, minors.*]

George Hobson, of Stanley.

(xv. j. 200 a.)

In Dei nõie Amen: the xxj day of December in the yere of o^{r} lord god m^{l}dlvjth. I George Hobson, of Staynley within the ꝑishe of Wakefeld, seeke in bodie & hooll of mynde and gud remembrance, maikith this my last will and testamente in maner and forme followinge. First I gyve and bequeathe my soull to God Almightie my Sayvor and Redemer, to oure ladie sanct Marye virgyne, and to all the celestiall companye in heaven, and my bodie to be buried in the churche yerde of Wakefeld. As for all my guddes and dettꝭ moveable and vnmoveable that I have or may have I gyve and bequeathe theme hoollie vnto Elsabethe Hobsone my wif, whome I maike and ordenne to be my full and onelie executrix, she to pay my dettꝭ and dispose for my soull as my truste is in her. Thes beyng witness, Sr James Brodebente, my curate, William Hobson, Thomas Thirkilbye, Robert Hesam & Willm Addamson, with other moo.—[*Proved* 12 *March*, 1556-7.]

JOHN WRIGHT, OF LOTHERTON.

(xv. j. 204 a.)

In the name of God Amen: the xiij day of Aprile in the yere of our lord god m^l^cccccclvj. I John Wright, of Lotherton within the ꝑishe of Sherborne, holl of mynd & of good memorie (lawde be to God), makithe my last will & testamente in maner & forme followinge. First I gine & bequeth my soull to Almighty God, to our blessed ladye sancte Marie, & to all the celestiall Companye of heven, & my body to be buried w^th^in the ꝑishe Churche yerde of all sanctꝭ in Sherborne. It' I giue & bequeth to the vicar of Sherborne to pray for me xij^d^. It' I gine to s^r^ Robert Blanche viij^d^. It' I gine to s^r^ Robert Taylyo^r^ ij^s^. It'm I giuc to Agnes my wif all my interest & righte that I haue of my fermhold in Lotherton. It'm to Xpofer Wright one yowe & one lambe. It' I giue to John Wright the son of Thomas Wryghte one yowe & a lambe. The Residewe of all my goodes vnbequest, my dettꝭ paid & legacies & my body honestly brought furthe, I gine to Agnes my wif, Thomas Wright & Wilfride my sonnes, whom I make & ordeyne myne executo^r^s of this my last will & testament. In witnes hereof, Sr Robert Blanche, curate, Lawrence Sysson, John Sysson & John Clellowe, with other.—[*Proved* 7 *Apl.*, 1557.]

ALICE STANSFIELD, OF OTLEY.

(xv. j. 204 a.)

In Dei nōie Amen: the viij day of Marche in the yere of our lord god m^l^ccccclvj. I Alice Stansfeld, of Otlay in the countie of Yorke, wydowe, holl of mynde & of good & ꝑfecte remembrance, maketh this my last will & testamente in maner and forme followinge. First I bequeth my soull to the mercie of my Redemer Ih'us Christe, & my bodie to be buried in the Churche yerd of Otlay aforesaid. Also I will that ij torches be provided by myne executors & be light in the tyme of the levac̄on of the sacrament at masse after my decesse. It' I will that eu'y of the Children of Thomas Dade & Thomas Smythe shall haue in money & in valo^r^ x^s^ a peice. It' I will that xx^s^ be giuen to the poore people of Otlay. It' I will that at my buriall a dirige & a masse be songe. It' I will that at my buriall ther be an honest dyñer by myne executors & suꝑvisors for my neighbours & freyndꝭ ther being present. It' I will that s^r^ Xpofer Waid shall haue vj^s^ viij^d^ for to saye certen masses for my husband soull & myne. Also I gine to Xpofer my son my best syluer spone & to Nycholas Dade & Jenet Smyth either of them a syluer spone & to the said Xpofer my son ij arkꝭ & an ambrye. Also I will that the said Xpofer shall haue & occupie all my ꝑte of grounde in Calostedꝭ so longe as I haue right therin payng therfor yerly to Alis Dade ij^s^ by yere. Also I giue to Jenet Smyth and Alice Dade all my houshold goodꝭ w^t^in the house. It'

I gine my Rayme'te & naprieware to be devided betwixt Agnes & Margret my doughters. It' I giuc to Ottę wif a peticote. It' to Besse Barker a cote doble lyned. It' I giue to Xpofer my son l^s owing by John Dycconson. It' I giue to John Dade & Anthony Smyth either of them vj^s viij^d. Item I giue to s^r Anthony Jakson my Curate iij^s iiij^d to pray for me. Also I make Xpofer my son, Thomas Dade & Thomas Smyth myne Executors of this my last will & testamente. And I desire Sr Xpofer Waid & John Dycconson to be supvisors of this my last will & they to haue either of them x^s for ther paynes takinge, desiring them of theire good Counsell to myne executors. His testibus, Antonio Jakson, clico, Xpofero Waid, clico, Johne Dycconson et Thoma Smythe.—[*Proved 7 April, 1557.*]

ELIZABETH COOK ALIAS ATKINSON, OF ADEL.

(xv. j. 204 a.)

In the name of God amen: the second day of M'che in the yere of our lord god m^lccccclvj. I Elisabeth Cooke als Atkynson, of the pishe of Addle, holl of mynde & pfecte of memorye (thankę be to almighty God), ordeyn & make this my last will & testament in maner and forme following. First I bequeath my soull to Almighty god, to the gloriose and blessed virgyn sancte Marie, & to all the blessed sanctę in heven, & my body to be buried wth in the Churche yerd of sancte John baptiste at Addle. It' I bequeth to the high altare xij^d for my negligent tithes. It' I giue to Thomas Bradforth my son in lawe on branded Cowe. It' to my doughter Agnes, his wif, on blake cowe & on sylu' spone & to them both my tacke of lyname & allandley closes during the terme of my yeres. It' I giue & bequethe to Thomas Bradforth the elder son to Thomas Bradforthe aforsaid on blacke whit headed cowe & j sylu' spone. It' I bequeth to Thomas Bradforth the younger brother son to the aforsaid Thomas the tacke of my fermhold in Addle during the yeres, on blacke cowe w^t cutt hornes, j counter, j presse, j ambrye, j gret arke, j sylu' spone. It' I giue vnto the doughter of Thomas Bradforth aforsaid on blacke quye, on sylu' spone, & if it fortune any of the said yong childer to dye vnder lawfull yeres of aige then I will that ther part or partes of this legacie remayn to the other yong children w^t in named. It' I giue to Isabell Speight my god doughter on ewe shepe. It' I giue & bequeth to Henrye Symson my god son on ewe sheipe. It' I giuc to Thomas Brigge thre shepe, on brasse pot, on pewder platter, on pewter disshe. It' I bequeth to Margret Scruton for her payns taken in all the tyme of my sekenes ij ewe shepe, on brasse pott, on pewter platter & on pewder dishe. It' I will that Thomas Bradforth thelder of the two children aboue mencioned shall haue my cowe w^t the one half of thencreasce whiche I did lett to on Robert Pikryng of Chappel toune, from the feast of thinvencõn of the crosse called sancte Ellen's day whiche was in the yere of our lord god m^lccccccliiij to th'ende of thre yeres than next following. It' I bequeath to Thomas Brigge my servant aforsaid on red quye stirke of a yere old & vpward. It' I gine to my brother s^r Willm Roger on whitheaded quye great w^t calf. Also I will that the said s^r Willm my brother haue the lettyng & thorder of the forsaid fermhold to the bringing vp of the said Thomas Bradfurthe the younger and to his vse or els the assignes of the said s^r Willm Roger to the vse of the said Thomas Bradfurth the yonger. It' I gine to Dorothee

Browne on ewe sheipe. It' I gine to Eliz' Redeall on ewe sheipe. The Residewe of all my goodę not bequethed, my dettę payd, my legacies pformed & my fun'all expens' discharged, I giue to my brother s^r William Roger aforsaid, whom I maike my full and lawfull executor of this my last will & testament to se it truly executed & fulfilled. Recordę of my will & testament, Thomas Browne, Robert Speight, Robert Ward, and Adam Speight, w^t other mo.—[*Proved* 7 *April*, 1557.]

JOHN SMITH ALIAS SCOTT, OF SAXTON.

(xv. j. 204 b.)

In the name of God amen: the xiiij day of January in the yere of our lord god m^lcccccl vj. I John Smyth, of Saxton, als Skott, holl of mynd & of good memorie (loved be god), ordans & makith my last will & testament in maner & forme following. First I giue & wytt my soull to almighty god, to our blessed Lady his mother, sancte Marie, & to all the celestiall company of heven, & my body to be buried w^tin the pishe Churche yerd of Saxton. It' I bequeth to the high alter xij^d. It' I bequeth to the Churche workę of the said Saxton xij^d. It' I bequeth to Thomas Scott my brother a quarter of barlye to be delyvered in the nexte yere after this. It' I bequeth to Leonard my son a bond wayne & a yocke of oxen. It' I bequeth to Anne my doughter a Cowe & x young sheipe. It' I bequeth to Alice Shippyn xx^s. It' I bequeth to s^r Willm Cowp iij^s iiij^d. It' I giue & bequeth to Margaret my wif all my land in Saxton lately purchased of Willm Hungate, Esquyer, during her naturall lif & after her decesse I will that the said lande shalbe equallie dyvided betwene Leon' my son & Anne my doughter & to ther beires for eu'. It' I bequeth to eu'y on of my god childer a yong lambe. The residewe of all my goodę vnbequest, my dettę paid & this my last will & testament well & truly pformed according vnto the trewe entent herof, I giue & will to Margaret my wif, Leonard my son & Anne my doughter, whom I ordayn & make my full executors of this my last will & testament for to bring me furth honestly & dispose for the helthe of my soull after ther discrecons. In witnes wherof, Willm Cowp, curate, Willm Lacocke & Ric' Skelton, w^t other.—[*Proved* 7 *April*, 1557.]

EDWARD WATSON, OF SOUTH MILFORD.

(xv. j. 204 b.)

In the name of god, Amen: I Edward Watson, of Southmylforth, beyng of good & pfcete memorye, do make this my last will & testament in maner & forme followinge. First I comende my soull vnto almighty god & to our lady sancte Marie & to all the celestiall company of heven, & my body to be buried in the pishe churche yerd of Sherburne wher it shall please god. First I giuc to the blessed sacrament ij^d. Also I bequeth to Ellen my wif one blak cowe northermer hodder of Royd lyeing in the moore furlonge. Also I bequeth to Jenet my doughter one quye stirke & my sheipe & I gine Luce ij sheipe & I giue to Henry, John & Roberte to eu'y on of them on sheipe. The residewe of all my goodę not bequethed, my fun'all made, I make Ellen my wif my holl executrix of this my last will & testament made the xxviij day of December in the yere of o^r lord god m^l.ccccc.lvj. Thes beyng witness', Henry Davye, Willm Halile, Lionell Lethom, Robert Hitlom, John Connyngworth.—[*Proved* 7 *April*, 1557.]

William Lee alias William Syme, of Harewood.

(xv. j. 205 a.)

In the name of God amen: the yere of our lord God m.ccccc.liiij, the xxix day of August. I William Le otherwise called Wiłłm Syme, w^tin the ꝑish of Harwood, makith this my last will & testament in maner & forme following. First I bequeth my soull to god almighty, & my body to be buried within the ꝑishe churche yerd of Alhallos at Harwood. Also I bequeth to my doughter v^s. I bequeth to her thre childer iij gymber lambes. The residewe of my gooḍ moueable & vnmouable, my detteꝭ paid and my body buried, I gine & bequeth to Isabell my wif during her naturall lif if my other chylder be so contented, if they be not so content my body buried I bequest the residewe of my parte to my said wif & farther I bequest to my said wif all my holl interest & possession of my tenement or fermhold during my yeres & if she fortune to dye w^tin the said terme I bequest the forsaid tēnte or fermhold vnto William Le my eldest son during my forsaid terme of yeres. I ordane & make my wif Isabell & Wiłłm my eldest son my executors for to accomplishe & fulfill this my laste will & testament. Thes witnesses, Xpofer Hird, Wiłłm Smalthar & Peter Wright, w^t other.—[*Proved* 7 *April*, 1557.]

John Tenant, of Methley.

(xv. j. 205 b.)

In the name of god amen: the xxij day of Marche in the yere of our lord god m^l.ccccc.lvj. I John Tenand, of the ꝑishing of Methelay, of holl myud & memorie, makith this my will of this man' following. The first I bequeth my saull to god almighty & to his blessed mother sancte Marie the virgyn & to all the sancteꝭ in heven, & my body to be buried w^tin the churche yerd of sanct Oswolde of the sāid Metheley. Also I bequeth to the most neideꝭ of the Churche xij^d. The residewe of my gooḍ I giue & bequeth to M'garet my wif, whom I make my laufull executrix to cōplemshe & fulfill this my said will according to the teno^r & intent therof. Witnes thervpon is s^r Laurēce Otteꝭ, chaplayn, Robert Gyge, John Laik & John Bryge.—[*Proved* 10 *April*, 1557.]

Alice Burgh, of Woodkirk.

(xv. j. 206 a.)

In the name of God Amen: the yere of o^r lord God m^l.ccccc.lvj & the xxiij day of December. I Alice Burgh, of the ꝑishing of Wodkyrke, holl of myud & of good remembrance, makeꝭ this my last will in man' & forme following. First I giue my soull to god almighty, till o^r lady sancte Marie, and to all the celestiall company of heven, & my body to be buried w^tin the Churche of Wodkirke. Also I giue & bequeth to the Churche of Wodkirke iij^s iiij^d. Also I bequeth towardꝭ the making of the Rowell iiij^d. Also I giuc to Wiłłm Facon^r & to Barbara his sister either of them one sheipe. Also I giue to Wiłłm Burghe my son son a wether. Also I giuc to my doughters Eliz. & M'garet either of them on sylu' spone. Also I gine to Robert Facon^r wif, my doughter, a grene gowne. Also I giue to M'garet my doughter, Wilfray Rayn^r wif, a candlestike, a charger, a mattres, a blanket, a shete & the worse cou'let. Also I giuc to Eliz' Blak-burne a peticote & on pewther dishe. It' I giuc to S[r] Ric' Robert, curat, xij[d]. Also I giue to Roger Fornes viij[d]. Also my dettę & my legacies paid & my fun'all expens' made at my buriall. The residewe of all my goodę moveable & vnmoueable I give vnto John Burghe my son, whom I make my full executor in the full pformacon of this my last will to dispose for my saull helth & all christian soulls as he shall thinke the best. Thes men beyng witnesses, S[r] Ric' Robert, Roger Fornes & John Lee, w[t] other. —[*Proved* 10 *April*, 1557.]

RICHARD SPROXTON, OF WAKEFIELD, YEOMAN.

(xv. j. 206 b.)

In Dei nõie amen: the first day of M'che in the yere of o[r] lord god m[l]ccccc.lvj. I Ric' Sproxton, yomã, of the pishing of Wakefeld w[t]in the countye of Yorke, of good & pfecte remembrance, seike in body, makith this my last will & testament as herafter followith. First I gine & bequeth my soll to God Almighty, to o[r] lady sancte Marie, & to all the blessed cõpany of heven,& my body to be buried w[t]in the churche or churche yerd of Alhallos in Wakefeld. Inprimis I bequeth to Agnes Sproxton my wif on blacke mare. It' I bequeth to Robert Sproxton my son on gray stag. It' I bequeth to John Queldayls wif, of Hull, on white headed quye ou' & besidę childę porcon. It' I bequeth to eu'y on of my childer children on lambe. It' I bequeth to Thomas Wrosse children x[s]. It' I bequeth to the said Robert Sproxton my son my best gowne & best doblet. It' I bequeth to Robert Risheforth my best Jaket. It' I bequeth to Willm Agland my second Jaket, a doblet, a paire of hose. It' I bequeth to John Andrewe my sleveles Jaket. It' I bequeth to Alice Hartley my gaberdyn. It' I will that Agnes Sproxton my wif shall haue the third parte of goodę moueable & vnmoueable, whom I make myne executrix. The residewe of all my goodę not bequethed I gine & bequeth vnto my children to be diuided emonges them by euen porcons. It' I make supvisors of this my last will M[r] Brian Bradfurth, gentleman, Robert Sproxton, my son, & John Poyle & they to se that this my last will be fulfilled. Thes beyng witnes, Willm Casson, Thomas Crakell, s[r] George Lee, John Powle.—[*Proved* 10 *April*, 1557.]

ROBERT HARTLEY, OF SHERBURN.

(xv. j. 211 a.)

In the name of God Amen: I Robt Hertlaie, of Sherburne, wholle of mynde & good Remẽbrance, thankę be to God, doth maike this my Last will & testamẽt in maner & forme folowing. First I bequith my soule to God Almightie & to all y[e] blessed cõpenye of heaven, & my bodie to be buried in y[e] churche yeard of Sherburne. Also I bequith to y[e] sacramẽt for my tythes forgotten iiij[d]. The Residewe of all my goodę, my dettę paid & my funerallę maid, I gyve to Jenet my wiffe & Willm Hertlaie my sonne, Edward, Alis, Grace & Jenett my childer, whom I maike myne executors & assignes of this my last will & testament. Thes being witnesse, S[r] Robert Blaunch, Willm King & John Shellowe. Dated the xiiij daie of Aprill, Anno d'ni millimo quingentesimo quinquagesimo septimo.—[*Proved* 28 *May*, 1557, *by the widow. Grant reserved to the children, minors.*]

Costen Crummock, of Farnley.

(xv. j. 211 b.)

In Dei nōie Amen. The xxix daie of Aprill in the yeare of o^r^ lord God a thosand syx hundreth fiftie & seaven. I Costen Crumhoc, of Fernelay in the cownte of Yorke, hole of mynde & of good & perfytte Remēbrance, doe ordeine and maike this my last will & Testamēt in mañ and forme folowinge. First I bequith my sowle to Almightie god my Creat^r^ & to Jesus Christe my Redem^r^, desiring o^r^ blessed Laydie & all the sainetę in heaven to pray for me that my Sowle may take place amongst ye electe people of God, & my bodie to be buried in sainete Katherine queare w^t^in the parishe churche of Otlaie & I will y^t^ my mortuarie & duties of the Church be paid according to the Custome of the cūtre. It' I will y^t^ my wiffe shall have the one halffe of my goodę & the other halffe to be as hereafter foloweth, that is to saie, to pore people & to the hie wais xx^s^. It' to my two doughters xx shepe & to my sonne James v powndę to be delyvered att the disscression of my supvisors. And also I will y^t^ my suñe Nicholas have a resonable parte of my said halffe goodę att the order of my said supervisors if he cā be cōtented therewyth & if he cā not be cōtented therwith then I will y^t^ he shall paie to my Executors ^xxtie^ merk wch he oweth vnto me. And I gyve to Walter Crumhoc two shepe & to his sonne one shepe. And I will y^t^ Thomas Crūhoc, sonne to my sonne Nycolas, have my lande in Brampton for ever. The rest of ye said second halffe I honestlie brought furthe therw^th^, I will y^t^ it shalbe devided amongst my said two doughters & my sonn Nicolas att ye ordre of my said supvisors. And I maike Margrett my wyfe my sole executrix of this my last will & testament. And I desire Thom's Angrom & Willm Robinson to be my supervisors of this my said last will & testament, And I gyve either of theim for their paynes iij^s^ iiij^d^. Thes being witnesses, Thomas Angrome, senior, Thomas Angrom, Junior, Ric' Colinson and Thomas Cave.—[*Proved* 28 *May*, 1557.]

Thomas Humblock, of Burton Salmon.

(xv. j. 211 b.)

In the name of God Amen: the first daie of M'ehe in the yeare of o^r^ lord god a. 1556. I Thomas Humblocke, of Burton, w^t^in ye parishe of Monkfriston, wholle of mynde & good of memorie, maikę this my last will & testamēt in maner & forme folowinge. First I bequith my soule to God Almightie, to our blessed Laidie Sainete Marie, & to all the celestiall cōpenye of heaven. And my bodie to be buried in my parishe churche yeard off Mūkfriston. Also I bequeath to the bolie Sacramēt viij^d^. Also I bequeath to iiij of John Robinson childer iiij ewe Lambes. Also I gyve to Christopher Attkinson an ewe & a lambe. Also I gyve to Alice Wood a lambe. Also I beq^th^ to John Atleburne one Close called Richardson Roidę during my leasse. It' I bequeath to s^r^ Ric. Jennyngę viij^d^. It' to John Metham iiij^d^. It' I gyve to John Humblocke my sonne one paire of kilne haires & a stepefatt. Also I will y^t^ when my wiffe mayries agayne y^t^ then John Robinson shall occupie two partę of my fermholdę & leases to ye behowffe & pfett of my childer during the termes in the said leases. Also I will y^t^ if my wiffe die before the lease wch I have of Thomas Gom'sall be expired that then the Residew of yeares nott exspente to remayne to John my sonne. Also I give to the said John Robinson one oxe stirke, whom I maike the supvisor of this my last will. The Residew of my goodę nott beq^{e}thed, my dettę paid, I gyve & bequeath to Agnes my wife & to my two children John & Ellen whom I maike my full executors of this my last will & testamēt. Thes being witnesses, s^{r} Ric. Gynnynge, my curatt, John Robinson, Thomas Shipperd, Henry Mitton, w^{t} other.—[*Proved* 28 *May*, 1557, *by the widow. Grant reserved to the children, minors.*]

PETER COOK, OF TONG.

(xv. j. 212 a.)

In nōie Dei Amen: the xx^{tie} day of Octob^{r} in the yeare of o^{r} lorde god a. 1556. I Peter Cooke, of Tonger, being seeke of bodie & wholle in memorie, maikę & orders this my will as foloweth. First I bequeath my soule to Almightie god, to o^{r} blessed Laidie sainete Marie, & to all ye glorious cōpenye y^{t} is in heaven, & my bodie to be buried in sanctyfyed ground att Birstall. The goodę y^{t} I have moveable & vnmoveable I gyve & bequith to my wiffe Alice & my viij children, whom I maike myne Executors. And if any of my children die before they come to aige then ye parte to be devided amongst the other y^{t} is aliffe after the customme of the cuntre. Witnesses, S^{r} Wiłłm Swanne, Maister Henrye Tempest, Thomas Cordinglaie, Bernard Hillous, John Broke, Wiłłm Wood, w^{t} other.—[*Proved* 5 *May*, 1557, *by the widow. Grant reserved to the children, minors.*]

ROBERT GAWKROGER, OF BIRSTALL.

(xv. j. 213 a.)

In the name of God Amen: the seconde daie of October in the yeare of o^{r} lorde God a m.d.lvj. I Robt Gawkroger, in the perishinge of Birstall, of wholle mynd, maketh my last will in forme folowinge. First I bequeath my soule to god almightie & to the cōpenye of our blessed Laydie sainete Marie & to all the sayn ctę in heaven, & my bodie to be buried in the churcheyeard of Birstall of the holie Apostles Peter and Pawle. First the tacke & leases of my howses w^{t} all other tackę of gronde that I have taken of John Brooke & Wiłłm his sonne I gyve them hollie to Isabell my wiffe, and also all my corne and cattell to bring vppe my children withall during her widowhed. And she shall gyve to everie one of my doughters vnmaried vj^{li} xiij^{s} iiij^{d} att suche tyme or tymes as they cā or shalbe able to occupie ytt. Also I gyve to my two yongest doughters Isabell and Alis, to either of them two ews & ij wethers over & above their childę porcons. And in case my said wiffe doo marie att any tyme, then all my said tackę & corne & cattelle & all other goodę shalbe devided by iiij men & my wiffe to have her third parte. And all the rest to my fyve doughters vnmaried, Margrett, Anne, Elisabeth, Isabell and Alice. It' I gyve to Jenett Jeffrason my doughter iij^{s} iiij^{d}. And to Wiłłm Jeffrason her sonne iij^{s} iiij^{d} to bie him an ewe shepe wythall. Finallie I maike Isabell my wiffe & my fyve doughters affore named my full executors after my decease & to dispose for my soule as they thinke best. Thes mē bearing witnesse, Wiłłm Walker, Wiłłm Walker, yonger, Wiłłm Gordall, Edmund Broke & Wiłłm Taillior.—[*Proved* 5 *May*, 1557, *by Margaret, daughter. Grant reserved to the other children, minors.*]

Agnes Glover, of Wakefield.

(xv. j. 213 b.)

In the name of God Amen: the ix daie of M'ch and in the yeare of o[r] lord God a m.d.lvj. I Agnes Glover, of Wakefeld within the Cowntie of Yorke, widow, of good and perfyte memorie, makith this my last will & testament in man' & forme folowing. First I gyve my soule to God Almightie & to our blessed laydie sainete Marie the mother of god and to all the holie & blessed cūpeny of heaven, & my bodie to be buried w[th]in the parishe churcheyeard of Allhallows in Wakfeld. It' I gyve & beq[th] to George Glover my sonne xiij[s] iiij[d] in money for the rest of his childꝭ porc̃on. It' I gyve & beq[th] to Thomas Glover my sonne xxvj[s] viij[d] in money for his porc̃on. The Residew of all my goodꝭ nott bequeathed I gyve vnto my thre doughters Alice Glover, Emmott Glover, and Jenett Glover, whom I maike executrysses of this my last will & they to have my goodꝭ devided amongst them by even porc̃ons. It' I will y[t] my funerall expenses shall be paid of my wholle goodꝭ. Thes being witnesses, Lawrence Borow, Mathew Browne & John Bradlaie, w[t] other moo.—[*Proved 5 May, 1557, by Alice and Jane. Grant reserved to Emmott, a minor.*]

Thomas Richardson, of Holme, Tong, husbandman.

(xv. j. 214 a.)

In nōie Dei Amen: The xv daie of September in the yeare of our lord god a m.d.lvj, that I Thom's Richardson, of Home, husbandmā, maikꝭ & orders this my Will in this man' & forme. First I bequeath my soule to Almightie god, to our blessed Laidie sainct Marie, & to all the glorious cōpenye y[t] ys in heaven, & my bodie to be buried in the churche earth of Birstall. It' I bequeath to the chapell of Tog[e] a pownde of wax. It' I bequeath to mine eldest sonne Nicholas the tacke of my howse. It' I bequeath to myne sonne Wiłłm the land y[t] that I bought of M[r] Henry Tempest. It' I bequeath to my sonne Richard an oxe besidꝭ his filiall porc̃on. The rest of my goodꝭ I gyve & bequeath to my wiffe Agnes & my thre children, whom I maike myne executors. Witnesses, Wiłłm Whithead, senior, Roberte Bawfett, Roberte Proctor & James Appleyeard, w[t] other moo as s[r] Wiłłm Swanne.—[*Proved 5 May, 1557, by the widow. Grant reserved to Nicholas, William, and Richard, sons, minors.*]

John Atkinson, of Kirskell.

(xv. j. 214 b.)

In the name of God Amen: the xxtie daie of M'ehe in the yeare of o[r] lorde God a m.d.lvj. I John Attkinson, of Kirskell in the parishe of Adle, husbandmā, seeke of bodie but whole of mynde & good Remēbrance, do maike my last will & testamēt in man' & forme folowing. First I beq'the my soule to almightie god my maker & my Redem', & my bodie to be buried in the churche earth at Adle & all other duties to be donne as the law doth require. Also my mynd and will is y[t] Elyzabeth my wiffe & my foure sonnes that is to say, John, Thomas, Richard, Wiłłm & Elyzabeth my doughter, shalbe my executors & have vse & possesse of my goodꝭ, moveable and vnmoveable, according as the Law doth require. Witnesses of this my last will & testament, Richard Hollingꝭ, James Rastricke, w[t] other moo.—[*Proved 6 May, 1557, by the widow. Grant reserved to the children, minors.*]

ROBERT *P*EASE, OF AUSTHORPE.

(xv. j. 214 b.)

In the name of god Amen: the xxij^tie daie Decēber & in the yeare of o^r lorde god a m.d.lvj. I Robt *P*eise, of Austhorpe w^th^in the parishe of Whitkirke, seeke of bodie & of perfyte Remēbrance, doo maike this my last will & Testamēt in maner & forme folowinge. First I beq^st^ my soule to god Almightie, to o^r blessed laidie sancte Marie, & to all the holie cōpenye of heaven, & my bodie to be buried w^th^in the churchyeard of o^r laidie of Whitkirke. Also I bequeath to the blessed Sacrament for tythes forgotten xij^d^. Also I bequeath to the church workꝭ xij^d^. Also I bequeath to Olyver Tottie an ewe & a hogge. The Residew of my goodꝭ nott bequest, my dettꝭ paid & my funerallꝭ deducte, I gyve to Jenett Peysse, Elene *P*eyse & Elizabeth *P*eyse, my doughters, whom I make myne Executryces. Also I will that Thomas Hemsworth, of Swillington, thelder, be the supervisor^r^ of this my last will. Thes men being witnesses, s' Robt Thomson, curatt, Willm Doeslaie, Henry Biwatter & Robt Hemsworth.—[*Proved* 6 *May*, 1557.]

WILLIAM READER, OF SWILLINGTON.

(xv. j. 214 b.

In the name of god Amen: the xxij daie of Januarie the yeare of our lord god a m.d.lvj. I Willm Reder, of the parishe of Swillington in the Cowntie of York, of good & pfytte Remēbrance, maikꝭ this my Testame't & last will in maner & forme folowing y^t^ is to saie, First I gyve & frelie betaike my soule to Almightie god, the blessed virgin o^r^ Laidie Sainct Marie, & to all the celestiall cōpenye of heaven, & my bodie to be buried in the churchyeard of thafforsaid Swillington. Also I bequeath to the anournamētꝭ of the said church viij^d^, and to Roger Reder my brother I gyve & bequest xij^d^, to my sister Agnes xij^d^. Further I will y^t^ Johan my wiffe have & occupie my fermhold during her lif naturall & after her deceasse my sonne John Reder have and occupie the same fermeholde. The Residew of all my goodꝭ not bequyte, my dettꝭ & funerall expenses maid & discharged, I gyve theim to Johan my saide wiffe, whome I maike the sole executrix of this my last testament to performe the saime as I have putt her in trust. Witnesses hereof, John Dawson, preest, John Fentymā, Henry Graywe, Christopher Tomson, w^t^ other moo.—[*Proved* 6 *May*, 1557.]

JOHN WHARTON, OF HELTHWAITE HILL, YEOMAN.

(xv. j. 255 a.)

In the name of god Amen: the vj^th^ daie of Februarie in the yeare of o^r^ lord God a thowsand fyve hundreth fyvtie & syx. I John Wharton, of Healthwathill in ye cowntie of Yorke, yomā, holle of minde & of good & perfyte Remēbrance, ordeine & maike this my last will & testame't in man' & forme folowing. First I bequith my soule to almightie God my creat' & to J'hus Christ my Redem', desiring o^r^ blessed Laidie & all ye celestiall cūpenie in heaven to praie for me y^t^ my soule maie take place emongst the electe people of god, & my bodie to be buried in my parishe church of Harwood where my frendꝭ thinkꝭ most mete & I will y^t^ my mortuarie & duties of ye churche be paid according to ye custome of ye Countrie. Also I gyve & bequith to Willm my second sonne in full recōpence of his childꝭ porcōn all my landꝭ in Helltwatehill, Dunkeswicke & Wetton to have & to hold to him & his heires for ever paying yearlie to

John myne eldest sonne during ye lyve naturall of ye saide John the sum̄e of fyve markꝭ & ye said Wiłłm nott to enter to ye said landꝭ nor paie ye said sum̄e of v m'kꝭ vnto Sibbell my wiffe doe either marie or departe to ye m'eye of almightie god, wch Sibbell shall have, occupie & enioy ye said landꝭ during her widowheed fynding ye said Wiłłm & John my sonnes meate, drinke & clotꝭ during her said wedowheede. Also I gyve & bequeathe to my Cosing George Wharton my right & interest of one lease wch I have of Christopher Redshaie in Nuton Walles during vij yeares, ye said George paying yearlye for ye same xvli to my executors & ye fedinge of one oxe yearly in ye garres of ye said ground during ye said vij yeares over & besydꝭ ye lordꝭ rente yearlie vpon cōdic̄on yt ye said George shall maike sufficient bondꝭ to myne executors for ye yearly payment of ye saide xvli the lordꝭ rentꝭ & other duties belongiñg ye same. And I will yt att ye ende of ye said vij yeares Mathew my sonne shall have & peaceablie enioy ye said lease of Nuton Walles wt all ye ꝑfittꝭ therof during all ye yeares in ye said lease cōteyned & then ye said George lovinglie & quietlie to leave th'occupac̄on therof. It' I gyve & bequith to my said Cosin George my parte interest & right of one lease wch Wiłłm Nevell, of Torksay, esquier, dyd demise to me the said John Wharton, George Wharton & Wiłłm Wharton & ye said George to have ye same during tenne yeares paying yearlie to myne executors tenne powndꝭ & ye feding of one cowe in ye said ground yearlie from Maie daie to Michelmas during ye said tenne yeares over & besides ye lordꝭ rentꝭ & all other chardges & duties belonging ye same. And ye said George to find & make sufficient bonndꝭ to myne executors for ye paymēt of ye p'misses & att ye ende of ye said tenne yeares I will yt ye said George shall leave th'occupac̄on therof & then my sonne Edward to enter, occupie & enioye ye same during all ye yeares in ye said Lease cōtenied, in full recōpence of his childꝭ porc̄on of my goodꝭ, ye said Edward paying yearlie xxs to John myne eldest sonne during his lyfe & ye said Edward lying sufficient suerties & bondꝭ to my executors for ye ꝑformance therof, and ye said xxs wt fyv m'kꝭ above rehersed to be paid to ye said John in full recōpence & satisfacc̄on of his childꝭ porc̄on & all other my landꝭ & tenementꝭ. And I will yt my dettꝭ shalbe paid of my wholle goodꝭ. And ferther I will yt ye said yearlie rentꝭ of xxvli wch my said cosing George shall yearlie pay to my executors shalbe paid as hereafter folowith that is to saie, xli yearlie to my wyfe for findinge of my children during tenne yeares & to Mathew my sonne, Dorythe, Jenett & Elyzabeth my doughters, xvli yearlie during vij yeares. It' I give to sr Thomas Walle & to sr Wiłłm Priston either of them xxd. It' I gyve to Thomas Herryson my best paire of hoose. It' my dettꝭ paid, my funerall expenses & legacies discharged, I gyve all my goodꝭ remaynyng of my parte to Sibble my wyfe, Wiłłm & Edward my soñes equallie to be devided amongst them, which Sibbell, Wiłłm & Edward I maike myne executors. And I desyre of Charitie Ric' Powle, clarke, & Lawrence Lyndlaie, gentlemā, to be supervisors of this my said will & testament. And I gyve to either of them xxs over & besidꝭ their charges for their paines. Thes being witnesses, Henrie Hebbletwhait, Wiłłm Wharton, Wiłłm Herryson, John Newsom, Thomas Herrison & Thomas Cave.—[*Proved 6 May, 1557, by the widow. Grant reserved to the sons, minors.*]

THOMAS YEADON, OF OVER YEADON.

(xv. j. 256 a.)

In the name of God Amen: the xij^th^ daie of Aprill in ye yeare of o^r^ lord god a. 1557. I Thomas Yeadon, of Over Yeadon w^th^in the Cowntie of Yorke, hoole of mynde & of good & p'fite remēbrance, thankꝭ be vnto almightie god, ordeneth, declareth & maketh this my last will & testament in maner & forme folowinge. First I gyve & bequith my soule vnto almightie god my maker & Redem' & to o^r^ blessed Laidie S. Marie & to all ye blessed cūpenye of heaven, & my bodie to be buried w^t^in the parishe church yeard of Gieslaie. Seco'dlie I gyve & bequith vnto Jenet Yeadon my wife & Thomas Yeadon my sonne my lease & my fermhold. The Residew of all my other goodꝭ moveable & vnmoveable, my dettꝭ paid & my funerall expenses maid ye daie of my buriall, I gyve them frelie & whollie vnto the said Jenett my wiffe & Thomas my sonne, whom I ordeine & maike my full executors of this my last will & testame't to dispose for my soules health as they shall thinke good. Thes being wittnesses, Willm Foster, Thomas Willson, w^t^ others.—[*Proved* 6 *May*, 1557, *by the widow. Grant reserved to the son.*]

WILLIAM HALL, OF HEDRICK, HAREWOOD.

(xv. j. 257 a)

In Dei nōie Amen: the xx^ty^ daie of March in ye yeare of o^r^ lorde God a m^mo^ d^mo^ lvij^mo^. I Willm Hall, of Hedricke w^t^in ye parishe of Harwoodde, being of good & p'fyte Reme'brance, maketh & ordeineth this my last will & Testament in this man' & forme folowing. First I bequith my soulle to god almightie, & my bodie to be buried in ye parishe church earthe of Allhallowes att Harwood. Also I gyve & bequeath to s^r^ Willm Preston to pray for my soule vj^s^ viij^d^. Also I gyve & bequeath to everie one of my sonne Roger Horner children one chist. Also I gyve to Marmaduke Horner one jacket of blew & one dublett of buckskinne. Also I gyve to Jenett Hall my s'vant one gymmer shepe. And all ye rest of my goodꝭ nott gyven nor bequithed, my dettꝭ paid & my funerall expenses dispached, I gyve & bequith to Roger Horner, whom I ordeine & maike my wholle executor for to occo'plishe & fulfill this my last will & testament. Thes being witnesses, Willm Smythson, Thomas Smith, w^t^ other moo.—[*Proved* 19 *May*, 1557.]

MARGARET INGLE, OF WEETON, WIDOW.

(xv. j. 259 a.)

In the name of God Amen. I Margrett Ingle, of Weton in ye parishe of Harwood in ye cowntie of Yorke, widow, seeke in bodie, wholle of mynd & of good & perfytte reme'brance, thankꝭ be god everlastinge, ye xx^ty^ daie of December in ye yeare of our lorde god a.m.d.lvj & in the thirde & fowrthe yere of ye Reignes of our Soveraingꝭ lorde & ladye Phillippe & Marie by ye grace of god King and queue of Englond, Spaine, France, both Cicilies, Jerusalem & Irelonde, Defenders of ye faith & Archduke of Austrie, Dukꝭ of Myllane, Burgonie & Brabante, Counties of Haspurge, Flanders & Tiroll, doth maike this my last will & testame't in man' & forme folowinge. Fyrst I comytt my soule vnto almightie God my maker & Redem' & to o^r^ blessed laydye S. Marie & to ye celestiall compenye of heaven, & my bodie to be buried w^{t}in my said parishe church yearde at Herwoodde. Also I gyve & bequyth to ye hie alter for forgotten tythes xij^{d}. It' I gyve & bequest to s^{r} Wiłłm Preston for a trentall of messes for my husband soule & myne x^{s}. It' I gyve & bequith to Wiłłm Ingle my sonne my Lease & whoolle interest of my fermhold & to enter to ytt according to ye custome of husbandrie. It' I gyve & bequeath vnto John Ingle my sonne xxxiij^{s} iiij^{d}. It' I gyve vnto Christopher Ingle my sonne xxxiij^{s} iiij^{d}. It' I gyve vnto Peter my sonne xxxiij^{s} iiij^{d}. It' I give & bequyth vnto Dorothe Ingle my doughter xl^{s} & my best sylver crookꝭ. It' I gyve & bequyth vnto Thomas Ingle an other of my sonnes xiij^{s} iiij^{d}. It' I gyve vnto Alexander Ingle xiij^{s} iiij^{d}. Also I will y^{t} this shall be well & trewlie paid to everie one of my chyldren above named over & besydꝭ their childꝭ porc̃on & partꝭ. It' I gyve vnto Jenett Skotte my doughter my best gowne. It' I gyve to ye said Jenett one great arke. It' I gyve and bequith vnto John Skotte her sonne a quye. It' I gyve & bequyth vnto Dorothe Ingle all my rayme't vnbequested. It' I gyve & bequyth vnto Robt Cloughe my Kinsmā vj^{s} viij^{d}. It' I gyve & bequyth vnto Wiłłm Cloughe my brother vj^{s} viij^{d}, whom I make supvisors of this my last will & Testament. The Residew of all my goodꝭ, my will fulfilled & my dettꝭ paid, I gyve vnto ye saide Wiłłm Ingle my sonne, whom I cōstitute, ordeine & maike my sole executor of this my last will & testame't. Hiis testibus, Wiłłm Clouge, Rawffe Ingle, cū allijs.—[*Proved* 31 *May*, 1557.]

———

Nicholas Lowkes, of Graystock, labourer.

(xv. j. 267 a.)

In Dei nōie Amen. The xiiij daie of Maie in the yeare of o^{r} lord God a m.d.lvij & in the third & fourte yeares of our moost dradde sufferandꝭ Philippe & Marie by the grace of god king & quene of Englond, France, Spaine, both Cicilies, Jerusalem & Irelonde, defendours of ye faith, etc., wytnesseth that I Nycholas Lowkꝭ, of Greastocke wthin the cowntye of Yorke, laborer, doth maike & ordeyne this my last will & testamēt as hereafter foloweth. First I bequyth my soule to Almightie god, our laidye saint Marie, & to all the blessed & glorious cōpeny of heaven, & my bodie to be buried w^{t}in the churchyeard of Normanton nie my predisessors. First I gyve for my soules health to the blessed Sacrament for tythes vnpaid xij^{d}. Also I gyve to Elisabeth my doughter & to Edward her sonne two coples of shepe. Also I gyve to Richard Hall one gray jackett, a paire of hoose cloth & my best dublett. Also I gyve to my sister Margarett one ewe & one lambe & to John Roger her husband my blacke jacket, my best hoose & one fustiā dublett and my best showes. Also I gyve to Alison Blome my servant one ewe & one lambe and finallie I gyve to Robt Tayliour, of Normanton, one olde xij^{d}, whom I desire to see my will fulfilled. The rest of my goodꝭ nott bequytt, my funerall expenses & chargꝭ maid, my dettꝭ paid & I honestlie brought furth, I gyve clearlie to M'grett my wiffe, whom I maike my full executrix for the terme of her lyfe & after her decesse to remayne to Elyzabeth my doughter to fulfill this my last will & testamēt according to my will & myud hereto affore written. Thes bearing witnesses, Wiłłm Brayton & Robt Tayliour.—[*Proved* 2 *June*, 1557.]

HUGH ATKINSON, OF CASTLEFORD.

(xv. j. 283 b.)

In the name of god Amen: the xix daye of M'che & in the yere of o[r] lord god m[l]ccccc.lvj. I Hugh Atkynson, of Castilforth, seike in body but holl of myud & perfecte of remembrance, makis this my last will & testament in this maner and forme followiñg, first I bequeth my soull to almighty god my only saveyor & redem[r] & to o[r] blessed lady sancte Marie & to all the celestiall companye of heven, & my body to be buried w[t]in the churche or churche earth of alhallows at Castilfurth. Also I bequeth to the holye sacrament for forgotten tithes xij[d]. Also I bequeth to Thomas Bullocke iij[s] iiij[d]. Also I bequeth to Willm Loage his bed that he lyes in & on blacke quye. Also I bequeth to John Hemynlay ij[s]. Also I bequeth to Robert Abbot ij[s]. Also I bequeth to Eliz. Hilton iij[s]. Also I beq[th] to Jenet Loage xvj[d]. Also I bequeth to Antony Roydes xij[d]. Also I bequeth to Thomas Atkynson, my son George son, xl[s]. Also I bequeth to Jenet Lawson ij brasse potte, v pece of pewther, ij sawcers, iij candlestycke & one salt whiche Alexander banke [*sic*]. Also I bequeth to John Amerson on blacke lether coyte & on blacke jaket. Also I bequeth to Hugh Lawson iij[li] vj[s] viij[d]. Also I bequeth to Isabell my wif my b[l]acke mayre & on yron chymney whiche standeth at Thomas Bulloke. I bequeth Briget Lawson on candlesticke with two flowres. Also I bequeth to John Rawson on wayne. Also I bequeth to M[r] Lawsons three doughters my iij best quysshyns. Also I bequeth to Peter Lawson & John Lawson either of them on sylu' spone. Also I bequeth to Mr. Lawson my son in law my two handed sword. Also I bequeth to my doughter Lawson on mellan basyn. Also I bequeth to Alexander Banke my wodknyf. Also I bequeth to his wif on chafing dishe & to his three children eu'y one of them on sylu' spone. Also I will that my wif be not trobled or hyndred of that pte of my goode whiche is her right to have. Also I make my executors Thoms Lawson, gent', & Alexander Banke, my sonnes in lawe, trusting that they will se me honestly brought furth at the day of my buriall & my bequeste & dette discharged & thes thinge truly gyven that I haue made mention of in my will & at there discretion to deale peny dolle or halfpeny dolle for the helthe of my soull, and thes thinges done they to haue that whiche will remayne of my goode. Also I giue to Eliz., my son George doughter, & to her mother on lode of slayte standing in my laith for the mending of the houses. Also I will that no glasse w[t]in my house or els where be removed w[t] my executors but to remayne to my beires & also I giue to Eliz', my son George doughter, & her mother the high table & the seattes on bothe sydes. Also I will that my lathe in Allarton be fynnyshed & made vp of my holl goode according to my promysse to my teñnte. I giue vnto Thoms Bulloke the intrest & right that I haue at Houghton of Heptonstall grond paying him therfore as I haue done yerly. It' I gine to Willm Shelito my maser. Thes witness', s[r] John Hall, W[m] Casson, Willm Hagger.—[*Proved* 11 *June*, 1557, *by Thomas Lawson. Grant reserved to Alexander Banks.*]

ALISON DENNIS, OF HUDDLESTONE, WIDOW.

(xv. j. 292 b.)

In the name of God Amen: in the yere of o[r] lord god m[l]ccccc.lvij, the xxvj day of Maye. I Alison Dynnys, of Hoddelston, widowe, late the wif of Henry Dynnys, beyng [holl] of mynd & seike in body, makꝭ this my last will & testament in man' & forme followinge. Firste I giue my soull to God o'ipotent & vnto all the celestiall company of heven, & my bodie to be buried in the churche yerde of Sherburne. It' I gine & bequeth to the blessed sacramente iiij[d]. I giue & bequeth to John Dynnys my eldest son half an acre of barly. It' I bequeth vnto Anne my doughter iiij sheipe & a blacke cowe & ij cou'lettꝭ & a paire of my best shetes. It' I bequeth to M'gret my doughter on brasse pott & ij sheipe. It' I bequeth to Eliz' my yongest doughter a pan of brasse, ij sheipe. It' I bequeth to Robert Dynnys my son ij sheipe. Item I bequeth to W[m] Dynnys my son a red whie & ij sheipe. It' I bequeth to John my son my cupbord, pot crokꝭ, a raken & my barres of yron in the chymney. The residewe of all my goodes not bequest, my dettꝭ & fun'all expenses paid, fynished & ended, I giue them vnto John Dynnys my son, whom I make my holl executor & he to ꝑforme & fulfil this my last will. In witnes herof, Richard Hemslay, curate & vicar ther, John Chelowe, w[t] other mo.—[*Proved* 15 *June*, 1557.]

THOMAS COWPER, OF LEEDS, YEOMAN.

(xv. j. 299 b.)

In Dei nōie amen: the xxix day of November in the yere of o[r] lord god m[l]ccccc.lvj. I Thomas Cowꝑ, of Leidꝭ w[t]in the countie of Yorke, yoman, of holl myud & good memorie, makith this my last will & testament in man' & forme following. First I bequith my saull vnto almighty god & to o[r] blessed lady sancte Marie & to all the sanctꝭ in heven, & my body to be buried w[t]in my ꝑishe church at Leedꝭ at my stall ende. Also I bequith to the blessed sacrament for tithes forgotten xij[d]. Also I give & bequith to Edward Cowper my son on ten'te or house & on litle ynge therto belonging nowe in the tenure of John Lynlay during my yeres & to the heires of his body laufully begotten & for lacke of heires of his body laufully begotten to retorne & remayne to Jenet Couꝑ my doughter & to her heires of her body lawfullie begotten. Also I giuc & bequeth to the said Jenet on cowe close now in the tenure & occupacōn of John Lynley & me the said Thomas, boundynge vpon lybberey called the oxe close during my holl termes of my leise. Also I giue and bequeth to Ric' Cowꝑ my son all my holl yeres & take of on house & on close nowe in the occupacōn of George Sander & to his beires of his body laufully begotten & for lacke of beires of his body to remayne to Eliz' Cowꝑ & to her heires. Also I gine to the said Eliz' my dought[r] my holl yeres title & intrest of & vpon on close nowe in the tenure & occupacōn of Roger Fawcet, ꝑeell of the forsaid oxe close w[t] all my tackꝭ, leas', title & intrest vpon certan clos's called lekeys as well belonging to the chantrie of Fernley as of landꝭ & medowes somtyme belonging to the late dissolued monasterie of the trinities of Yorke & for lacke of beires of the said Eliz' to remayne to Jenet Cowꝑ & to her beires. Also I will that the rest of my ꝑte, all costꝭ & charges of my buriall & probacōn, to remayne to Jenet my doughter. Also the said leaces doth remayne in the handꝭ of Roger Fawcit on cove't lease given out of the p'or & covent of the trinities of Yorke, also other ij leases made by the honorable lord Monteglc & s[r] Gabriell Crofte, chantre preist, & on lease of Chippyndaill. Also I make Isabell my wif & Eliz' my doughter my holl & full executrices of this my last will & testament to pay my dettę & to bring me furth according to my will. Also I will that my closes pay the rentę eu'y on of them vj^s viij^d. Also I giue & bequeth to Isabell my wif my holl take & leise of my house whiche I nowe do dwell in during my yeres. Also I make supvisors of this my last will, s^r John Mathewe, Thomas M'tyu, Roger Fawcet, Robte Atkynson. Also I giue & bequeth to Richard Cowp my son xl^s & it to be paid of the first rentę of the tenement whiche is nowe in the holdinge of John Lynley to his bringing vp. Also I will that Robert Ball, of Dewsbery, shall pay xl^s to Nicolas Seker of the first rentę after my decesse whiche I the said Thomas borowed of him. Also I will that Edward Cowp haue gou'no^r reule of Jenet Cowp & Eliz' & all ther goodę & takę & he to se for the same according as my trust is in him vnto such tyme as they com at age. Also I will that ther be paid yerly to s^r John Mathewe & his depute after his deth during xx yeres, ij^s out of John Lynley fermhold in discharging of my conscience. Thes being witnesses, Ric' Cloudley, Roger Fawcet, Robert Atkinson, w^t other.—[*Proved 2 July, 1557, by the widow. Grant reserved to the daughter, a minor.*]

THOMAS LEE, OF WESTERTON.

(xv. j. 316 b.)

In Dei nõie Amen: the xxx^ti daye of the moneth of Aprill, the yeare of our lord god a thowsand fyve hunderith and vij. I Thomas Lee, of Westerton in the pishinge of Woodkirke, hole of mynd and of good and pfitt remembrance, maikę this my present testamente concerninge herein my last will in maner and forme followinge that is to saye. First I cōmend my soull vnto Allmightie god my maker and redem', and my bodie to be buried within the pishe churche yearde of Woodkyrke, where it shall please almightie god the best. Also I gyve and bequeath vuto the church of Woodkirke towardę bying of a nornamentę to the same iij^s iiij^d. Also I gyve vnto my wif one bedd. Also I gyve and bequeath vuto eu'y one of my children, Dorithe, Isabell, Alice, and Elisabeth, to eu'y one of them a bedd. Also I devide my goodę in thre ptes, that is to witt, the fyrst ptc to maike my fun'all expenses, the secound to my wif, the third to my childer. Also I gyve and bequeath vnto Richard my brother a doblett and a jacket. Also I gyve and bequeath to John Lee of Ardeslawe my brother one jacket. Also I gyve and bequeath to Agnes my wif, Dorothe, Isabell, Alice, and Elisabeth, the reu'con of my leace of all the yeares that is to spend at the daye of my death. The Residewe of all my goodę moveable and not moveable not legate, my fun'all expens's maid the daye of my buriall and thes my legacies and dettę paid and discharged, I gyve vnto Agnes my wif, Dorothe, Isabell, Alice, and Elisabeth, whome I do maike my full executors of all my goodę within my house and without, my will so pformed. Thes men bearinge wytnes, sir Richard Robert, curate, John Lee, John Burghe, and John Haldworth, whome I do maike ou'sears and supvisors apon this my last will & they to see yt fullie pformed. Yeven the daye and yeare aboue wryten. Also I will that if George Lee my brother or any child of his bodie lawfullie begotten cū over to thes myne executors afforsaid, I will that they delyver vnto hym or them so comynge lawfullie viij^s.—[*Proved 26 July, 1557, by Agnes, widow, Dorothy, Isabel, and Alice, daughters. Grant reserved to Elizabeth.*]

THOMAS BOTHOM, OF WAKEFIELD.

(xv. j. 317 a.)

In Dei nōie Amen: the fyft daye of June in the yeare of lord god a thowsand fyve hunderith fiftie and seven. I Thomas Bothom, of the ꝑish of Waikefeld, seke in bodie and hool of mynd and good remembrance, makith this my last will and testament in maner and forme followinge. First I gyve and bequeath my soull to god allmightie my savyo[r] and redemer, to oure laidie sanct Marie Vyrgyn, and all the holie companye in heven. And my bodie to be buried in the churche yeard at Waikfeld. Item I gyve and bequeath to John Bothom my father one jackett and a lether dublett and a ewe and a lambie. And also to my mother, his wiff, a ewe and a lambe. The Residewe of all my goodꝭ, cattellꝭ, and leases that I haue I gyve and bequeath them hoollie to Jane Bothom my wif, whome I maike and ordayne to be my full and onelie executrix, she to dispose for the health of my soull and to se my children brought vp and to haue ther partes accordinge to the valyation of my goodꝭ. Thes beinge wytnesses, Sir James Brodbent, my curate, Brian Cartmell, Wiłłm Haldisworth.—[26 *July*, 1557.]

THOMAS ARNOLD, OF WAKEFIELD.

(xv. j. 317 b.)

In the name of God Amen: the xth daie of Julie in the yeare of our lord god a thowsand fyve hunderith fyftie and seaven. I Thomas Arnald, of the ꝑishe of Waikefeld within the countie of Yorke, cupper, of good and ꝑfytt memorie, thankꝭ be to god, makith this my last will and testament as hereafter followithe. First I gyve and bequeath my soull vuto allmightie God my maker and redemer and to oure blissed ladie sanct Marie the mother of god and to all the blissed companye of heaven, and my bodie to be buried within the ꝑishe churche yeard of all hallowes in Waikefeld. Item I bequeth vnto Thomas Arnald my sone one fether bedd in the ꝑlor with all thingꝭ ꝑtey'inge vnto it with vijth peces of pewther vessell and one latten candilsticke and ij sawcers. Item I gyve and bequythe vnto George Arnalde my son a bedde in the parler wythe all thynge partaynynge vuto yt and one chafynge dyshe. Item I gyue and bequythe vuto Jenat Burye my doughter one fleckt bede in the chamber wythe all thynge partaynynge vnto yt and one chafyngedyshe, the Resydewe of all my pewder vessell not bequyathede I gyue vuto George Arnalde my son and to Jenat Burye my doughter to be devydede betwyxte them by even porcyons. Item I gyve vnto John Arnallde my brother one grene jackyt and a chamblete dublet. Item I gyve vuto Amerye Vaveser my servante one blacke gowne and a felt hatte. Item I geue vnto Hewgo Robynson my s'vante a blewe jacket and a buttonde cappe. Item I gyne vnto s[r] George Lee a mette of wheate. Item I geve vuto George Arnalde my son and to Jenat Burye my doughter my lease of ij closses at wyll lone heade durynge the yeares after my dissease that ar not expyrede. Item I wyll that George Arnalde my son shall haue all my toyles ꝑtaynynge to my occupation. Item I gene vnto Jenat Burye my doughter all my brewynge vessell. The Resydewe of all my goodꝭ not bequyathede, my dettes and funerall expensis payde, Item I gyne and bequyathe vnto Thomas Arnalde, George Arnalde, and Jenat Burye, my chyldrynge, to be devydede emonge them by even porsyons, whome I make my executors of thys my last wyll. Also I make supvysers of this my last will, Willm Casson and Richarde Lowes. These beynge wytnesses, John Dyconson, Xpofer Kyrke, s[r] George Lee, wythe other.—[*Proved* 26 *July*, 1557.]

RICHARD LEWIS, OF PONTEFRACT.

(xv. j. 317 b.)

In Dei nōie Amen: the vij[th] day of May in the yeare of our lorde God a thowsande fyve hundrythe fyftye and seven. I Richarde Lewis, of Pontefracte, hole of mynde and of good remembrance, makethe this my last will and testamente in maner and forme folowynge. Fyrst I geve and bequythe my soule vnto almyghtye god and to our blessed lady sancte Marye and to all the holy companye of heaven, and my bodye to be buryede in the churche yearde of Alhalowes in Pomfracte. Also I bequeathe to Katheren my wyf my howse in Cawode wythe all the landes and all thynges ther to belongynge for the terme of her naturall lyfe accordinge to my comandment in my maredge, and after the disceace of the said Katheryn my wyfe to remayne to George Lewis my youngest sonne to hym his heyres for ever. Also I bequyathe to Richard Lewis my sonn for a foull contentacon of his childe parte xxxx[s] that Edwarde Houngate of Bramham owyth vnto me yf he be contente to take it thankefullye, and if not to remayne to my executors, for I take yt of my charge that he bathe had yt of me in pennyworthe twentye markes that he owythe vnto me. The Residew of my goodę not bequyathed, my dettes paide, my funerall expensis made the day of my buryall, I gine them frelye to Katheryn my wyfe, whom I make my full executors of this my last will and testamente, and I desyre Lyonell Roleston my father in lowe and Nycholes Mavlevareye, gentleman, and James Roleston, yoman, to be supvysers of this my last will and testamente, and they to haue my sonn George in ther governance wythe landes, leases, and goodes vntyll he be twentye yeares and one of aige. Thes beynge wytnesses, Lyonell Roleston, Robert Shawe, Wyllm Tyasse, Willm Westroppe, Roberte Spynsse, John Roleston.—[*Proved* 26 *July*, 1557.]

JOHN ROGER, OF METHLEY.

(xv. j. 318 a.)

In Dei nōie Amen: the xij[th] day of November in the yeare of our lorde god a thowsand fyue hundrythe fyftye and eyght. I John Roger, of Methleye, of good memorye, thankes be to god, makeythe this my laste wyll and testamente in maner and forme folowynge. Fyrste I bequyathe my sowle to God Almyghtye my creator and redemer and to our blessede ladye sancte Marye and to all the holye companye of heaven, and my body to [be] beryede wythe in the churche yeard of sancte Oswalde of the said Metheleye. Item I bequyathe to the most nedes of the churche ij[s]. The resydewe of all my goodes not bequyathed, the full costes and charges borne at my buryall, I geve to Jenat my wyfe, whome I make and ordayne my lawfull executor. Thes beyng wyttnesses, syr George Tayllyer, chaplyn, Roberte Gyge, John Mies, Thomas Mytley & John Oytes.—[*Proved* 28 *Nov.*, 1558.]

EDMUND *P*ARKER, OF ROTHWELL HAIGH, YEOMAN.

(xv. j. 318 b.)

In the name of God Amen: the xxiiij[th] daye of Apryll in the yeare of ur lorde god a thousande fyve hundrythe fyftye and sevven. I Edmonde P'ker, of Roithewell haie wythein the ꝑishe of Roithwell and countye of Yorke, yoman, lyenge in extremys, beyng of hole myud and ꝑfyte remembrance (thanks be vnto god), do constitute, ordayne and make thys my laste testamente wherein is declarede my laste will in maner and forme folowynge. Furste I bequythe my soule to the mercye of almyghtie god my creator and Redemptor, to the blessed virgyn Marye, and all the sanctes in heaven, and my deade corps or bodye to be buryede wythe in the Churche yearde of thafforesaide Roithwell foranempste the saide churche porche. Also I wyll that my house shalbe kepte together one hole yeare after my discease as yt is at this daye. Also I geve and bequythe to euery one of my iij doughters thre poundes sex shillyngꝭ and eighte penns, And also eu'y one of them one quarter of rye corne to be delyverede to theym before the feaste of sancte Mychell tharchangell nexte comynge. Further I will that the howse that I now dwell vpon wythe the olde Riveles grave wodde and the new launde shall goo together, fortye shillinges Rente that George Dobson haithe nowe in occupacon onelye exceptede, wiche said fortye shillinges rente I will that the said George Dobson have yt styll durynge my lease payinge therfore the saide rente. Also I will that Francis Byrkedall shall haue one lytle close wiche Edmonde Fenton occupyede withe one ꝑte of one other close wiche Adam Byrkdall dyd occupye durynge my lease payinge therfore yearlye [*blank*] And further I will that the carre wythe olde lande and Kyrkenabbe shall goo togethers. And then I will that Wiℏm P'ker my sonn shalbe in chose whether ꝑte that he will take. Also I gyne and bequythe my lease of Haggestoncliffe to the sonns of George Dobson, Lawrence Sponge, and Thomas Cowꝑ. Also I geve and bequythe to the mendynge of the hyghe waies betwyxe Leedes and Waikefelde in the carr lone thyrtyne shyllinges and four pence. Also I geve and bequyathe to Robert P'kere one nagge. Also I will that my fun'all expences be maide of all my hole goodꝭ. Also I will that twentye shillingꝭ rente shalbe taken fourthe of the byrke nabbe for a nobyt, masse & derige to be downe yearely for my sowle healthe, and the money that shalbe spared to be delte vnto the pore people. The residewe of all my goodꝭ and cattells not bequyted, my dettꝭ, fun'all expences, and legaces before expressed discharged and payde, I will that Margaret *P*arker my wyfe and Wiℏm P'ker my sonn haue them and order them at their discression for the healthe of my sowle, whome I make and cōstitute thexecutors of this my p'sent last will and testamente. Also I desyre Syr John Hagger, preste, the vicar of Rothwell, John Ashelay, Hemeswor of gaynerie, and Gylƀte Dobson, of Oulton, to be supvisors of this my last will and testament, and eu'ry one of them to haue for ther paynes takynge thyrtyne shillinges & iiij[d]. Thes beynge wytnesses, syr John Hagger, clarke, Vicar of Rothewell, John Asheley, Thomas Hemsworth, and Gylberte Dobson, wythe other moo as Francis Byrkedalle.— [*Proved* 20 *July*, 1557.]

Richard Harrison, of Stanley.

(xv. j. 328 a.)

In the name of God Amen: the viijth day of June in the year of our lord god 1557. I Richard Harryson, of Standley in the ꝑyshe of Wakefelde in the countye of Yorke, being of good and ꝑfett memory, laud and prayse be vnto allmyghtye god, make and ordayne this my presente last will and testament in man' and forme followynge, that ys to say. Fyrst and pryncypally I comend my soull vuto Allmyghtye god my maker and redemer, to our lady St Mary the virgyn, and to all the holy company of heauen, and my body to be buryed in the ꝑyshe churche yerde of Wakefelde aforesaid. It' I bequeathe to Thomas Arnall the yonger three ewes, thre lambes, one whye styrke, the greater Ambrey whiche standethe in my house, and iij^{s} iiij^{d} in money. It' I bequeathe to Thomas Arnall thelder vj^{s} viij^{d} in money. It' I bequeathe to Anne Johnson one ewe, one lame. It' I gine and bequeathe to Mr Bryan Bradforde my landę lorde my best oxe or beast at my house. The rest and residewe of all my goodę and cattalls before not bequeathed nor gyven, my dettę and fun'all expenses thereof paid and done, I giue and bequeathe vnto Agnes my wyfe and Bryan Harryson my sonne, equally to be devided betwixte them. And I ordayne, constitute, and make the said Bryan my sonne my hooll and full executor of this my presente last will and testament. And I make, ordayne, and constitute the said Bryan Bradforde the suꝑvisor of the same to se allthingę hearin contayned well and trulye fulfilled and ꝑformed accordingly. Thes beynge wytnes, John Clarkson, John Gryme, Richard Browney, George Thompson, w^{t} others.—[*Proved* 29 *Sept.*, 1557, *by Agnes, the widow, guardian of Brian, the son, a minor.*]

William Stockall, of Monkhill, shoemaker.

(xv. j. 328 a.)

In the name of God amen: the xxvjth day of July in the year of our Lord 1557°. I Willm Stockall, of Mon[k]hill, shoumaker, hooll of mynde and god remembrance, makethe this my last will & testament in this maner and forme followinge. Fyrst I comend my soull vnto the handę of allmyghtye god, and my body to be buryed wythin the churche yerd of all hallowes in Pontefract. It' I bequeath to John Stockall children a yew and a lambe emongę theme, and to John Atkynson childer a yew and a lambe emongę them, and to Jennet my doughter a yew and a lambe. It' to Isabell my doughter a landyron after the decesse of Agnes my wyfe. It' I giue and bequeathe to John Stockall my sonne fouer markę in money or in other stuffe or in household go[o]d, and after the decesse of my wyfe the take of my house. It' I giue to Elsabethe my daughter wch is John Atkinson wyfe xx^{s}. It' to the hye alter viij^{d}. The rest of all my goodę not bequeathed nor gyven, my children porcons paid and my dettę paid, I giue them frelye to Agnes my wyfe, Jennett, Isabell, and Agnes my doughters, whom I make my full executrices. In witnes wherof, Sr Richard Rediall, clarke, Sr Alexander Caraver, curate, Robert Blesseby, Wyllm Atkinson, and Thomas Glewe, wth other moo.—[*Proved* 29 *Sept.*, 1557, *by the daughters, Agnes, the widow, being dead.*]

RICHARD HOLLINGS, OF KIRSKELD, WHEELWRIGHT.

(xv. j. 332 a.)

In the name of God Amen: The vj^th^ day of August in the yer of our lord god 1557. I Richard Holingℯ, of Kirskelde wthin the countye of Yorke & of the pishe of Adle, whelewright, seke in body and hooll of mynde and of good remembrance (thankℯ be vnto allmyhtye God), makethe this my last will & testament in man' & forme followinge. First I giue and bequeathe my soull vnto Allmyghtye God my maker & to my redemer Jesu christ, besecheninge our blessed lady St Marye and all the blessed company of heauen to pray for me that my soull may take place amongest the electe and chosen people of god, and my body to be buryed within my pishe churche or churche yeard of St John the Baptiste of Adle. It' I giue & bequeath vnto John Lofthus all my tymber felde and vnfelde wthin the felde of Burdon and also xxtie gauge of speakes. Also I giue and bequeathe vnto Steven Stable xxtie gauge of fellowes and a blake stagg & a reede quye and a blake stott. It' I giue vnto Jennet my wyfe the hooll interest & goodwill of my farmeholde duringe her lyfe naturall, and after her decesse I giue yt vnto John Lofthous, and if yt shall please God to call hym to his mercye then I giue and bequeathe the same vnto Henry Lofthous. The residew of all other my goodℯ moueable and vnmoueable vnbequeathed, my dettℯ paid and my fun'all expenses maide the daye of my buriall, I gyve them frelye and hollye vnto Jennett my wyfe, whome I ordayne and make my full executrix of this my last will and testament to dispose for my soull healthe as she shall thinke good. Thes beinge witnes, Willm Gill, John Lofthous, Willm Wayte.—[*Proved 15 Sept.*, 1557.]

GEORGE PIKARD, OF OTLEY, YEOMAN.

(xv. j. 332 a.)

In the name of God Amen: The xxixth of August in the year of our lord God 1557. I George Pykerd, of Otley in the countye of Yorke, yoman, do ordayne and make this my last will and testament in maner and forme followynge. First I bequeathe my soull to the mercye of allmyghtye God & my redemer Jhu christ, beseching our blessed lady St Marye and all the celestiall company of heauen to pray for me that yt may take place emongest the elect people of God, and my body to be buryed wthin the churche yeard of Otley nigh vnto the palmecrosse. It' I will that my mortuarye be paid accordinge to the lawe. It' I will that my goodℯ be devided into thre ptℯ, one pte to my wyfe, another to my selfe, and the thirde to my children. Also I bequeathe all my interest, title, and possession of my farmeholde and my take therof to Margarett my wyfe duringe her lyfe naturall, and after her deathe vnto George my sonne yf he can optayne the landeslord favor. Also I giue vnto the said George my son one counter and also a swerd and a buckler, and to Effay P'ker my doughter one ambrey whiche was her owne. Allso I make Margaret my wyfe, Effay P'ker my doughter, Richard, Tho., and George, my sonnes, Alyce and Agnes my doughters, my executors of this my last will and testament, my dettℯ to be payd of my hooll goodℯ, my fun'all expenses, legacies, and other duties to be paid of my pte of goodℯ. The residewe of all my pte of goodℯ I gine vnto my said wyfe Margaret and my said children.

Thes beynge wytnes, S[r] Anthonye Jackson, clerke, Thomas Dunwell, of Otley, Willm Steide, and Willm Dickson.—[*Proved* 15 *Sept.*, 1557, *by Margaret, the widow, Richard, George, Alice, and Agnes. Grant reserved to William and Thomas, Euphemia renouncing.*]

JOHN *P*ERSON, OF METHLEY, YEOMAN.

(xv. j. 333 a.)

In the name of God Amen: the xxvij day of Julye in the year of our lord God 1557. I John *P*erson, of Metheley in the countye of Yorke, yoman, pfett in mynd and memorye and seke in body, makethe this my last will and testament in maner and forme followinge. Fyrst I bequeathe my soule to the holye and glorious Trinytie of heauen and to the blessed and holy S[t] Marye the virgyne and mother of god, the second pson in trinitye, and my body to be buryed w[th]in the pyshe churche yerd of Methley, evermore trustinge and in stedfast beleve throughe the glorious and paynefull passion of o[r] lord Jhu chryst to be one of thos chossen & electe children of God at the last resurrection and dredfull day of Judgement, and to company wythe o[r] holy father Abrahm, Isaac, and Jacobe, and all other the holy company of heauen. Allso I gyve and bequeathe to Willm *P*erson my son in full recompence, satisfaccon, and contentation of his chyldę porcon, fouer jackettę, iiij dublettę, two payre of whyte hoose, one mattres, one coverlett, one payre of sameron shetę, ij olde angells of golde, one grete Iron chymney, one gret brasse pott, one axe, one hatchett, one browlynge yrne, twoo yron spettę, the one broken, two yron toughwethes, one ambrey, two chystę, one grete balde meare, one whyte nagg, and one rede whye wythe calve. Also I gine and bequeathe to Elisabethe my daughter in full recompence and satisfaccon of her childę porcon ix[li] in golde and silver, two kye, the one called whytehorne and the other nyghtgaill, two brasse pottę, thre dublers, thre pewther dishes, one mattres, two cou'lettę, one payre of lynne shetes, one payr of harden shettę, two bolsters, two pillowes, two pilloberes, too towells, one shorte girdle wythall that belongę therto, and two cuple of ewes and lambes. Also I bequeathe to Robert Kirbye one ewe lambe. Allso I bequeathe to Isabell Kyrkbye one ewe lambe. Allso I bequeathe to George Kyrkbye one dublett, one payre of over worne hoose. Allso I bequeathe to Wyllm Kyrkebye one blacke jackett wythout sleves and one bukskyn dublett. Also I bequeathe to eu'y one of my godchildren ij[d]. Allso I will that Agnes my wyfe yf yt happen or forton the brigg called the newe brige to be remoued and maid newe shall pay or cause to be paid for the remendinge as ys aforesaid xiij[s] iiij[d]. Also I wyll yf the said Agnes my wyfe do clayme, challence, and recover the thirdę of all my landę that then my said sonne Wyllm *P*eerson shall haue the hooll lease of certayne groundę wythin Rothwell and also the halfe lease of meddopp to hym and his assigns, and also yf the said Agnes my wyfe stande and be contented wythall thos landę whiche I haue appoynted vnto her and do nether clame, challence, then recover the thirdę as ys beforesaid, I will that the said hooll lease and halfe lease as ys beforesaid shall holy remayne to the said Agnes my wyfe, to Jennett and Margery my doughters and to ther assignes. The residew of all my goodę not gyven then bequested I gine and bequeathe to the said Agnes my wyfe, Jennett and Margerye my doughters, whome I make my lawfull executrices to dispose for the healthe of my soull as they shall thinke most mete and convenyent. Thes beynge wytnes, Robert Nallson, Robert Gige, Robert Warde, and Willm Pratt.—[*Proved* 16 *Sept.*, 1557, *by the widow. Grant reserved to daughters, minors.*]

NICHOLAS DOBSON, OF LOFTHOUSE.

(xv. j. 333 b.)

In the name of God Amen: The xxvjth of Januarie in the year of our lord god mdvclvj that I, Nycholas Dobson, of lofthouse of the pyshe of Rothewell, of hooll mynde and pfett remembrance, dothe constitute, ordayne, and maike hearin this present worlde my last will and testament in the maner and forme hearafter followynge. Fyrst I giue and bequeathe my soull vnto God Almightye and to our blessed lady saynt Mary and to all the holye company of heauen, and my body to be buryed wthin the churche yearde of the blessed Trenytye of Rothevell. Allso I gine and bequeathe vnto the blessed sacrament for tythes and oblacons forgotten viijd. Also I bequeathe and assigne all my hooll farmeholde after my deathe vnto Anthony Dobson and Raufe Dobson my sonnes and they to occupye yt joyntlye together; also yt ys my will and mynde that my dettę whiche I do owe be payd of my hooll goodę to the vttermost penny. Also I bequeathe to John Dobson my sonne one yewe and one lambe in full contentacon of his childe portion. Allso I bequeathe to James Dobson my sonne one yewe and one lambe in full contentacon of his childe portion. Also I bequeathe to Steven Dobson my sonne xxs in full contentation of his childe porcon. Allso I bequeathe vnto Isabell Remyngton my doughter the wife of John Remyngton vjs viijd in full contentation and satisfaction of her portion; also I bequeathe to Alys Remyngton [*blank*] doughter one yewe and one lambe. Allso I bequeath to Jennett Dobson my doughter iiijli in full contentacon and satisfaction for her childe portion. Allso yt ys my mynde and wyll that my executor shall pay vnto Robert Helvisse xvs whiche I have in kepinge of his chylde portion at suche tyme as he shall come to lawfull yeres of aige. Allso the residewe of all my other goodę not bequeathed moueable and vnmoueable, my dettę paid, fun'all expenses mayde, I gyve and bequeathe vnto Antony Dobson and Raufe Dobson my sonnes, whome I make my full and laufull executors, and they for to transpose some pte therof for the healthe of my soull as they thinke the best. In wytnes hearof I the foresaid Nycholas Dobson vnto this my last will I haue setto my marke the day and yeare abouesaid. In the presence of Thomas Gamyll, Rauffe more, Thomas Apleyerd, John Talyer, and wytnesses.—[*Proved* 16 *Sept.*, 1557.]

THOMAS SWANSON, OF WAKEFIELD.

(xv. j. 333 b.)

In the name of God Amen: the first day of September in the year of our lord God 1557. I Thom's Swanson, of the pyshe of Wakefeilde, of hooll and pfett remembrance, makę this my last will and testament in maner & forme followynge, fyrst I bequeathe my soull vnto allmyghty God and to our lady saynt Mary and to all the blessed company of heauen, and my body to be buryed in the churche yerde of Allhallowes in Wakefelde. Also I bequeathe vnto Thomas Swanson one ewe hogg. Allso I wyll that my dettę be payd of my hooll goodę. The residew of my goodę not gyven, my dettę paid and fun'all expenses mayd, I giue them to Richard Swanson, Willm Swanson, George Swanson, and Nycholas Swanson, whome I make my full executors of this my last will and testament. Thes beynge [wytnes], Lyonell Barker, Willm Boillynge, John Hyll, wth other.—[*Proved* 26 *Sept.*, 1557.]

Thomas Clapham, of Wakefield.

(xv. j. 334 a.)

In Dei nōie Amen: the seconde day of November in the year of our lord God 1556. I Thomas Claph'm, of Wakefeld, seke in body and hooll of mynde and good of remēbrance, make this my last will and testament in maner and forme followinge. First I giuc and bequeathe my soull to God Allmyghtie, to our lady St Mary, and to all the celestyall company in heauen, and my body to be buryed wythin the churche yerde at Wakefelde. It' I gyve to Water Claph'm my sonne the som̄e of x^s^ and one blake colte, and yt to stande for hys childę porc̄on. The residewe of all my goodę I giue them to Isabell Claph'm my wyfe, whome I make and ordayne to be my full and onlye executrix, she to pay my dettę and dispose for my soull as my trust ys in her. Thes beynge witnes, s^r^ James Brodbentt, my curate, Jeffraye Richardson, John Killingbeke, Lyonell Clyffe, and Thomas Parke, wythe other moo.—[*Proved* 26 *Sept.*, 1557.]

John Dawson, of South Milford, husbandman.

(xv. j. 336 a.)

In the name of God Amen: the xijth day of August in the year of our lord God m^d^ccccclvij. I John Dawson, of southe Mylforthe, husbandman, hooll of mynde and seke of body, beynge of good and pfect m̄emorye, makes thys my last wyll and testament in maner and forme followynge. Fyrst I bequeathe my soull vnto God Allmyghtye and vnto the gloryous and blessed virgyn saynt Marie and vnto all the celestiall company of heauen, and my body to be buryed in the pishe churche of Sherburne. Also I bequeathe vnto the highe alter of the said churche xij^d^. Item I bequeathe vnto John Richardson my son in law one quarter of barlye. It' I bequeathe vnto Robert Dawson my sonne one quarter of barlie. Item I bequeathe vnto Richard Richardson the sonne of the aforesaid John Richardson one yowe. Item I bequeathe vnto Jennett Dawson one yewe. Item I bequeath vnto eu'y one of my sonne Thomas Dawson children one yewe a pece and vnto s^r^ John Talier iiij^d^. The residewe of my goodę not gyven nor bequest, my dettę and fun'all expenses paide, fynyshed and ended, I giue and bequeathe them vnto John Dawson, Mergaret Dawson, and Anne Dawson, my children, who I do ordayne and make my executors of this my last will and testament. In wytnes hearof, Sr Richard Hemsley, vicar ib̄m, Thomas Barton, Thomas Sykes, John Chellowe, wythe other moo.—[*Proved* 28 *Sept.*, 1557, *by John and Margaret. Grant reserved to Anne.*]

JOHN GODFREY, OF ARMLEY, HUSBANDMAN.

(xv. j. 336 a.)

In the name of God Amen: the xxj^th day of M'ehe, Anno D'ni 1556. I John Godfray, of Armeley in the countye of Yorke, husbandman, beynge of hoole mynde and pfett memory, makethe this my last wyll and testament in man' and forme followynge. Fyrst I gyve my soull to allmyghtye god and to our lady saynt Marye and to all the saynte in heauen, and my body to be buryed in my pishe churche yeard of saynt Peter at Leede. Also my dette shalbe paid of my hoole goode. Also my goode shalbe devided in thre pte, one pte I gyve to my wyfe, a nother to my children, and that that remaynethe of my pte, my fun'all expens's discharged and dette paide, I giue vnto Isabell my wyfe, whome I make hooll executrix of this my last wyll and testament. Allso I giue vnto Isabell my wyfe my lease or interest of my farmeholde durynge her wedoheade, and yf yt chance that she marye agayne, than I will that my children shall haue yt to ther proper vse. Thes beynge wytnes, Sr Xpofer Brodley, vicar of Leede, Xpofer Sampson, John Walker, and Wyllm Cawdray, wythe others. Also I make Xpofer Sampson and my mother Eliz. Godfray, supvisors of this my last wyll.—[*Proved* 28 *Sept.*, 1557.]

JOHN SPINKE, OF CASTLEY.

(xv. j. 336 a.)

In Dei nōie Amen: the fyrst day of August in the year of our lord God m^dccccclvij. I John Spynke, of Castley wythin the countye of Yorke, of holl mynde and pfett memorye but seke of body, laude and prayse be to God, do make my last wyll and testament in manner and forme followinge. Fyrst and pryncipally I yelde & bequeathe my soull to Almyghtye God my maker and redemer, to our lady saynt Mary, and to the hole celestiall company of heauen, and my mortall body to be buried wth in the churche earthe of Leythley. It' I gyve for my mortuarie as the lawes requyrethe. It' I giue and bequeathe to Henry my sonne one battell axe and to Edward my sonne my swerd. It' I bequeathe to the said Henry and Edward my sonnes all my plowes and ploughe geare together wythall my waynes, cowpes, yocke, teymes & harrowes, and all other thinge apptenynge and belongeing the said plowghes and waynes. It'm I giue and bequeathe to Jennet my doughter one blacke cowe of the fyrst calfe. It' I giue to Margaret my doughter one dou' whye. Item I gyve to Isabell and Eliz. my doughters ether of them one quye. Wher the right worshipfull maister Henry Arthington owethe vnto me for one quarter oite vj^s, I gyve and bequeathe to the said Mr Arthington the said vj^s, humblye requyrynge hym to be good m^r to my poore wyfe and children wythe his good counsell at suche tymes as they shall stande nede therof. The residewe of my goode, my dette paid and my fun'all expens's discharged, I giue to Eliz' my wyfe and to my chyldren equallie to be devided emongest them. It' I constitute, ordayne, and make Eliz. my wyfe, Henry and Edward my sonnes, myne executors of this my last will. Thes beynge witnesses, Sir Thomas Helme, prest, my curate, Richerd Waid, Robert Day, John Dybb, Marke Thompson, wth other moo.—[*Proved* 28 *Sept.*, 1557.]

THOMAS HARDWICK, OF POTTERNEWTON, GENTN.[1]

(xv. j. 360 b.)

In the name of God Amen: the iijth day of June in the thyrde and fourthe yeares of the Reignes of sou'aigne lord and lady Philipp and Marye by the grace of God kinge and quene of England, Hispane, France, both Cicilies, Jer'lem, and Irelonde, Defenders of the faythe, Archedukꝭ of Austrie, Dukes of Myllane, Burgunde, and Brabant, Counties of the Haspurge, Flanders, and Tyrolls. I Thomas Hardweke, of Potternewton in the countie of Yorke, gent., beynge hole of mynde and in good and ꝑfett remembrance, thankꝭ be vnto allmyghtie God, and knowynge the vncertayntye of lyfe, dothe make this my last wyll and testament in manner and forme followinge. Fyrst I gine and bequeath my soull to allmyghtye God my creator and Redemer, trustinge that I bothe body and soull throughe the merytes of Chrystꝭ deathe and passion shall haue eu'-lastynge lyfe, I giue and beq'athe my body to be buryed wythin the ꝑyshe churche at Leedes or in any other churche where yt shall please God to call me to his mercye. Item I giue and bequeathe xx^{li} laufull Inglyshe money to be distributed emongest the poore people dwellinge and inhabytinge wythin the ꝑyshe of Leedꝭ and Ilkeley in manner and forme folowynge, that ys to say, yearly durynge the space of fower yeares to the poore people of the ꝑishe of Leedes, every yeare fyve markꝭ, and to the poore people wythin the ꝑyshe of Ilkeley, eu'y yeare durynge the sayd fower yeares $xxxiij^{s}$ $iiij^{d}$. Item I giue and bequeathe to my sonne and hayre Thomas Hardwicke my cheyne of golde and the som̄e of a hundrethe poundes in golde to be delyu'ed vnto hym by my executors at suche tyme as he shall accomplyshe the aige of $xxij^{o}$ yeares towardꝭ the furnysheynge of hys house. Item I giue to Katheren Hardwicke my doughter one sylver bowle, a sylver copp, a flatt sylver pece, a lytle sylu' salte, and sex sylver spones. Item I giue to the said Katheren my doughter all suche som̄es of money as Francꝭ Pasley dothe owe vuto me at this day by a byll or by dede oblygatorye or otherwayes, whiche som̄e ys twoo hundrethe markꝭ and fortye thre poundꝭ. Also I giue to the sayd Katheren Hardwycke so muche money as shall maike the same extende and amou'te to the som̄e of fower hundrethe markꝭ in full contentac̄on satisfacc̄on, and payment of her thyrdꝭ parte & porc̄on. Item I giue to Edythe my welbeloued wyfe the som̄e of a hundrethe markꝭ in golde and sylver vpon condyc̄on that she wythe the sayme shall pursue the lawe wythe effecte agaynste the sayd Frauncys Paslewe for all suche som̄es of money as he dothe owne vnto me the sayd Thomas Hardwycke at this daye, and not to agree wythe the said Francys Pasley otherwyse then the lawe wyll. Also I wyll that the resydewe of all my playte before not gyven shalbe equallye devided betwyxte the sayd Edythe my wyfe and Thomas Hardwicke my sonne, and Thomas ꝑte to be delyu'ded vuto hym at suche tyme as he shall accomplyshe the full aige of xxij yeares. Item I giue to Edithe my wyfe the twoo ꝑtes of all my landes wythin Potternewton or els wheare wythin the countye of Yorke vnto suche tyme as my son Thomas come and accomplishe the full aige of $xxij^{tie}$ yeares upon

(1) He married Edith, daughter of Costan Bampton. His son Thomas married Ann, daughter of Lyon Reresby. Their estates in Potternewton were eventually inherited by William, Earl Cowper. See pedigree Thoresby's *Ducatus Leod.*, 2nd ed., p. 121.

condiĉon that she duringe the said tyme do keep her wedowheade, and then I wyll that at suche tyme as my said sonne Thomas do accomplyshe the said aige of xxij yeares that my wyfe shall haue the thyrde ꝑte of my landꝭ over and besydes her owne lande aswell copyholde as freholde whiche she hathe wythin the countye of Yorke. Also I wyll the other thyrde ꝑte, beynge the Resydewe of all my said landꝭ, go to the chefe lorde or lordꝭ of whome the sayd landꝭ ar holden durynge the nōaige of my said sonne Thomas Hardeweke towardꝭ his fyndinge and bringynge vpp accordinge to the lawes and statutes of this realme. Allso I giue to my father in lawe Costan Bampton my satan dublett, and to my welbeloued mother my blacke wursett gowne furred wythe conye. Also I giue to my suster Jennet Garthefurthe fyve markꝭ, to my syster Margaret xx^s^. It' I giue to my brother Wyłłm Hardweke my beste blacke gowne faced wythe sarsnytt, and I giue to my sayd brother Wyłłm and my suster his wyfe ether of them one angell of golde. It' I gine to Syr Wyłłm Brame xx^s^. It' I giue to Margaret Hardwycke my brother doughter fyve markꝭ and to Robert Hardweke her brother brother [*sic*] fyve markꝭ. Also I giue to Margaret Garthfurthe my suster doughter other fyve markꝭ towardes the p'ferment of ther maraiges. Allso I giue to Wyłłm Hardweke sonne of Thomas Hardweke, of Horsforthe, decessed, vij^li^ to be taken of thyshewes and profettꝭ of his landꝭ over and besydes his chyldes ꝑte and bryninge vpp in learnynge and to be gyven hym at suche tyme as he shall come to full aige. Item I gyve to Wyłłm Vavasour my s'unte xxx^s^, and to Robert Hardweke thelder my s'unte xxx^s^. Also I gyve to Alexander Pasley my servant xx^s^. Also I giue to eu'y one of my s'untꝭ vj^s^ viij^d^, Rychard Ellis, Thomas Ellis, and Margaret Ellis excepte, whom I giue to everye one of them xl^s^. It' I giue to my brother John Estley my blacke gowne furred wythe connye. Allso I will that yf my syster Estley do over lyve my brother Estley and me, that then I will that Edithe my wyfe and Thomas my sonne shall fynde her meate, drynke, fyer, chamber, and other thinges necessarye of ther costes and charges duringe her naturall lyfe. Allso I giue to s^r^ Arthure Darcye my mayster the soṁe of x^li^ vpon condiĉon that Wiłłm Vavasor my s'unte ymediatly after my deathe shall ryde to London and requyre the said Sr Arthure Darcye to gett and optayne the wardshippe of my sonne at the kingꝭ hande, and my wyfe to beare the charges of suche soṁes of money as the said s^r^ Arthure shall disburse for the optaynynge and gettinge of my said sonne, so that she may haue the wardshipp of hym at her pleaso^r^. And the said s^r^ Arthure to haue the sayd x^li^ declare onlye for his paynes takinge. The residewe of all my goodꝭ vpon stottꝭ, stottꝭ kyne, shepe, and all other maner of yonge nowte whatsoever they be at Marley, Potternewton, Stankꝭ, and Roydꝭ, as all other householde goodꝭ, bedding, pottꝭ, pañes, and other hustilment of householde whatsoever they bee, and all dettꝭ wch at this day I am owinge, I give vnto Edithe my wyfe, whome I maike my full and sole executrix of this my last wyll and testament, so that she pay all legacies mentyoned and before expressed in this my present will and also all other dettꝭ wyche by the order of the lawe I ought to paye. Also I giue to Sr Xpofer Bradley, vicar of Leedꝭ, x^s^. Also I make John Mydleton and Francys *P*almes, Esquiers, suꝑvisors of this my wyll, And I gyve to ether of them for ther paynes takinge xx^s^, trustinge that they will se the same p'formed. In wytnes wherof I the said Thomas Hardweke to this my p'sent will haue setto my seale and subscribed my name the day and yeares aboue wrytten. Thes beinge wytnesses, S[r] Xpofer Bradley, vicar of Leedes, Willm Vavaso[r], Robert Hardwicke, Richard Adcocke, John Androwe, and Thomas Jeffrayson, wythe others.—[*Proved* 21 *Oct.*, 1557.]

LAWRENCE LYNDLEY, OF LEATHLEY, GENTN.[1]

(xv. j. 370 b.)

In the name of God amen: the xxiijth of Maij, mccccclvij. I Laurance Lyndley, of Leathley in the countye of Yorke, gent., beynge of pfect mynde and memorye, thankę be to allmyghtye God, do ordayne and maike thys my last wyll and testament in maner and forme followynge. Fyrst I gyve and bequeathe my soull to allmyghtye God my maker and redemer, and my body to be buryed in Xpian mens buryall wher yt shall please God to call me to his mercye. Allso I giue and bequeathe to Elisabethe my wyfe my hooll interest and lease of Leeds myl[n]es and th' occupacon therof vntyll suche tyme my sonne John Lyndley come to thaige of xxiiij yeres, to helpe her to brynge vpp all my chyldren. Item I gine and bequeath to Elisabethe my wyfe my interest and lease of Deane grange. Item I giuc and bequeathe my Lease of Leatheley to my said wyfe durynge the terme of yeares yet to come to bryng vpp my said chyldren wythe. Allso I wyll that my said wyfe shall yearlye frome hencefurthe at the feast of Ester contente and pay to Thomas Hardwicke, gent., and Richard Boothe to the vse and behalfe of my chyldren, that ys to say, Francys Lyndley, Henry Lyndley, Wyllm Lyndley, and Margaret Lyndley, the some of twentie markes of laufull money of Englande to be equallye devided emongest them, when they or any of them shall come to the aige of xxj[th] yeares. And that my sayd wife wyth sufficiente suerties wythe her shall stande bonden to the said Thomas Hardweke and Richard Boothe for the payment of the sayd some of xx[tie] markę to be trulye contented and paide eu'y yeare at the said feast of Ester to the sayd vse as then learned counsel shall devise. And I will that all my said goodę and cattalls beyng devided in three ptę (viz.), the fyrst part for my selfe to beare my fun'all expenses and charges, the seconde for my wyfe, and the thyrd pte to be equallye devided amongest my chyldren Frauncys Lyndley, Henry Lyndley, Wyllm and Margaret Lyndley. Also I wyll that the Residewe of my parte, my fun'all expenses borne, be disposed in maner and forme followynge, viz., To Margaret Lyndley my doughter vj[li] xiij[s] iiij[d]. To Francys Lyndley my seconde sonne xl[s]. To Henry Lyndley & Wyllm Lyndley my two other sonnes ether of them xl[s]. Allso I wyll that the said Thomas Hardwicke and Boothe shall yearlye receyve the hooll yeares rentę of all my copye holde lande in Leedę and Leedę Woodehouse, or els wher w[th]in the countye of Yorke to the vse of my sayd children vntill they come to thaige of xxj[tie] yeares. Item I gyve to Richarde Boothe, of Leedę, all my freeholde lande in Leedę aforesaid for ever. Item I giue and bequeathe to Vmfray Hodgeson my s'unte th'occupacon of one close in Leatheley called Myre close durynge his lyfe wythe out my thinge payinge therfore. Item I giue and bequeathe to Sir Ed-

---

(1) Son of Ch[r]istopher Lyndley, whose will is p[r]inted *ante*, vol. xix, p. 29.

warde Lyndley, preist, his houses and teñte that he dwellethe vpon durynge his naturall lyfe wytheout any thinge paynge therfore to singe and pray for my soull at Lethley or els wher. It' I ordayn and maike Francys Palmes, of Lyndley, esquyer, and Thomas Hardwicke, of Newton, gent', Mathew Redman, gent', and Elisabethe my wyfe myne executors of this my last wyll and testament. Item I ordayne and maike Cuthbert Layton, knyght, my vncle in lawe, Richard Boothe, and Thomas Lyndley, yomã, supvisors of this my last wyll and testament. Item I giue to Thomas Lyndley my cosyn v^{li} wythe my gray horse beare beynge. Item I giue to Richard Booth, of Leedꝭ, my brother in lawe, v markꝭ for ther paynes to be taken hearin. Item I giue and bequeathe to the churche of Leathley xx^{s}. Item I gyve and bequeathe to be distributed amongest the poore people wythin the ꝑishe of Leathley xx^{s}. It' I will that my executors receyve the profettꝭ and yearly rentꝭ of all my socaige landꝭ in Leathley, Farnley, and Shadwell, or els wythin Ingland for the ꝑformance of this my last wyll durynge the nõaige of John Lyndley. The residue of all my goodꝭ not bequeathed, all my dettꝭ and fun'all expens' paid, I giue to myne executors. In wytnes of this my last will and testament I haue subscribed my name wth myne owne hande the yeare and day abouewrytten. Wytnesses hearof, Sir Cuthbert Layton, knyght, Sir Robert Knyght, prest, Thomas Lyndley, Raufe Burrell, Xpofer Emerson, Xpofer Ackson, Robert Fawkener, Robert Kendall, and Henry Martyn, wth other. Lawrence Lyndley.—[*Proved* 23 *Sept.*, 1557, *by three executors, Thomas Hardwicke being dead.*]

RICHARD WHARTON.[1]

(xv. j. 371 a.)

In Dei nõie amen: in the year of our lord God m^{d}ccccclij, [*blank*] day of Februarij in the first year of the Reigne of our sou'aigne lady Marye by the grace of God of Englande, France, and Irelande queue, &c. I Richarde Wharton, beinge in hooll mynde and of good memorye but seke in body, dothe ordayne & maike this my last wyll and testament in maner and forme followynge. First I bequeathe my soull to allmyghtie God, our lady saynt Marye, and to all the celestiall company in heauen, and my body to be buried in the churche or churche yerde wher yt please Allmyghtie God to call me to his m'eye. Item I giue and bequeathe vnto my brother Edward all my hool tytle and inter[e]st that I haue by vertue of one Lease in Bryreyflatt vpon this condicõn, that he the said Edward shall content and pay vnto James Wharton my brother as p'eell of this my last will xl^{s}. And also vnto John Wharton son of the sayd Jaymes as of my bequest xxvj^{s} viij^{d}, and the same to be paid wthin two yeares next and ymediatlye after my decesse. Allso I wyll and bequeathe vnto my cosyn George Wharton the some of fowerscoore poundꝭ, all my hooll tytle, right and interest that ever I had of all my landꝭ in Newton, the whiche said some of lxxx^{li} the said George coueñntethe to pay vnto me or vnto myne executors or assignes, and the same to pay all my dettꝭ and legacies of this my last wyll, and the remaynder therof to remayne in the handꝭ of myne executors. Item I gyve vnto fyve chyldren of Alex-

(1) Son of Thomas Wharton, of Leathley, for whose will see vol. xix, p. 218, *ante*.

ander Reyme eu'y of them vj^{s} viij^{d}, and eu'y one of them to be others hayres. Item I gyve vnto my brother Nycholas iij^{li} vj^{s} viij^{d}. Item I gyve to iiij children of my brother James eu'y of them vj^{s} viij^{d}, and vnto Wyłłm his base sonne iij^{s} iiij^{d}. Item I giuc vnto sex chyldren of my brother Mawes eu'y of them vj^{s} viij^{d}. It' I gyve vnto myne aunte Banester doughter iij^{s} iiij^{d}. Item I gyve vnto Sandr' Elletwhart iij^{s} iiij^{d}. Item I gyve and bequeathe vnto my brother Casson, G'ce my suster hys wyfe, and Isabell ther dought^{r}, iiij^{li}. Item I giue and bequeathe vnto my brother Moyses and Agnes my syster his wyfe iij^{li}. Item I giue to yngram Moyses x^{s}. Item I bequeathe to Myles Bradley my kynseman x^{ls}. Item I giue vnto my brother Syr P'cyvall my bay gelding. Item to eu'y of my godchildren xij^{d}. Item to the poore folke of Leathley at the discretyon of myne executors v^{s} iiij^{d}. It' I gine to litle John Steide xij^{d}. Item to Agnes Jenkynson wyfe to Xpofer Browne xiij^{s} iiij^{d}. Item I giue to Xtopher Bampton iij^{s} iiij^{d}. Item I gyve to the churche of Leathley for the mantenance of Gods s'vice iiij^{s}. Item to the highe wayes ther iiij^{s}, yt to be distributed wher my cosyn Lyndley, my brother Moyses, and my brother James shall thynke most nedefull. Item I gine to eu'y of Sadler children xij^{d}. Item I gine to George Sadler man xx^{d}. Item I giuc to Grace Tele and her children vj^{s} viij^{d}. Item I gyve to Wyłłm Morehouse iij^{s} iiij^{d}. Item to Elene Stockdaill iij^{s} iiij^{d}. Item to Wyłłm Stockdaill yonger I gyne iij^{s} iiij^{d}. Item I giue to Thomas Dūwell xij^{d}. Item to Thomas Couper, of Casteley, ij^{s}. Item I gyve to the poore folk in Castley ij^{s}. It' I giue my hostes Warde v^{s}. It' I gine to John Cawdrowe and Elsabethe his suster v^{s} betwixte them. It' I giue to M'gerye Cooke xij^{d}. Item to John Bradley that was my hostes s'unte vj^{d}. It' I glue to Bery wyfe of Stayne burne iiij^{d}. It' to Thomas Wharton my brother Edward sonne iiij^{li}. Item I gyve and bequeathe vnto George Wharton my cosyn vj^{li} xiij^{s} iiij^{d}. Item to my brother James I gyve xx^{s} and my bay nag. It' I gyve to John Wharton, James sonne, xx^{s}. It' I wyll and com̄ende George Wharton and my brother Edwarde as they wyll answere to pay iiij^{li} x^{s} for me wheras I haue bydden them. It' I gyve to Peter Wharton vj^{s} viij^{d}. It' to Edward Wharton my gray mayre. Item I gine to my brother Moyses my fillye. The Residewe of all my goodꝭ not bequeathed, my dettꝭ paid, my fun'all expenses maide, I giue vnto my brother Edward and my brother Moyses to se all this my last wyll be fulfilled, whom I ordayne and make myne executors. I[n] wytnes wherof to this my last wyll I haue setto my signe manuell the day and yeare abouesaide. Thes berynge wytnes, Thomas Faux, Peter Wharton, John Cawdro, Myles Bradley, and John Wharton, wythe other, Nycholas Reyme, Richard Pearson, Wiłłm Mathewe, Alexand^{r} Hopton.—[*Proved 28 Sept., 1557, by Edward Wharton, Moses renouncing.*]

Myles Mawson, of Snowden, Weston.

(xv. j. 371 a.)

In Dei nōie amen: Anno D'ni miłłimo qui'quagesimo septimo, terc̄o Augusti. I Myles Mawson, of Snadon of the ꝑishe of Weston, whole of mynd and memory, ordenethe and makethe this to be my wyll and testament in forme as dothe followe. Fyrst I bequeathe my soull vnto Allmyghtye God my maker and redemer, and my body to be earthed wthin the churche yerde of Weston. It'm I wyll that my goodę be devided in three ptę accordinge to the lawe, that ys, one to my selfe, seconde to my wyfe, and my thyrd pte to my thre doughters. Item I giue to my curate in discharge of my conscience for tythes forgotten xx^d^. The residewe of my goodę, ordinaries, fun'alls & legacies discharged, I gyve vnto my thre doughters, and I make Isabell my wyfe, Margaret, Agnes, and Elsabethe Mawson, my doughters, thexecutors of this my last wyll and testament, and I hartelye desyre my landę lorde and Robert Richardson to be supvisors of this my said wyll. Wytnessethe, Martyn Wardeman, my curate, John Lyndley, gentleman, Robert Richardson, Edward Mawson.— [*Proved* 27 *Sept.*, 1557.]

JOHN BOSWELL, OF SHERBURN.

(xv. j. 371 a.)

In the name of God Amen: The xiiij^th^ day of August in the year of our lord God m^d^ccccclvij. I John Bosswell [of Sherburn—*Act Book*], hooll of mynd and seke of body, beynge of good and pfett memorye, makę this my last wyll and testament in maner and forme followynge. Fyrst I bequeathe my soull vnto God allmyghtie and vnto the blessed virgyn our lady saynt Marye and vnto all the celestyall company of heauen, my body to be buryed in the churche porche of Allhallowes even agaynst sant Mayng quere dore. I bequeathe to the churche workes for lyenge ther ij^s^. Item I gyve vnto the said churche [*sic*]. Item I gyve vnto the sayd church wardens to lye one stone of mee iij^s^ iiij^d^. Item I bequeathe to hym that wrytes my name of the sayd stone xx^d^. Item I bequeath vnto the hyghe alter xx^d^. Item I wyll that yf yt shall chance that ever saynt Antony light goo vpp and be founde agayne that my executrix shall gyve thervnto iij^s^ iiij^d^. I wyll that yf yt shall chance me for to dye at thys tyme that Thomas Stedman and Thomas Hallane yf he marye my doughter shall haue two ptę of my donge hill and one flatt called claye flatt wth one acer called Dame Agnes Raws for to sett the seyd dong one. Item I bequeathe vnto Alys my wyfe the thyrde parte of my said dounge hill wth one acre called goore acre. I bequeathe to Thomas Stedmā vj^s^ viij^d^. Item to Effam hys wyfe vj^s^ vj^d^, and vnto eu'y one of his chylden iij^s^ iiij^d^. I bequeathe vuto John Loundisdaill my sonne in lawe xl^s^ whiche he ded clame gyven acquyttance vnto my executrix for the same. I bequeathe to Agnes Talier my s'unte one mette of wheate and a wyndle of malte wythe mythe [*sic*] my wyfe rewarde. I bequeathe to Robt Felde the yonger xvj^s^ whiche ys in his fathers handę to fynde hym at schole. All the residewe of my goodę not gyven nor bequeathed, my dettę paid and fun'all expenses fynyshed, paid and ended, I gyve vuto Agnes my wyfe, whome I make my hole and full executrix of thys my last wyll and testament. Item that she shall gyve vnto my doughter Agnes in maraige x^li^ vj^s^ viij^d^, and my brother psons rewarde for her chyldę portion. Item I wyll that my executrix shall pay vnto the said Agnes my doughter and Thoms Allyne yf that he marye her iij^li^ w^th^in two yeares seu'allye at the feast of Trenytie w^che^ iij^li^ ys in the handę of Symon Barmbye of the holl some of x^li^ whiche he owethe vnto [me]. The Residewe of the said x^li^ aforesaid, iij^li^ paid as aforesaid, I giue vnto Ales my wyfe. Item I bequeathe vnto my brother mayster pson Hall one pese of golde of the some of x^s^, and I gyve vnto my sonne Mr. Thomas Bosswell one colte. Item I wyll that my said brother and my said sonne shalbe sꝑvisors of thys my last wyll hartely desyrynge them to be good vnto my wyfe. Wytnesses, Sir Rychard Hemsley, John Charley, Thomas Stedman, John Gylson.—[*Proved* 28 *Sept.*, 1557.]

Agnes Sykes, of South Milford.

(xv. j. 371 b.)

In the name of God Amen: The fyrst day of August in the year of our lorde God m^{d}ccccclvij. I Agnes Sykes, of southe Mylforthe, hooll of mynde, seke of body, beyng of good ꝑfett memorye, makethe this my last wyll & testament in manner and forme followynge. Fyrst I bequeathe my soull vnto God allmyghtye, to our lady saynt Mary, and all the celestiall companye of heauen, my body to be buryed in saynt Thomas queare in the churche of Alhallowes. I bequeathe to the blessed sacrament vj^{d}. I bequeathe to Robert Flansall one cowe. To Jenne Flansall one cowe. I wyll that my best bed be sold and xiij^{s} iiij^{d} be bestowed in dirige and masse for to be done for my soull & all chrysten soules, and other xiij^{s} iiij^{d} to be bestowed of the poore people in wheat brede and good aile. I gyve to Anne Tomplynson one greate brasse pott. Allso to Luce Tomplynson two cou'lettꝭ and one mattres. All the rest of my goodꝭ that Thomlynson hathe in hys handꝭ to be distributed amongest his children. I bequeath to John Sykes my best Arke. The Residew of all my goodꝭ I gyve to Thomas my sonne and Jennett my doughter, whome I make myne executors of this my last wyll. I wyll that Thomas Lethome and Henry Lethome shall be the sꝑvisors of this my last wyll for the behofe of my doughter Jennett and ether of them to haue xij^{d} for ther labors. I bequeathe to Henry Lethome one coverlett. I bequeathe to Jennett Flansall my best gyrdle, one payre of beadꝭ. I bequeathe to Luce Thomplynson one payre of beedꝭ, one gyrdell nexte to my best, and my best gowne. I bequeathe to Jennett one kyrtle, a gowne, a coũter, a coborde, a longe borde, one paynted clothe in the hall, also a kymnell, a kneadinge troughe, and one horse. The residewe of my goodꝭ vnbequeathed I giue to Thomas my sonne and Jennett my doughter, whome I maike myne executors. I bequeathe to Richard Hemsley a towell of new clothe. Wytness^{s}, Ric' Hemsley, Thomas Lethome, John Dowson, Henry Lethome, Thomas Sykꝭ.—[*Proved* 28 *Sept.*, 1557.]

Thomas Wilkinson, of Allerton.

(xv. j. 371 b.)

In the name of God Amen: In the year of our Lord god a m^{d}ccccclvij, the ^{xxtie} day of August. I Thomas Wylkinson, of Allerton wthin the ꝑyshe of Kepax, beynge of hoolle mynde and of good and ꝑfect memorye, makethe this my last wyll and testament in maner and forme followynge. Fyrst I bequeathe my soull to Allmyghtye God, to our lady saynt Marye, and to all the blessed company of heauen, and my body to be buryed in the ꝑyshe churche yeard of our lady in Kepax. Item I giuc and bequeathe to my sonne Thomas my farmeholde at Wytt wood durynge the yeares in my lease in full contentacõn of his chyldꝭ porcõn, and my wyfe to sawe the hardcorne ther, and Thomas my sonne to agre wythe her for the same, and he to enter to the said farmeholde at Wyttwood after chrystenmas next ensuynge and then to gyve his mother a gen'all quyttance. Also I wyll that Katheren my wyfe haue my farmeholde at Allerton as longe as she kepethe her wedowe to bringe vp my children wythall. And yf she marye then I will that one of my sonnes haue yt whiche John Ridiall and Thomas Fremã thinkę most meyte for it, and to bring vpp his bretheren and susters vnto they come to laufull aige. Item I wyll that Wyllm Longefeilde and hys wyfe and the longer lyver of them haue all suche landę wch the said Wm Longefelde hathe thoccupacon of at this present tyme belongynge to my farmehold. The residewe of my goodę not bequest, my dettę paid and my fun'all expenses discharged, I gyve to Katheren my wyfe, whome I make my full and sole executrix of this my last wyll and testament. Thes beyng wytnes, John Ridiall, Thomas Freman, and Willm Longefeilde, wythe other moo.—[27 *Sept.*, 1557.]

CHRISTOPHER FIELDE, OF WAKEFIELD, MERCER.

(xv. ij. 37 a.)

In the name of God amen: The viijth day [of] Julie in the year of our lord God 1557 and in the fourthe and fyft yeares of the Reigne of our sou'aigne lord and lady Philipp and Mary by the grace of God kinge and quene of Englande, Spayne, France, bothe Cicilies, Jerusalem, and Ireland, Defenders of the faythe, Archedukę of Austria, Dukę of Myllane, Burgunde, and Braybant, Counties of Haspurge, Flanders, and Tyrolls. I Chrofer Feylde, of Waikefelde in the countye of Yorke, mareer, hooll and sounde in body and of good and pfett remembrance, laude and prayse be gyven to God, do ordayne, constitute, and make this my last wyll and testament in maner and forme hearafter followynge. Fyrst I giue and comende my synfull soull into thandę of my savior and redemer Jesus Christe, throughe whose most paynefull deathe and bytter passion I truste of all my synnes to haue free p'don, and my body to buryed wythin the pyshe churche of Wakefelde as nyghe vnto the place wher my wyfe was buryed as convenyentlye may be. And I wyll that my executors shall cause a troughe stone wythe a remembrance of my selfe, wyfe, and chyldren in pycketures of brasse to be set vpon and layd vpon the grave as shortlye after my buryall as they may convenyentlye.[1] Allso I wyll, give and bequeathe vnto Eliz. Watkynson my daughter, now wyfe of Henry Watkynson, one hundrethe poundes. Also I wyll, gine and bequeathe vnto Katheren Atkynson my doughter, now wyfe of Richard Atkynson, one hundrethe markę. Also I gine and bequeathe vnto Anne Browne, doughter of the said Katheren, xli, and vnto Beatrice Thepland vli, and vnto eu'y other of the chyldren of the said Elisabeth Watkynson that she nowe bathe levinge at the day of the date and makinge of this my last wyll and testament fyve markę to be paid to eu'y of them by my executors as they shall come to ther full aiges of xxjth yeares or otherwyse be maryed. Also I gine and bequethe vnto Eliz. Atkynson, doughter of the sayd Katheren, vli, to be payd by my executors when she shall accomplishe her full aige of xxjth yeares or els maryed. Also I gyve and bequeathe vnto my brother Nycholas Feylde yf he be lyvynge the some of vli. Allso

---

(1) See Walker's *Cathedral Church of Wakefield*, p. 211.

I wyll, giue and bequeathe vnto Edward Crawshawe xx[d], and vnto Wyllm Hamelay fyve markę, and vnto Roger Jowett and Nycholas Jowett ether of them xx[s]. Allso I wyll eu'y of my syster children shall haue vj[s] viij[d] apece, Roger Jowet and Nycholas excepte, P'cyvall Feilde xx[s], and vnto Eliz. Morgane, layte wyfe of Xpofer Alane, xx[s], and vnto mynchewe the capper of Nontwiche x[s], and to Robert Graue xl[s] yf he be in my s'uice the day of my deathe, and to eu'y one of my other s'untę vj[s] viij[d]. Allso I wyll that my executors shall yerly by the space of three yeares after my deathe dispose emongest the most poore and nedye people w[th]in the towne of Waikefelde every yeare the some of fyve markę, and allso I wyll that my executors by the discretion of my supvisors hearafter named shall wythin one yeare nexte after my deathe bestowe in eu'y of the thre stretes in Wakefelde the some of fyve poundę towardę the amendement of the pavement. Allso I giuc and bequeathe vnto Xpofer Hamylyn fyve markę. Also I giue vnto Mathewe Feilde my sonne my salte wythe a cover of sylver doble gylte. Also I bequeathe vnto Henry Watkynson a flatt pece of sylver peell gilte, and vnto Katheren Atkynson my doughter a standynge pece of sylver pcell gylte. Also I bequeathe vnto my sonne Mathewe wyfe a drinkinge cupp of sylver wythe a cover p'eell gylte. Allso to Xpofer my sonne a small mayser. The residewe of all my goodę, cattalls, and dettę before not gyven nor bequeathed, after my dettę and fun'alls paide & discharged, I gyue vnto Mathewe Feilde my sonne and haire, whome I do ordayne, constitute, and make my sole and onlye executor of thys my last wyll and testament, and he to dispose the same at his discretion. And furthermore I do ordayne, constitute, and make Henry Gryce, gentleman, Wyllm Feilde, my brother, and John Asheley, of Thorpehall, yomā, the supvisors of thys my last wyll and testament, and vnto eu'y of them I give and bequeathe the some of fyve markę and a gowne. In wytnes wherof unto this my present last wyll and testament I the said Xpofer Feylde haue subscribed my owne name, the day and yeres aboue wrytten. In the presence of the sayd Henry Gryce, Willm Feilde, John Ashlay, and others.—[*Proved* 18 *Dec.*, 1557.]

Alice Saxton.

(xv. ij. 49 b.)

In the name of God Amen: I Alice Saxton, the xxij[th] day of June in the year of our lord God 1557, do make this my last will and testament in maner and forme followynge. Fyrst I bequeathe my soull vnto allmyghtye God, to our lady Marye, and to all the sayntę in heauen, and my body to be buryed in the churche yerde of saynt Peter at Leedes. Inp'mis I bequeathe to Xpofer Saxton my sonne xl[s]. It' to Wyllm Saxton my sonne xx[s]. It' to John Saxton my sonne vj[s] viij[d]. The residewe of all my goodę vnbequeathed I giue to Thomas Saxton and Henrye Saxton my sonnes, whome I make my full executors of thys my last wyll and testament. It' I giue and bequeath to Cicilie Saxton my doughter vj[s] viij[d] and a belte. It' to Richard Saxton my sonne vj[s] viij[d]. Thes beynge wytnesses of the same, Wyllm Wylson, thelder, Wyllm Wyllson, yonger, Rauffe Sympson, withe other mo.—[*Proved* 1 *Dec.*, 1557.]

JAMES WOODROFFE, OF PURSTON JACKLINGE, GENT.

(xv. ij. 53 a.)

In the name of God Amen: the xxx^th day of August in the year of our Lorde God a m^d v^c lvij. I James Woodroffe, gent., of Pryston Jacklynge and of the pyshe of Fetherston, seke in body but hole of mynde, thankę be to God, dothe ordayne and make this my last wyll and testament in maner and forme followynge. Fyrst and principally I giue and bequeathe my soull to God allmyghtye my maker and redemer, to his blessed mother o^r lady saynt Mary, and to all the celestyall company of heauen, and my body to be buryed in the Lady quere of the churche of Fetherston near whear as my two wyves were buryed. Item I giue vnto the hye alter to be prayed for and for tythes forgotten yf any be xij^d. The residewe of all my goodę and cattallę, my dettę paid and I honestlye brought furthe, I gine and bequeathe to Richard Woodroffe and his children, whiche Ric' I make my full executor. Thes wytnes, Edward Wormall, clerke, Nyeholas Eu'yngham, Robert Heptonstall, and Nycholas Shelytoo, thelder, wythe other moo.—[*Proved* 13 *Dec.*, 1557.]

WILLIAM DUFFAN, OF HOUGHTON.

(xv. ij. 53 b.)

In the name of God Amen: The last day of October, Annis regnor' Phillippi et Marie Regis et Regine quarto et qui'to. I Wyllm Duffan, of Houghton wythin the countye of Yorke, hole of mynde and of good remembrance, make this my last will and testament in maner and forme followynge. Fyrst I bequeathe my soull vnto allmyghtye God and to the prayer of the blessed virgyn Mary and all the holy company of heauen, and my body to be buryed within the pyshe churche yerde of Castelfurthe. Item I bequeathe vnto Thoms Huscrofte xx^s. Item I bequeathe vnto Willm Batlay xx^s, and ether of them to be well arayed of my owne proper goodę. Item I wyll that Edwarde Huscroft cast in all suche quieke good as he had of me at his maraige or synce and then to be one of my children. Item I wyll that John Duffan my doughter three quarters of barlye over and besydes her childę porcon. Item I giuc to Anne Batlay my syster one mette of wheate. Item I giue to Robert Huscrofte one ewe and one lambe. Item I wyll that my goodę be equallye devided in thre ptę, and my wyfe to haue one pte, and my children an other pte emongeste them, and the thyrde to remayne to pay my dettę and bequestę and to discharge my fun'all expenses, and yf any remaync I wyll that yt be equallye devyded emongest Jennett my wyfe, John Duffan and Thomas Duffan my sonnes, Edward Huscroft my sonne in lawe, and Elsabethe Duffan my doughter, whome I ordayne and make executors of this my last will and testament. [Witnesses], Robert Bradforthe, Robert Flemynge, and Wyllm Nellson.—[*Proved* 13 *Dec.*, 1557. *Grant reserved to Thomas Duffan.*]

WILLIAM HYDE, OF PONTEFRACT, BUTCHER.

(xv. ij. 53 b.)

In Dei nōie Amen: The xiij^th day of September in the year of our lord God 1557. I Willm Hyde, of Pontefract, butcher, seke in body, hole in mynde and pfett in remembrance, makethe this my last wyll and testament in maner and forme followynge. Fyrst I giue and bequeathe my soull to God Allmyghty my maker and redemer and to the blessed company in heauen, and my body to be buryed wthin the churche yerd of Allhallowes in Pontefract. It' I giue to John Pynderson vjs viijd. It' I giue to Anne P'lington xxs. It' I giue to Anne Hyde xvjs. It' I giue to Eliz. Hyde, to Margerye Hyde, to Thomas Hyde, and to John Hyde, iijli emongest them. It' I giue to Alison Hyde my wife my house in Baxstergayt for the terme of her lyfe, and yf nede requyre to sell yt provided allways that yf she do mary that then the house shall not be solde but remayne to Thomas Hyde my sonne and to his hayres for ever after her decesse. It' I giue to Richard Baytson my gray gowne. It' I make Thomas Everington, Bonyface Savege, Richard Baitson, the supervisors of this my last wyll to se that yt be fulfilled and kepte. All the reste of my goodę vnbequeathed, my dettę paid, my fun'all expenses maide the day of my buryall, I giue to Alyson my wyfe, whome I make and ordayne my sole executrix. Wytnesses hearof, Anthony Flemynge, clerke, Thomas Pearson.—[*Proved* 13 *Dec.*, 1557.]

George Dymonde, of Wakefield, clothier.

(xv. ij. 53 b.)

In the name of God Amen: The year of our lorde God a thousand fyve hundrethe fyftye and seaven and the xijth day of September. I George Dymonde, of Wakefelde wythin the countye of Yorke, clothyer, seke of body and of good and ꝑfett remembrance, do ordayne and make this my last testament and wyll in maner & forme followinge. Fyrst I comende my soull into the handę of allmightie God my redemer and saviour, to our blessed lady saynt Marye, and to all the sayntę in heauen, and my body to be buryed wthin the churche of Allhallowes in Wakefelde. Also I bequeathe vnto the blessed sacrament for all forgotten tythes xijd. The residewe of all my goodę moveable and not moveable I gine vnto Eliz. my wyfe & my children whiche I make my full executors, they for to discharge my debtę and my fun'all expenses and for to dispose for the healthe of my soule and all Xpian soules. Also I make Olyver Dymonde, thelder, Robert Dymonde, and Gylbert Dymonde, suꝑvisors of this my wyll and testament. Thes beynge wytnesss, Sir Richarde Seyll, prest, Sr William Baull, prest, John Burrye, John Ray, yonger.—[*Proved* 13 *Dec.*, 1557, *by the widow. Grant reserved to the children, minors.*]

William Naylor, of Woodkirk.

(xv. ij. 54 b.)

In the name of God amen: the vijth day of October and in the year of our lord god 1557. I Wyllm Nayler, of the ꝑishe of Woodkyrke wythin the countye of Yorke, clothyer, seke in body and hooll in mynde and of good memorye, makethe this my last wyll in maner and forme followynge. Fyrst I bequeathe my soull vnto allmyghtie god, our Lady saynt Mary, and to all the hole company of heauen, and my body to be buryed wythin the churche yerd of our Lady at Woodkyrke or els whear yt shall please allmyghtie god to call me vnto his mercie, &c. Item I giue to the churche towardę buyinge of a chalesse xijd. Item I bequest to Thomas my brother a jackett, a dublett, a payr hoyse and my best capp, and viij^s of money. Item I bequeath to John my brother a jakett of shepe color, a lether dublett, a payr of hoyse, a payr of showes, a payr of my best sheares, two shyrtę, and xvj^s of money. Allso I wyll that John my brother haue hys cowe agayne, whiche ys in the handę of James Grene wyfe, and I giue hym myne expenses whiche comethe to xvj^s. Item I giue to Bryan Adcoke my best dublett, and to his wyfe a shete, and to Jenet my syster a pan or els x^s. Item to John Webster my best jackett. It' to the poore people w^th^in the pyshe of Wodkyrke ij^s iiij^d. Residewe of all my goodę not gyven and bequest I giue them to Katheren my wyfe and my childe (yf she be wth chylde), whome I make my full executors. Wytnes of the same, Laurence Nayler, Thomas Bradlay, and John Burghe.—[*Proved* 13 *Dec.*, 1557, *by the widow. Grant reserved to unborn child.*]

AGNES SAWER, OF SHERBURN, WIDOW.

(xv. ij. 84 a.)

In Dei nõie Amen: The xviijth day of August in the year of our lord God a thousand fyve hundreth fyftye and seven. I Agnes Sawer, of Shereborne, wydowe, hole of mynd and memorye, doo ordayn and constitute and make thys my testament and last wyll in manner and forme hereafter folowyng. Fyrst I gyve and bequethe my Sowle vnto Allmyghtye God whoo suffered deathe apon The Crosse for the redempcion of me and all synfull Creaturs, and my Bodye to be Buryed wythin the pysshe Churche yeard of Shereburne. It'm I gyve and bequeth to the blyssed Sacrament xij^d. It'm I gyve and bequyth to the vicar my Curett iij^s iiij^d. It'm I gyve and bequyth to Sr Robert Blaunche iij^s iiij^d. It'm I gyve to Syr John Tayllyer ij^s. It'm I gyve and bequeth to Alys Herlyng my doughter xx^s. It'm I gyve and bequythe to my doughter Jane Holdell xx^s. It'm I gyve and bequythe to Elysabeth Holdell my doughter xx^s. It'm I gyve to Jenett my doughter xx^s. It'm I gyve to John Holdall my son vj^s viij^d. It'm I gyve to Agnes Holdell, my son Robert doughter, vj^s viij^d. It'm I gyve to my brother Henrye Wylson vj^s viij^d. It'm I gyve and bequethe to Wyllyam Herlyng my son in law one bay mare. It'm I gyve to my syster Margarett Horburye iij^s iiij^d. It'm I gyve to Thomas Barmbye, Stepham Hebden, and John Hebden, beyng wytnesses hereof, to euerye one of theyme iiij^d. The resaydeu of my goodę moveable and vnmoveable here vnbequeathed I gyve and bequethe vnto Lawrence Holdell my sone and Agnes Holdell my doughter, whom I doo ordeyn, constitute, and make my Executors of thys my testament and laste wyll, and also I doo make Mr Vicar and Thomas Morret the super vysors hereof. Thes beyng wytnesses, Syr Rychard Emsleye, vicare, Thomas Morret, Thomas Barmbye, Stephan Hebden, and John Hebden, wyth others.—[*Proved* 1 *Dec.*, 1557.]

THOMAS WARD, OF OVER YEADON.

(xv. ij. 84 a.)

In the nayme of God Amen: The iiij^th day of Marche in the year of our lord God 1556. I Thomas Ward of Oueryeadon wythin the peryshyng of Gyeslay, seke in bodye, perfyte of mynd and memorye, do make my last wyll and testament as hereafter foloweth. Fyrst I bequeath my soull to

God Almyghtye, to the blessed vyrgyn Marye, and to all the holye Companye of heauen, and bodye to be buryed within the paryshe Church of Seynt Osswold at Gyeslaye. It'm I wyll that all my goodꝭ quieke and deade be deuyded into iij partꝭ, of the whych iij partꝭ I bequeyth one parte to Alys my wyff, The second part to my children, and the thyrd part to myselffe, the whych thyrd part, my funerall Chargꝭ deducted frome the same, I bequeath to my chyldren equallye to be devided emonge theym. Also I wyll that Alys my wyff have the vse of my fermhold enduryng her wedohede to the bryngyng vp of my Chyldren. Also I wyll that the said Alys my wyfe haue the ordre of my chyldren and ther porcyons, yf she do not marye, vnto they cume to lawfull age. And yf yt fortune the said Alys to marye at any tyme then I wyll that Wyllyam Ward my sonne or any other of my sonnes whiche than shalbe myne eldest sonne lyvynge, shall haue my farmhold. Also I do make Alys my wyfe and my chyldren my executors, provyded always that yf Alys my wyf ether do marye at any tyme, or yf she be called oute of thys world to God's marcye, before my eldest sonne than lyvyng be xxj yeares of age, then that John Yeaden, of Westcarlton, my landlord, and Thomas Mershall, of Westeshholt, my brother in law, as my most trustye and faithfull frendꝭ, haue and vse my farmehold for the most profett of the bryngyng vp of my Chyldren vnto my eldest sonne cum to lawfull age as ys aboue sayd, p'vided also in lyke maner y^{t} yf the sayd Alys eyther do marye or dye before my Chyldren cum to lawfull age, than the aboue named John Yeadon and Thomas Marshall haue the order of my chyldren and ther porcyones vnto the sayd chyldren cum to lawfull age, at whyche lawfull age I charge the sayd John and Thomas to delyuer my farmhold to my eldest sonne than lyvyng and hys po[r]tyon, also and to my other chyldren all such goodꝭ as the sayd John and Thomas hayth or had receyved for the same any thyng in thys wyll to the contrary notwythstandyng. Also I wyll that my lease and intreast of the stonne howse wyth two naut gayth in the lee feld, one garthe called pryor garth, and all such land as doth belong to the same stonne house, be delyvered by the dyscretyon and consent of the aboue named John and Thomas to such on of my chyldren as they shall thynke most to haue ned therof at lawfull age. Also I bequeyth to the Church workes at Gyeslay iij^{s} iiij^{d}. Also I wyll y^{t} all such sommes of money as I haue payd before hand for rentꝭ of my farmhold and stonne howse to my landlord John Yeadon or Wylffryd Colyer be as my other goodꝭ and be devyded as ys abouesayd. Recordꝭ, Wiłłm Boys, ꝑson, Chrystopher Sugden, Wyłłm Ilcocke, Wyłłm Foster.—[*Proved* 6 *Dec.*, 1557, *by the widow. Grant reserved to the children, minors.*]

MARGERY BRAMHAM, OF LEDSTONE.

(xv. ij. 84 b.)

In the name of God Amen: The xvijth day of Novembre In the year of our lord god 1557. I Margere Bramham of Ledstone, being of holle mynd and of good memorye, makethe this my last wyll and testament in maner and forme followynge. Furst I bequyethe my soule to almyghtye God, to oure Laydye Sanct Mary, and to all the Celestiall Companye of heaven, and my bodye to be buryed in the Churche yerde of our ladye in Kepax. Itm. I bequeythe to the blyssed sacrament ther xij^{d}. Also

WS - #0007 - 200123 - C0 - 229/152/8 [10] - CB - 9780332963983 - Gloss Lamination